COMPUTER
SOLUTIONS
for
BU

COMPUTER SOLUTIONS

for

Planning and Implementing
a Successful Computer Environment

BUSINESS

Doug Dayton

PUBLISHED BY
Microsoft Press
A Division of Microsoft Corporation
16011 NE 36th Way, Box 97017, Redmond, Washington 98073-9717

Library of Congress Cataloging in Publication Data
Dayton, Doug, 1951 –
Computer solutions for business.
Includes index.
1. Business—Data processing.   2. Computers—Purchasing.
I. Title.
HF5548.2.D377   1987   651.8   87-23957
ISBN 0-914845-98-5

Printed and bound in the United States of America.

1 2 3 4 5 6 7 8 9 MLML 8 9 0 9 8 7

Distributed to the book trade in the
United States by Harper & Row.

Distributed to the book trade in
Canada by General Publishing Company, Ltd.

Distributed to the book trade outside the
United States and Canada by Penguin Books Ltd.

Penguin Books Ltd., Harmondsworth, Middlesex, England
Penguin Books Australia Ltd., Ringwood, Victoria, Australia
Penguin Books N.Z. Ltd., 182-190 Wairau Road, Auckland 10, New Zealand

British Cataloging in Publication Data available

Project Editor: Ron Lamb   Manuscript Editor: Rebecca Pepper   Technical Editor: Bob Combs

To Terry L. Smith

Contents

Acknowledgments

I would like to thank Susan Lammers and my editors at Microsoft Press for their help and encouragement.

I would also like to thank Microsoft Corporation and the RealWorld Corporation for letting me use samples of their reports and data entry screens as examples throughout *Computer Solutions for Business*.

The names of companies used as examples throughout this book have been changed to maintain everyone's sense of humor.

Introduction

In my work as a marketing representative for IBM and later as an independent consultant, I have found that many of my customers and clients did not know how computers worked or how computers could work for them. Although many of them were motivated to learn about computers, they did not have the time or desire to become computer engineers.

Most reference books on computers and information processing are not easy to read and are not oriented toward the concerns of business people. Buyer's guides are usually out of date by the time they are published, and they do not help the business person make judgments about system requirements for a specific situation.

This book is not a buyer's guide; it provides the background you need to make intelligent decisions about automating your business. Here you will find answers to your questions about the process of computerization:

- How do I determine whether it makes sense to automate my company?
- What effect will office automation have on my company's structure and personnel?
- Can I justify the cost of automating my office?
- What kind of computer system should I buy?
- How do I select and negotiate with system suppliers?
- How do I install and implement an office-automation system?

Computer Solutions for Business will help you evaluate your office-automation requirements and determine whether you can cost-justify an automated system for your business.

Section I

Planning for Office Automation

Until you understand the basics of how computers work and what they can help you do, it is difficult to make an informed decision about automating your company's office procedures.

This section helps you determine your needs and describes how to find a computer system that meets them.

Chapter 1 describes the sorts of tasks that can be automated. Several case studies illustrate the right and wrong ways to go about adding a computer system to your business.

In Chapter 2 you analyze your office procedures to find areas that could benefit from computerization. Chapters 3 and 4 give you guidelines for evaluating business software and hardware.

Finally, Chapter 5 helps you choose a system supplier.

Computers in Business

Al Brown owns Northwest Floors. He has been in the floor-covering business for 18 years and has built the small family operation into a profitable $1.5-million-per-year company.

When Al decided to investigate purchasing a computer, he really wasn't sure what he would do with one. He knew that many other small businesses were finding it profitable to automate, and he wanted to know if computers made sense for his company.

Like most business people, Al felt that he was in touch with day-to-day operations. However, as business grew, overseeing operations took more time. He decided to see if a computer could help him be more productive and save his company money. Al analyzed each area of his business and found that he could use help managing his outstanding receivables.

In the floor-covering business, as in most other resale operations, profitability is closely tied to cash management. Many of Northwest Floors' customers had to wait 90 days for their own bills to be paid, so Northwest Floors' invoices were often extended to 120 days. Al reasoned that, with more than $100,000 in outstanding receivables at any given time, the accounts-receivable department was the most logical area to automate first. He used a simple payback analysis to cost-justify the acquisition of a small computer system.

Paula Lyons had been doing the bookkeeping for Al for the past three years. Al knew that Paula would need to be firmly committed to the automation project for it to be successful. He approached Paula with the idea of automating the accounts-receivable department and was delighted to learn that Paula realized the importance of computers in the accounting field and that she was excited about the opportunity of learning more about them.

Paula enrolled in an introductory college extension class on computers, and she asked Al to send her to an accounting software seminar offered by a local computer consultant. Encouraged by Paula's enthusiasm, Al delegated the task of automating the accounts receivable department to her.

After six weeks, Paula had successfully made the transition to an automated accounts-receivable system. At that point, Al decided to explore the possiblity of installing an accounts-payable module. He found that he could easily justify the acquisition of an accounts-payable software program. Al then confirmed the feasibility of implementing the application with Paula. She was able to install the accounts-payable module over a three-day weekend.

I asked Al what he felt was the most important reason for his successful computer installation. He quickly answered, ''That's easy; it's because my people like it and want to use it…and because I told them that if the system didn't work out we were all going to have to spend more time collecting bills and pushing papers!''

Northwest Floors' experience points out a number of key factors in the successful implementation of computers in small businesses. First, a computer system should not be implemented until you have done a payback analysis based on the specific tasks that will be automated. Northwest Floors' computer paid for itself in less than three months. Second, and perhaps most important, there needs to be a positive, encouraging attitude from top management. The personnel in the organization must be made to feel secure about their ability to learn how to work with the computer, and they must feel that their jobs will not be eliminated. Finally, if additional tasks are to be automated, they should be phased in slowly to give everyone time to learn to work with and take advantage of the new system.

Derik, Peterson, and Crouch, Attorneys at Law

John Derik learned at his law firm's weekly staff meeting that the secretaries were threatening to quit if another clerical person wasn't hired "immediately!" At the time John's firm had three partners, several legal assistants, and three full-time secretaries. He did not want to hire additional secretaries because he knew that although the company's work load fluctuated, the real bottleneck was in the typing area.

John called a local computer store to find out more about computers and word processing. He learned that a word-processing system would reduce the time it took to create a new document by about half. The major benefit of a word-processing system, however, was that his secretaries could be about ten times as productive when they modified documents and generated contracts and legal forms from boilerplate text.

The computer representative's survey revealed that the secretaries were spending over half their time typing and retyping briefs and other documents. John used the simple formula in Chapter 6 to determine that a word-processing system would pay for itself within six months.

John's firm leased a microcomputer system with word-processing software and a laser printer. The monthly cost was slightly less than $400. With the increased productivity of his clerical staff, John did not need to hire another full-time typist. The new system also greatly increased office morale by bringing the firm, as his assistant remarked, "into the twentieth century." John estimated that the word processor saved his company more than $15,000 in direct labor costs the first year.

If your business produces many typed documents, or if it produces different versions of standard documents over and over, the most cost-effective area to automate may be your typing work. A word-processing system, like an accounting system, can often be justified by using a payback analysis. You may also find that such a system produces intangible benefits, such as greater job satisfaction among your staff.

Laurence Electronics

Laurence Electronics is a major defense contractor. Blaine Gorski supervises its marketing engineering group and is responsible for all government bids. This can be very difficult and time-consuming work, and

Blaine wanted to investigate whether computers would be able to help his group bid on projects more effectively.

Blaine had read in industry trade magazines about job-costing software packages that run on microcomputers. He went down to a local computer store to find out more about this type of system. Unfortunately, although the sales people were courteous and seemed to understand computers, they didn't know anything about the defense-contracting business. Blaine realized that he needed to find a system supplier who understood his specific requirements as well as computers.

Blaine called several friends to find out what kinds of job-costing systems their companies were using. One friend enthusiastically recommended a major computer supplier that had helped his company automate. Blaine called the computer firm's marketing representative and was invited to a job-costing software seminar.

Blaine discovered that Tom, one of his senior engineers, was very upset by the idea of working on a computer. Tom had never worked with microcomputers and wanted to stick with their manual job-costing procedures. Blaine decided that the best way to win Tom over was to get him involved in the planning process. Tom had designed their current manual system and was, Blaine felt, well-qualified to evaluate an automated system. Blaine also knew that unless Tom's concerns were overcome, resistance from less-senior members of his staff who emulated Tom might kill the project.

When he began to look at the available systems, Tom found that computer technology had progressed in the 23 years that he had been out of school. Basic computer operations had become much simpler; by reading through the documentation he was able to get a good understanding of the features and capabilities that each job-costing system offered.

As Tom learned more about automation, he overcame his fears about computers and began to view them as powerful office tools. He realized that, rather than replacing the engineers in his group, the computers would allow the engineers to spend more time doing creative problem-solving for their customers.

The automated job-costing system that Blaine and Tom decided to purchase allowed their group to generate job estimates automatically from standard costing data that had been entered into the system. This sped up the process so much that Blaine's group was able to bid on four contracts in the time it formerly took to respond to one request for quotation. Because all the marketing engineers used the same cost database, their information was up-to-date and their bids were more consistent from one job to the next. This helped Blaine track key contract requirements and estimate his competitors' margins.

The microcomputers and software that Blaine and Tom selected cost less than $350 per month. This allowed them to save more than $4,000 per month in labor costs and to increase their division's sales by bidding on more jobs. Blaine's boss was especially pleased with the professional-looking graphs and charts that the software was able to prepare automatically from data that had been entered for customer bids.

Blaine, like most other departmental managers, had to sell the idea of automating job costing to his boss. He prepared a thorough payback analysis to justify the acquisition, and then he drafted a request for proposal to help several computer companies address his specific requirements. Chapter 5 and Chapter 6 show you how to prepare these documents.

As these examples demonstrate, the costs of office automation can be justified when automation helps generate higher profits or decrease business expenses by helping control operations. The key to sucessful office automation, however, is having your management and personnel committed to the project.

Why Do Businesses Automate?

The telephone, the automobile, and the copy machine are some of the tools we use to automate our businesses. We are familiar with how these tools work, and we have integrated them, often unconsciously, into our daily tasks. Although we are dependent on these tools, we feel that their value more than compensates for the risk we take in relying on their performance.

Many companies are finding that computers are just as critical to their success as these other tools. Most business people today feel pressure to computerize their operations. Knowing which areas to automate is difficult, however, because most business people do not understand how computers work and how they can be smoothly integrated into their day-to-day operations. They do not know how to evaluate the advantages and potential risks of office automation.

The primary reason that business people explore office automation is to help them manage problem areas within their business. Poor sales performance, mismanaged inventory, large outstanding receivables, and excessive personnel costs are the most frequent business problems. Some of the other factors that encourage automation are rapid business growth, increased competition, rising business expenses, and social pressures.

Unfortunately, management often expects computers to be a quick fix for fundamental business problems like these. Although office automation is rarely a panacea for the myriad ills that can plague a mismanaged or poorly financed business, it can help improve productivity and operating efficiency in many areas, including the following:

Poor sales performance. Sales analysis reports can help management determine where the problem lies.

Too much or the wrong type of inventory. Inventory-analysis reports allow management to track inventory more closely and eliminate slow-moving items from stock.

Large outstanding accounts receivables. Automated accounting systems provide up-to-date credit information on customers' accounts and offer timely and accurate invoicing.

High overhead due to excessive personnel. Automation can improve corporate communications, help in the scheduling and management of projects, help eliminate redundant or repetitive office tasks, and help increase business revenues.

Too large an investment in fixed assets. Timely financial reports help management make better decisions as to how and when to allocate company resources.

"Lost" information. Corporate growth leads to departmentalization of tasks and eventually to tiers of management. As the layers of management are put into place, routine communications become more formalized. This often results in important information being lost before it can be acted upon. An automated office-information system can help your business respond to growth by providing a workable intracorporate communications channel.

Automated competitors. In many areas, such as the travel, banking, and insurance industries, it has become necessary to make heavy investments in office automation to remain competitive.

Inability to respond to government agencies. Each year more and more reports and forms must be filed with city, state, and federal regulatory agencies and with the ever-present Internal Revenue Service. Holding down these expenses may be reason enough for you to automate different office procedures.

Social pressures. Many business people feel that modern, effective business practice demands computerization. In fact, some executives feel more comfortable if they have computer terminals on their desks, even if they do not know how to use them.

Fortunately, computers are not difficult to understand. You no longer have to make a major investment of your time before you can use a computer effectively. In fact, some business microcomputer systems can become functional office tools the day they are installed.

As computers have become easier to use, less expensive, and more reliable, they have been adapted to a wide range of office automation applications. Office productivity and general accounting programs have been installed on over 10 million microcomputer systems. You will be able to take advantage of the experience of other users as you automate your own business.

The Power of the Computer: Management Reports

The "currency" of business is information. To make effective business decisions, management must have accurate, timely information. Computers can help you automate the collection, processing, and distribution of information within your organization.

In a computerized information-processing system, data regarding, for example, the performance of your company's different departments is entered, or input, into the computer, where it is processed. You receive the computer's output in the form of reports, which you can analyze to help you determine where to allocate your company's resources. The "output" of management is decisions.

This processing of information is known as a management information system, or MIS. Management information systems help management make informed decisions.

Figure 1-1 shows a diagram of the MIS cycle. Let's follow a production run through this cycle. The data to be entered into the computer is the number of a given product sold in a month.

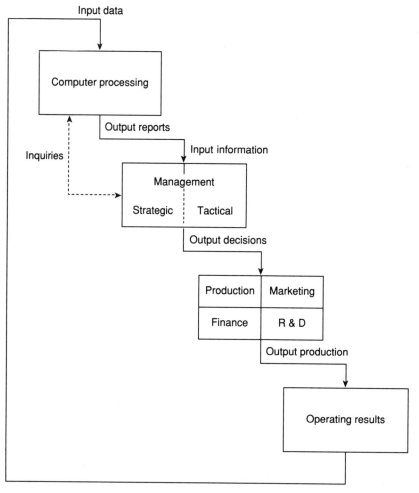

Figure 1-1.
The management information cycle.

The computer processes the sales data and produces a sales report as output. This report helps management decide how many more of the product to build during the next production cycle.

As the second batch of the product is sold, the new sales data is entered into the computer and new sales reports are produced that allow management once again to make timely, informed decisions about how and where to allocate corporate resources.

Computer-generated management reports can provide timely information about the status of virtually every department within your organization. These management reports focus your attention on the areas within your organization that require additional support and provide an objective measure of individual, group, and overall corporate performance. Although this information can usually be generated manually, it is often so time-consuming to do so that the reports either don't get done or arrive too late to be of much use.

Figure 1-2 shows an example of an inventory report. These reports can help you see which items are overstocked so that you can reduce the price or take other steps to correct the problem. Without such reports, it might be months before you noticed that a particular product was overstocked.

Figure 1-3, on the next page, shows an aging-receivables report. These reports, together with on-line credit checking, can provide you with the information you need to make informed decisions about extending credit to your customers. Unless you have timely credit information, you run the

```
RUN DATE: 1/1/99              MUFFIN INCORPORATED
-----------------------------------------------------------------------
            I T E M   S T O C K   S T A T U S   R E P O R T
-----------------------------------------------------------------------
      ITEM # RANGE: ALL
         VENDOR #: ALL
 PRODUCT CATEGORY: ALL

 BACK ORDER CONTROL CODE (BOC): B = OK TO BACK ORDER  N = NOT OK TO BACK ORDER
    R = ITEM HAS HIT REORDER LEVEL  O = ITEM IS OUT OF STOCK
-----------------------------------------------------------------------
 ---ITEM----------  PRICE/  PRICE  AVERAGE QTY ON REORDER  QTY   BOC    VALUE
 # DESCRIPTION      25 LBS.   #2    COST    HAND   LEVEL    COM        (QTYxCOST)

 1 BLUEBERRY MIX    24.67   22.57  12.12     20      10      0    B      242.30
 2 BRAN MIX         13.65   12.60   7.24     60      50      0    B      434.10
 3 ENGLISH MIX      19.95   17.85  10.54     42      30      0    B      442.51
 4 CORN MIX         45.15   41.47  23.50    120      25      0    B     2820.00
 5 MACADAMIA MIX    16.80   14.96   8.14     55      45      0    B      447.43
 6 RAISIN MIX       48.30   45.93  25.53      2      10      0    B       51.06
 7 HONEY MIX        17.85   15.75   9.26    145      25      0    B     1341.98
 8 CHEESE MIX        1.99    1.20   0.45    750     200      0    N      333.75

 8 ITEMS      1 AT REORDER LEVEL      0 OUT OF STOCK      TOTAL   6113.12
                                                                 ==========
```

Figure 1-2.
An inventory report.

```
RUN DATE: 1/1/99                MUFFIN INCORPORATED
--------------------------------------------------------------------------
A C C O U N T S   R E C E I V A B L E   S U M M A R Y   A G I N G   R E P O R T
--------------------------------------------------------------------------
AGED AS OF:   3/31/99   DOES NOT INCLUDE ITEMS PAST AGING DATE
   CUSTOMER # RANGE:    200        TO        300
 CUT-OFF BALANCE DUE:   ALL
CUT-OFF AGING PERIOD:   ALL
--------------------------------------------------------------------------
DOCUMENT TYPE:    I = INVOICE    P = PAYMENT    C = CR MEMO    D = DR MEMO
                  B = BALANCE FORWARD    F = FINANCE CHARGE

---CUSTOMER-----------    BALANCE    ------AGED CUSTOMER BALANCE (DAYS)---------
#   NAME        BAL-MTH   CR-LIMIT   CURRENT    31-60     61-90     OVER 90
--------------------------------------------------------------------------

200 21ST CENTURY BAKERY  $10235.20   $108.09 $10127.11    $0.00     $0.00
             OPN-ITM     $20000.00

300 BEVERLY HILLS BAKERY  ($835.00)  ($835.00)   $0.00    $0.00     $0.00
             BAL-FWD     $50000.00
```

Figure 1-3.
An aging-receivables report.

risk of alienating good customers or extending too much credit to customers who are poor credit risks.

Perhaps the most useful marketing aid is the sales analysis report, an example of which is shown in Figure 1-4. These reports give you better

```
RUN DATE: 1/1/99                MUFFIN INCORPORATED
--------------------------------------------------------------------------
           S A L E S   A N A L Y S I S   B Y   C U S T O M E R
--------------------------------------------------------------------------
---CUSTOMER-----------        ----------- % OF    COST OF    GROSS  % OF  MARGIN
#   NAME / CITY,STATE         SALES       SALES    SALES    PROFIT PROFIT  %
001 ELLIOT BAKERY        PTD     0.00     0.0%      0.00      0.00   0.0%  0.0%
    GLENDALE          CA YTD   500.00     1.4%    250.00    250.00   2.2% 50.0%

010 HARRIS BAKERY        PTD     0.00     0.0%      0.00      0.00   0.0%  0.0%
    SAN DIEGO         CA YTD     0.00     0.0%      0.00      0.00   0.0%  0.0%

030 W.J. MUFFINS         PTD     0.00     0.0%      0.00      0.00   0.0%  0.0%
    LOS ANGELES       CA YTD     0.00     0.0%      0.00      0.00   0.0%  0.0%

040 WASHINGTON BAKERY    PTD  7000.00    64.3%   4000.00   3000.00  68.4% 42.9%
    DALLAS            TX YTD  7000.00    19.0%   4000.00   3000.00  25.9% 42.9%

050 SPACE BAKERY         PTD  1050.00     9.6%    535.00    515.00  11.7% 49.0%
    NEW YORK          NY YTD  1050.00     2.8%    535.00    515.00   4.4% 49.0%

100 NEPTUNE BAKERY       PTD   600.00     5.5%    345.00    255.00   5.8% 42.5%
    SANTA MARINA      CA YTD   600.00     1.6%    345.00    255.00   2.2% 42.5%

200 21ST CENTURY BAKERY  PTD  2240.75    20.6%   1623.05    617.7   14.1% 27.6%
    SAN FRANCISCO     CA YTD 27699.31    75.2%  20137.87   7561.64  65.3% 27.3%

300 BEVERLY HILLS BAKER  PTD     0.00     0.0%      0.00      0.00   0.0%  0.0%
    LOS ANGELES       CA YTD     0.00     0.0%      0.00      0.00   0.0%  0.0%

600 ARIEL BAKERY         PTD     0.00     0.0%      0.00      0.00   0.0%  0.0%
    LOS ANGELES       CA YTD     0.00     0.0%      0.00      0.00   0.0%  0.0%

  9 CUSTOMERS
          TOTALS        PTD 10890.75   100.0%   6503.05   4387.70 100.0%
                        YTD 36849.31   100.0%  25267.87  11581.64 100.0%
```

Figure 1-4.
A sales-analysis report.

control over your sales and distribution channels and can help you evaluate where you need to focus your company's resources.

Avoiding the Pitfalls of Automation

Feature articles in *Business Week, Fortune,* and other popular magazines have warned that office workers whose jobs have been automated are not necessarily more productive than those who are still using manual systems; in some instances, they say, productivity might even be reduced. These articles cite several key issues that can lead to stagnant or decreased office productivity. Let's look at each of these issues in turn to see how preinstallation planning and effective project management can ensure a successful and profitable computer installation.

Underuse of the computer system. If your cost justification for a computer system is based on the tasks that will be automated, it does not matter what percentage of the workday the computer is used. The important thing is that those tasks are now performed faster and more efficiently. However, buying a computer in the hope that someone in your organization will take the time to use it for something productive is simply inviting a waste of a resource. You need a clear plan for how the computer will be used and a schedule for changing over to the automated system.

Underutilization of a resource, whether it is personnel or office automation equipment, must be perceived and addressed by management. Successful office automation requires that management have a basic understanding of computer technology and of how computers interface with existing manual office systems.

Creation of reports or tasks that negate the benefits of automating other tasks. It is important periodically to reevaluate all reports and paperwork generated within your organization. Even computer-generated paperwork takes time to produce. Look for ways to reorganize or eliminate unnecessary or unprofitable activities.

Automation of activities with low payoffs. Good planning will help you determine which areas of your company you should computerize and where automation will result in the greatest payback. As a general rule, activities that are complex and that are done infrequently are easier to do manually than with a computer. Computers are best at doing simple, repetitive, relatively straightforward tasks.

Computers can do only exactly what they are programmed to do. Although they can be programmed to make simple value judgments, such programming is usually not worth the effort it requires. Thus, many management activities are best carried out by human beings. Automation brings the greatest return in tasks involving the storage and retrieval of large amounts of data and ones in which the key elements are rapid processing, numerous calculations, and absolute accuracy.

For automation to be effective, your organization needs to have implemented standard procedures. If many of your policies have in the past been managed by exception, you will need to standardize computer-related office functions to adapt to the limitations of computer systems. For example, your company may offer different products or different pricing to different customers on the basis of the mood of your sales manager during the workday. If you want to take advantage of automated inventory management and billing, your sales manager is going to have to accept standard company policies. Computers can be programmed to provide favorable terms to a particular customer under certain circumstances, but a computer cannot make the kind of arbitrary management decisions that your sales manager may make.

Avoiding Computer Disasters

Without good preinstallation planning and ongoing management support, office automation can be unprofitable and, in extreme cases, disastrous. LRK Distributors decided to jump right into "computerization" with more optimism than common sense.

LRK Distributors

LRK Distributors was extremely angry with its computer supplier. Its management called in a consultant to sort out the mess and get things back on the right track. It quickly became apparent that what LRK really wanted was an expert opinion as to whether it had reasonable grounds to sue its system supplier! Expert or not, the consultant came well equipped with opinions.

It turned out that LRK had spent three weeks gathering and entering data into its new system. Unfortunately, a power surge during a storm had erased portions of the computer's memory. As you might have guessed, no one had thought to make another copy of the system's files on tapes or disks. The data was gone for good; it had to be reentered manually and then rechecked, causing a three-week setback.

It would not have been such a calamity, except that everyone was so enthusiastic about the new system that they had done a ''crash'' conversion and did not maintain their existing manual system during the first few weeks of operation. No one had anticipated that there would be any problems beyond ''fine tuning'' the system. When the consultant asked, no one could say exactly what fine tuning was.

There were even more problems! After learning how to make backup copies of the files, LRK began to rebuild its customer database. Things went smoothly, except that the customer software lumped the customer name together in one field, instead of breaking it down into first and last name. This made it impossible to find a particular customer's file without a customer number, which had to be looked up manually. With about 6000 customers, manual lookup made using the system painfully slow. The consultant added a last-name field to the database, reentered the customer names, and got LRK and its supplier back on speaking terms.

The people at LRK were very positive about office automation, but they got a bit ahead of themselves. If management had done more preinstallation planning and training, the operators would have learned the importance of making regular backup copies of the files. If their systems analyst had taken the time to double-check the data fields in their database, they would have avoided having to reenter their customers' names. And if they had run their manual system in parallel with the new automated system, they would have decreased their chances of losing any important information or of impairing day-to-day business operations as they made the transition to their automated system.

LRK suffered a setback, but now it is happy with its system. Like many other companies that have chosen to automate, LRK found that its learning curve was longer and steeper than had been anticipated. However, LRK's management was committed to its new automated system, and its perseverance paid off.

Learning to work with computers requires a great deal of patience. People expect computers to make their lives easier, not more complicated. To reap the benefits of automation, however, you and your staff will need to invest the time to learn to operate your system properly.

Automation and Your Personnel

Your personnel are the key to a successful conversion to an automated system. If they are involved and enthusiastic, you can be confident that you will be able to move forward with office automation. If they do not want to implement an automated system, you can be equally sure that your conversion will be plagued with problems. You will need to be sensitive to your own intracorporate politics and to resistance toward any organizational change.

It is very important to be supportive of your staff and to help them overcome their concerns about office automation. Many people have conscious or unconscious fears that computers will take their jobs, or that a machine can do their jobs better than they can.

A recent study conducted by George Mason University indicated that over 10 percent of professionals and managers suffer from "technostress." This type of stress occurs when a person must incorporate computers into his or her work. The study also found that about 3 percent of the entire work force suffers from "cyberphobia," or fear of computers. This can cause both mental and physical symptoms and may require extensive counseling.

You can do several things to help your staff overcome its anxiety about office automation. A well-thought-out training program is the best way to acquaint your employees with the new computer system and to raise their confidence in their ability to master it. Also, by implementing your system in planned phases you will be able to reduce or eliminate much of the stress associated with the learning of new skills.

You might want to purchase several computer games and encourage your employees to play with them. Computer games are just like video arcade games and can help people overcome the anxiety they feel when they "meet" a computer for the first time. However, after your staff has become comfortable with the system, you should erase the games and hide the disks in your wall safe. Playing computer games is fun and can become a very time-consuming habit.

If it is not your intent to have any layoffs, you should reassure your staff of this. It is also helpful to remind everyone that computers are designed to help them accomplish boring, repetitive tasks. Your employees should think of the computer as a business tool that they can use to make their jobs more productive and more interesting.

Some people in your organization are bound to resist change, but most will be excited about the opportunities that automation will offer them. Many people view working with a computer as a chance to learn something new, make themselves more valuable to their company, or increase their chances for promotion. Take the time to recognize individuals in your organization who are interested in working with computers.

Automation and Your Customers and Suppliers

Another challenge that you will face as you begin the transition to an automated system is presenting your automation as a benefit to your customers and suppliers. Emphasize the improved service that automation will allow you to offer your customers, and sell the organizational strengths of automation to your suppliers; this will help convince them that your new procedures are worth putting up with during your learning period.

If the transition to an automated system is not handled well, it can create serious problems. For example, although it often takes years to build a customer's trust, it takes only a few billing mistakes to lose that confidence and loyalty. Your transition to automation will require everyone's patience as your employees, your customers, and your suppliers learn about and adopt your new procedures and policies.

Computer Acquisition as a Business Proposition

Like most business executives, you are probably concerned with how computerization affects the bottom line. You want to know the tax implications, the impact on your business' cash flow, and the payback period for a positive return on your investment. Buyer's remorse will not set in if there are sound financial reasons for automating your business and if the system you choose is capable of meeting realistic expectations.

Before you commit to automating one or more of your business procedures or tasks, you must satisfy yourself that the potential rewards outweigh the possible risks and liabilities. You should consider automation only if you feel that it will result in reduced expenses or increased profits or if it is an investment that will provide future business opportunities.

Unfortunately, it is not intuitively obvious where or when automation is justified for different business activities in different organizations. In one organization it may be beneficial to automate the inventory-control system. In another company it may be unprofitable to automate inventory-control but extremely cost-effective to automate job-costing or payroll. The following chapters provide the information and techniques you need to evaluate the costs and benefits of office automation.

2

Determining Your Office Automation Needs

As you evaluate the possible benefits of computerization, the question to ask yourself is not, "Do I need a computer to help me run my business?" but, "Will it pay to automate one or more of my business activities?" Framing the question in this way will help you to set realistic expectations for office automation. Computers can automate tasks that you are already performing manually and can also provide the means to perform additional tasks that you would like to accomplish but cannot because of limited resources.

To determine which tasks are good candidates for automation, you need to take a detailed look at your existing manual systems. The largest gains in productivity are often obtained by the automation of complex, labor-intensive procedures. As a general rule, the more people there are involved in a procedure, the more difficult it is to evaluate the benefits of automation. This chapter describes a straightforward process that you can use to determine which areas of your company would profit from automation.

You will learn to analyze your procedures by completing a form that I call a "story" worksheet for each task. These worksheets will give you a detailed picture of the who, what, when, where, and why of a given activity. You will then use these worksheets to create flowcharts that depict the flow of data and information through your business. Once you have done this, you will analyze the worksheets and flowcharts to see if you can streamline your system in any way by reorganizing or eliminating activities. You will also find out how much it costs you to carry on each activity so that you can determine later whether it is worthwhile to computerize. Finally, you will see how to draw up a list of the features that a software package must have to meet your needs.

An Overview of the Planning Process

The process of planning for automation involves a thorough review of your current business procedures and a careful analysis of the costs involved in automating those procedures. The remainder of this section takes you step by step through this process. At the end you will know where computers can benefit your company and how long it will take for a computer system to pay for itself.

1. Create a story worksheet for each task or procedure that you are thinking of automating.

2. Diagram each task or procedure with a flowchart.

3. Analyze the story worksheets to see how efficient your current system is.

4. Estimate the current cost of each activity to establish a basis for a payback analysis.

5. Draw up a list of the features that you require in an automated system to help you evaluate different software and hardware systems.

6. Make preliminary decisions about software and hardware and choose a system supplier so that you can come up with an estimate of the cost of automation.

7. Work out a payback analysis that shows which tasks can be automated profitably and how long it will take before the system pays for itself.

8. Establish priorities for the activities you want to automate.

You will find that the process of planning and implementing an automated office system is not a linear one. You may wish to begin gathering information on available software and hardware before drawing up your feature list, for example, or you may want to read more about the different types of printers and display monitors before beginning your preliminary hardware selection. Take some time to skim through the rest of this book before you begin working through the planning steps. That way you will become familiar with the scope of the discussion and will know where to look for information.

One important chapter that falls later in the book is Chapter 8. It describes the process of automating a business from the early planning to the actual implementation. Turn to that chapter if you want to see what types of concerns are in store for you.

Creating the Story Worksheets

The best way to determine how automation can help your company is to put together the "story" of each task or procedure that you are thinking of automating. To help you gather all the information you need to analyze each task, I have developed a form that I call the "story" worksheet, shown in Figure 2-1 at the end of this chapter. Complete a separate story worksheet for each task or procedure that you think might be worth automating. Figures 2-2, 2-3, and 2-4, also at the end of this chapter, show examples of completed worksheets.

The set of story worksheets you develop will provide a framework that will help you analyze your current business situation. You will use the worksheets to determine what your automated system must be able to do and exactly what manual functions and operations it will replace. They will also help you establish a base cost for your manual operations.

Name of Activity

Write a brief title at the top of the worksheet to identify the activity it describes. This allows you to find the worksheet you want quickly, especially if you are creating worksheets for a number of different tasks.

Who Is Involved?

Determine who in your company is doing each task in the procedure you are considering automating. List the name and job title of each person involved.

You may find that people have become involved with tasks that have little or nothing to do with their formal job descriptions. In fact, the people responsible for actually doing the work often apportion or structure it in ways very different from the formal system devised by their managers.

After the worksheet is complete, ask the people involved to sign off on it in the space provided. Reading the worksheet will prepare them for procedural and organizational changes, and their signatures will show whether they agree with its description of what they are supposed to be doing.

What Is the Activity?

Next you need to describe the activity, whether it consists of writing up a sales invoice, ordering a part from the warehouse, or reproducing a copy of a contract that is on file. This section is the core of the story worksheets. From it you will develop a flowchart that illustrates the process.

First list the inputs, the data that is required for the task. Then describe the task itself, telling what is done to the inputs. Finally, give the results, or outputs, of the task: What do you have once the task is completed?

For many business activities, part of the output produced is information that will eventually be compiled in a management report. Now is a good time to begin thinking about the types of reports and other information you need to manage your business effectively. For example, you may require a report that summarizes your company's sales by region, or you might need to know how much business was done with a particular vendor or with a particular inventory item. Only you and your other information managers know what information is necessary for you to operate successfully.

Where Does It Occur?

In this section you need to evaluate how and where your company processes information. Indicate where the activity takes place and where the output it produces goes once the activity is completed.

It is essential that the people in your organization receive the information they need to do their jobs in a timely, coordinated manner. Manual office systems usually require information to be transferred from one department to another in the form of paper documents (sometimes referred to as hard copy by computer types). This causes a delay before the information on the document can be processed by the other department.

Flowcharts

Computer consultants—experts who study an organization's current procedures to see how and where automation can be effective—often use *flowcharts* to describe different activities in an organization. These charts are a powerful tool for gaining an overview of a system or procedure.

Flowcharts usually follow an "input-process-output" model. For each business activity that you are considering automating, your flowchart should show the key inputs, the process needed to accomplish the task, and the outputs of the activity. This is why the story worksheets include input, process, and output subheadings. Figure 2-5 gives a sample flowchart for an accounts-receivable process. Other flowcharts can be found in Chapter 13.

To create a flowchart, draw a box for each element of the activity. Use a separate box for each type of input, for each step of the process, and for each type of output. Connect the boxes with arrows showing the flow of information. You can use one shape for all of the input, another for all of the steps in the process, and so forth. If you are interested in producing neat, professional-looking flowcharts, buy a flowchart template at an office supply store.

Flowcharts can help you see how the information that is communicated to different areas of your company is produced. This can help you reorganize your office systems for maximum efficiency. Use flowcharts in conjunction with the story worksheets to help you visualize each process that you are thinking of automating.

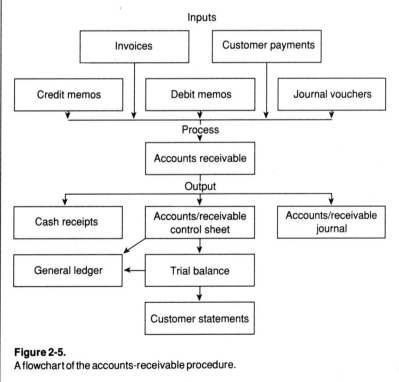

Figure 2-5.
A flowchart of the accounts-receivable procedure.

Automated office systems can sort and organize data electronically, so that several different departments can access the data.

When Does It Occur?

Here you should indicate when and how often a task is performed. Activities that are performed on an exception basis or that occur very infrequently generally do not produce cost savings when they are automated. Daily routines or procedures that rely on extensive paperwork or clerical support generally are best suited to office automation.

Why Is the Activity Done?

When office procedures are reviewed, management is often surprised to find that certain activities that have become part of the routine are no longer necessary or are already being accomplished in other areas of the organization. Analyze your story worksheets carefully to see exactly why different tasks are being done. You may find that some habits have outlived their usefulness.

How Can Automation Improve Efficiency?

In this section you should evaluate how automation could improve the productivity of your organization. You might find that it would be profitable to automate some or all of a department's activities, or you may discover that reorganizing or eliminating activities from your existing manual system would be best for your organization.

Analyzing the Worksheets

Now that you have gathered information on the tasks you might automate, you are ready to spend some time analyzing your findings. Examine the story worksheets and flowcharts to make sure your system is as streamlined and efficient as possible. Interacting routines and procedures can usually be broken down into smaller tasks. Simple, well-defined procedures are easiest to automate.

It may be necessary to reorganize your business procedures or work flow in order to implement an automated system. There are no set rules to help you here. You will need to assess the value of each step and activity to determine whether your current systems offer a reasonably efficient way of getting the job done.

As you found in the ''why'' section of the worksheet, many reports and procedures remain in place out of habit. Shaking off old habits that no longer serve a purpose can revitalize an operation. Automating an inefficient system or unnecessary tasks may simply cause further confusion and loss of productivity.

On the other hand, your analysis of the worksheets may turn up reports or procedures that are lacking in your current manual systems. You may also find that automation will help you to implement some processes that would be too time-consuming to perform manually.

Estimating Activity Costs

As part of your analysis of the story worksheets, you should put a price on each activity that reflects how much it currently costs you to perform that task manually. This cost is a crucial part of the payback analysis you will do later to see whether it is worthwhile to automate that activity.

Begin by examining the inputs, processes, and outputs on the story worksheet. How much does each cost you? Estimate the time spent by each person involved in the task. You can express this as a number of hours per day, week, or month or as a percentage of total work time. Then multiply your time estimate by the person's hourly wage or annual salary. Regardless of how you calculate the time spent, your final figure should be the current annual cost of the activity.

If you are thinking of switching from an outside bookkeeping service to an in-house automated accounting system, simply list the amount you pay per year to have your books done. (For an example of a payback analysis, see Chapter 6.)

Preparing a Feature List

Once you have completed your story worksheets, you can begin to create a *feature list*. This is simply a list of the features an automated system must have in order to interface with your current manual office systems and provide you with the information you need to manage your business. Creating a feature list is time-consuming, but it will help you find an automated system that handles *all* of your company's needs.

You will find that some features are absolutely necessary and that others, although they may be desirable, are ones that you can live without.

I call these required (R) and desired (D) features, respectively. For example, in your company, the ability to account for back orders may be a required feature, whereas having a data field to store your customers' purchase order numbers may be desirable but not required.

Chapter 12 and Chapter 13 provide skeleton feature lists that you can use to put together your own feature lists for specific accounting and office productivity tasks. (Office productivity software includes programs for word processing, file management, financial analysis, and project management.)

Figure 2-6 shows a sample feature list for software to handle the accounts receivable for a typical distribution business. The format shown in

Function	Required/ Desirable	Available in System 1	Available in System 2
Handle balance forward	R		
Handle open items	R		
Perform standard 30-/60-/90-day aging	R		
Permit variable aging periods	D		
Calculate finance charges	R		
Support multiple divisions	R		
Support multiple companies	D		
Automatically post invoice totals from order processing	R		
Handle month-end reporting	R		
Do exception reporting	D		
Post cash and partial payments	R		
Handle discount accounting	R		
Handle payments on account	D		
Support multiple data-entry terminals	R		
Support laser printers	D		
Support networked microcomputers	D		
Support color display monitors	D		

Figure 2-6.
Sample feature list for an accounts receivable application.

the figure allows you to indicate which features are available in the different software packages or hardware solutions you are evaluating. This will give you an objective comparison of the different systems.

Taking the Next Step

By now you should have a good picture of your existing office procedures and what they cost and some idea of the features you need in an automated system. Your next step is to estimate the cost of a system that will meet your needs. To do this you must go through the process of selecting software and hardware and choosing a system supplier. These topics are discussed in the next three chapters.

As you will see, the cost of automation involves much more than the price you pay for software and hardware. Training and service are only two of the other costs you need to consider. Once you have an estimate of all the costs involved in your automation project, you will be ready to do a payback analysis to see what areas of your business you can profitably automate and to establish priorities for automation.

Name of activity:

WHO is involved?

_____   _____

_____   _____

_____   _____

_____   _____

_____   _____

WHAT is the activity?

INPUTS to the task:

PROCESS—the actual task:

OUTPUTS from the task:

WHERE does it occur?

Figure 2-1.
The story worksheet.

WHEN does it occur?

WHY is the activity done?

HOW can automation improve efficiency?

Expected Impact of Automation:

Management Approvals for Modification or Automation of Current Systems:

Feasibility: (knowledgeable in-house person, system supplier, or consultant)	**Cost Effectiveness:** (financial manager)
Reasonability: (department manager)	**Final Approval:** (the boss)

Figure 2-1. *(continued)*

Name of activity:
Process customer orders

WHO is involved?

John Bugler, sales representative   Bill Peters, warehouse supervisor

Patty Scene, sales representative   Mary Pelnick, accounting records

Trudy Roberts, sales representative   Tom Brown, department manager

Tom Pelenton, warehouse picker   Al Brown, the boss

Bob Young, warehouse loader, driver

WHAT is the activity?

INPUTS to the task:
All customer orders.

PROCESS—the actual task:
The order is entered, the customer's credit is checked, and a four-part
order form is generated.

OUTPUTS from the task:
Customer invoice
Picking slip
Packing slip
Shipping slip

WHERE does it occur?
The order form is filled out by a sales representative in the sales department.
The sales representative is responsible for doing a credit check before any
merchandise is shipped.
The customer invoice is sent to the billing department.
The picking slip is sent to the warehouse and then to the billing department,
where it is matched with the invoice before a final statement is sent to
the customer.
The packing slip is sent to the warehouse to be sent to the customer along
with the order.
The shipping slip is sent to the warehouse to be given to the freight carrier
when the order is shipped.

Figure 2-2.
Sample story worksheet for the order entry department of Northwest Floors.

WHEN does it occur?

Whenever a customer orders merchandise.

WHY is the activity done?

To generate the paperwork that is necessary to deliver merchandise
to customers.
To generate the input necessary for the accounting department to bill
customers accurately for merchandise that is shipped.

HOW can automation improve efficiency?

A sales representative could use a computer to generate a four-part form when
a customer order is received. The form would include the customer invoice
and the picking, packing, and shipping slips.
The computer could perform credit checking automatically by calling up the
customer's file and checking the outstanding balance.
A computerized order-entry system could automatically generate picking
slips in a logical sequence to improve the productivity of the pickers
in the warehouse.
A computer could update the back-order file immediately when necessary
and could automatically print a card to notify the customer of an
expected delivery date.
Daily sales journals could be updated immediately for posting to the general
ledger, and both the accounts receivable and inventory files could be updated
automatically when an order was received.
A computerized order-entry system could generate input for sales analysis
reports and sales commission reports.

Expected Impact of Automation:

Sales personnel will save time because the paperwork involved in order
writing will be reduced.
Picking in the warehouse will be faster and more accurate.
Orders will be internally easier to track.
Paperwork for customer billing will be processed faster.
Collection of receivables will be faster because customer invoices will
go out faster.
Accounts receivable and inventory files will be more accurate and up-to-date.

Management Approvals for Modification or Automation of Current Systems:

Feasibility: William Stone, Good Guy Consulting	**Cost Effectiveness:** William Brown, financial officer
Reasonability: Thomas Brown, department manager	**Final Approval:** Al Brown, the boss

Figure 2-2. *(continued)*

Name of activity:
Typing correspondence and legal documents

WHO is involved?

John Derik, attorney	Maury Hope, paralegal
Frank Sharp, attorney	Pauline Shultz, office manager
Alan Profit, attorney	Sherry Lobell, typist
Patty Cerino, attorney	Dana Lindmann, typist
Trudy Schwartz, paralegal	Tricia Peddle, administrative assistant

WHAT is the activity?
Typing and editing all correspondence and legal documents.

INPUTS to the task:
Handwritten, dictated or boilerplate correspondence and legal documents.

PROCESS—the actual task:
Correspondence and legal documents are dictated or handwritten by one
of our attorneys. The handwritten notes, modified boilerplate, or tapes are
put into the typing queue. Urgent responses are always expedited. Documents
are then typed, proofed, edited, and returned to the requesting attorney
for changes or approval.
All standard contract and document boilerplate is retyped and refiled each
time it is used.

OUTPUTS from the task:
Typed, edited, and proofed correspondence and legal documents.

WHERE does it occur?
In the clerical area.

Figure 2-3.
Sample story worksheet for word processing at Derik, Peterson and Crouch.

WHEN does it occur?

Virtually every legal document is processed by the clerical staff
and then resubmitted to an attorney for changes or approval.

WHY is the activity done?

Documents must be submitted in a standard format for the courts.

HOW can automation improve efficiency?

All boilerplate text could be stored in electronic files. The word
processor could modify the boilerplate as necessary. This would
eliminate the need to retype entire forms and documents. This would
save over 75 percent of the time we currently spend retyping standard
contracts and documents.
Revisions and edits could be done over 50 percent faster using a word
processor than using manual typewriters.
Fewer typos and corrections on our documents would create a more
professional image for our firm.

Expected Impact of Automation:

Our existing clerical staff could handle our firm's anticipated clerical
needs over the next fiscal year.
The turnaround time for documents could be reduced to one working day
for over 90 percent of all typing requests.
Our clerical staff would enjoy their work more since they would be able
to spend less time retyping documents.

Management Approvals for Modification or Automation of Current Systems:

Feasibility:	**Cost Effectiveness:**
Bill Thomas, System Supplier, ABC Computer Co.	John Derik, Managing Attorney
Reasonability:	**Final Approval:**
Pauline Shultz, Department Manager	John Derik, Managing Attorney

Figure 2-3. *(continued)*

Name of activity:

Job Costing and Bidding

WHO is involved?

Blaine Gorski, Department Manager

Tom Browning, Senior Staff Engineer

Ingred Ramirez, Engineer

Patricia Cooper, Engineer

Alan David, Engineer

WHAT is the activity?

Each request for quotation (RFQ) or request for proposal (RFP) must be
responded to in a timely, accurate manner.

INPUTS to the task:

Past costing data.
Current customer requirements.

PROCESS—the actual task:

A review team responds to each RFP or RFQ. One technical support engineer
and one project manager are assigned to each project.
The department manager supervises all activities and approves all cost
estimates and proposals.

OUTPUTS from the task:

The output of the bidding process is a bid response tailored to the
prospective customer's specific requirements.

WHERE does it occur?

The work is usually done in-house, unless site visits are required to help
interpret the customer's requirements.

Figure 2-4.
Sample story worksheet for Laurence Electronics.

WHEN does it occur?

The department is usually involved in responding to five or more outstanding RFPs or RFQs. The average response currently requires between 15 and 20 man-days of work to complete.

WHY is the activity done?

All proposals and bids must be accurate and competitive. Bids that are too high will be lost to competitors, bids that are too low will result in insufficient profitability on awarded jobs.

HOW can automation improve efficiency?

Automation would allow us to store our existing cost data in one database. All of our engineers would be able to use the same data. Using up-to-date costing information would allow us to bid more aggressively.
An automated system would help check for errors and improve the accuracy of our bid responses.
Cost estimating software would allow us to calculate the required time and materials for each activity. This would reduce bid preparation time significantly.
The program would also help us create the documentation necessary to support our bid responses.

Expected Impact of Automation:

Our staff will be able to respond to more RFPs and RFQs.
Our bids will more accurately reflect our current costing structures.
Our engineers will be able to spend more time working directly with our customers on pre-bid sales activities.

Management Approvals for Modification or Automation of Current Systems:

Feasibility:	Cost Effectiveness:
Frank Milcott, V.P. Information Services	Harold Hausemann, Executive V.P.
Reasonability:	Final Approval:
Blaine Gorski, Department Manager	Harold Hausemann, Executive V.P.

Figure 2-4. *(continued)*

3

Selecting Business Software

This chapter helps you evaluate and select the business software that will best meet the needs of your business. Because many software packages run only on specific hardware configurations, you should select the software you will be using *before* you choose any hardware.

In selecting business software, you must take several factors into consideration:

Functionality. Does it offer the features and capabilities you need? Does it parallel your current office procedures?

Performance and usability. How easy is it to install and learn? Is it fast enough for your needs?

Support. What types of training materials does the manufacturer offer? Can you call the manufacturer with questions? Are any products (books, tutorials, and so forth) available from third parties?

These issues are discussed in more detail in the sections that follow. The subject of support will come up again in Chapter 5. The last part of this chapter helps you decide whether off-the-shelf software or custom software will best meet your needs.

Discussions of specific features of office productivity and accounting software can be found in Chapters 12 and 13.

Evaluating Features and Capabilities

The most common complaint of business people who have installed a computer system is that the system is unable to perform a function that they either require or desire it to do. Make sure that the application software you choose provides the features and capabilities, or functionality, you need to automate the work that you have been doing manually.

It is easy to overlook things that make an otherwise excellent program useless for your specific needs. Just because most companies do something in a particular way does not mean that the particular software you are evaluating uses the same reasonable approach. You will have to read the program's documentation carefully and in most cases actually run an application yourself to get an idea of a program's features and limitations.

If the documentation for a program does not explicitly state that it will do something, the only safe assumption is that the feature or option is *not* included. For example, a company that is distantly related to LRK Distributors discovered that their general ledger program did not provide any way of consolidating the financial reports from their different divisions. This was discovered after the company had already installed the program and used it for eight months. They were furious with the program, with their supplier, and ultimately with themselves. You can easily avoid this problem by carefully comparing a program's features with the features that you specified in the feature lists you developed in Chapter 2.

You also need to evaluate whether the software will work well with your other office systems. If the software you choose does not closely parallel your current manual office systems, you will have to change the way you do things.

Another consideration, if you have already begun thinking about hardware, is whether the application software that you select will work with your current or proposed hardware configuration and with hardware and software packages that you anticipate adding to your system in the future. For example, many so-called IBM-compatible software products are not supported on IBM's Token Ring local-area network. If you think you might install a network of this type in the future, you need to confirm that the software that you select will work on it. The bottom line is that you should not assume that the features or capabilities you require are included in different software products.

Performance and Usability

Although functionality is the main factor in the selection of software, you also need to consider how easy it will be for you to install and use the applications you are evaluating. Ideally, software should be easy to use and learn, work perfectly, and interface, or link, properly with all related applications. Unfortunately, software often requires many hours of training, works correctly almost all of the time but may have "bugs," or programming errors, and usually does not work well with other software.

Well-designed software applications are written to be as *intuitive* to use as possible. Intuitive applications closely parallel the manual functions that are being automated and provide logical and easy transitions as the user moves from one activity to another.

Well-designed programs also provide a logical, easy-to-understand *user interface*. The user interface is the part of the program that the user

---

Do Computers Make Mistakes?

GIGO stands for "garbage in, garbage out." If bad information or data is entered into your computer system, your reports and files will be corrupted. As in a manual system, such mistakes must be corrected or your data and reports will be inaccurate. Most of the "computer errors" that you hear about or even experience firsthand are really data-entry errors made by human beings.

Assuming that there are no bugs in your system and that you have entered the correct data into your program, you can be almost 100 percent sure that your data will be computed accurately and that the results will be correct. Error rates for computer chips are now as low as less than one in one hundred million computations. That is orders of magnitude better than most accounting services!

The only way to verify that your system has absolutely no programming errors is to test it under literally every possible condition. Program developers run software known as "test suites" that are meant to do this; this software automatically checks programs for errors that would be difficult or impossible to find manually. Many popular business application programs do have minor programming errors, however. In most cases, the only thing you can do about bugs is report them to the software developer and hope that the company can track them down and eliminate them.

If other businesses have been running the same application program on the same hardware that you plan to implement, and they have not had any problems, your system will probably be free of any serious bugs. Most popular off-the-shelf general-accounting programs and office-productivity tools have been installed on thousands of computer systems and are well tested.

sees and interacts with; it consists of screens and command prompts that allow data entry and screens that present processed data to the user.

Most business programs have *menu screens* that offer lists of choices with which the user can direct the program to execute tasks or enter data. (See Figure 3-1.) Another type of user interface presents a *command line* at the bottom of the interactive work area. A command line allows the user to enter commands that direct the program to perform different functions. (See Figure 3-2.)

Both types of interface have advantages and disadvantages. The advantage of menus is that they are easy to learn. The disadvantage is that once you learn the system, menus will slow you down. Command languages are usually more difficult to learn but allow more rapid program execution. Some well-designed software uses both menus and command languages. (See Figure 3-3.) This allows users to go through the menus when they are learning the program and enter commands after they have mastered the program.

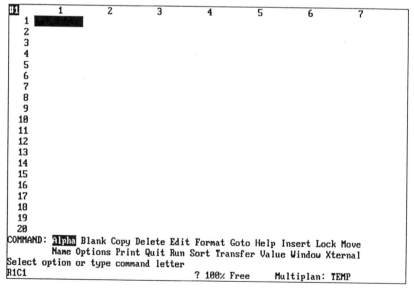

Figure 3-1.
An example of a menu screen in Multiplan.

```
A:\>
```

Figure 3-2.
An example of a command line in MS-DOS.

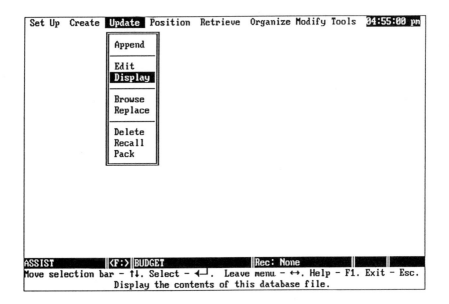

Figure 3-3.
Examples of a menu (top) and command line (bottom) in dBASE III.

Some software developers have designed their programs to emulate the user interface and special program commands of the most popular office productivity applications. This allows users who are experienced with "standard" application programs to learn new programs faster. For example, several developers of word-processing software have copied WordStar's text-formatting commands. They feel that duplicating this well-known user interface will help them market their products to the hundreds of thousands of WordStar-trained office workers.

Graphics-based application environments, such as Apple's Macintosh computer and Microsoft's Windows software, treat the computer screen as a "desk." On the desk are *icons*, or graphic symbols that represent software tools and programs that the user can select and execute using a pointing device known as a *mouse*. For example, a telephone, representing a telecommunications program; file folders, representing data files; and other icons, such as calendars or calculators, can be selected. Applications appear on the screen as discrete tasks in separate windows. A graphics-based application environment makes working with different software packages easier and more intuitive. Figures 3-4 and 3-5 illustrate this type of environment.

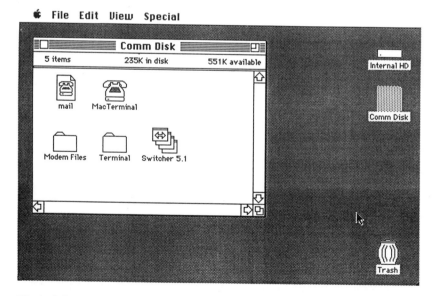

Figure 3-4.
An example of the graphics-based environment of the Apple Macintosh.

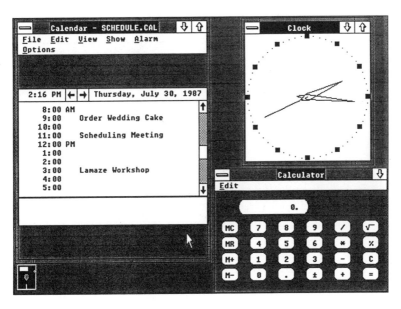

Figure 3-5.
An example of the graphics-based environment of Microsoft Windows.

The trade-off is that graphics-based applications usually run a bit slower than text-based applications. This is because graphics programs are usually larger and more complex and because the computer system takes more time to "paint" the graphics images on the screen. Microcomputers using the latest microprocessors and graphics coprocessor chips can make up for the additional processing overhead of graphics applications and provide a good *system response time*. System response time is the amount of time it takes for the computer to respond to a command. A good system response time means that your system appears to process your data instantaneously and is always ready to accept your next program command.

At this point, the computer industry has not agreed on a standard graphics-based user interface for application programs. End users must learn different sets of commands for each program that they want to use. Microsoft's Windows environment has received the most support in the business microcomputer market and will probably become the standard microcomputer interface as it is adopted by more computer manufacturers and software developers. Integrated graphics application environments are discussed in more detail in Chapter 12.

Support

Support for a software package includes all of the information that helps you install and learn to use the program. The amount of learning time needed before a person can use the program will be an important factor in the cost analysis you perform in Chapter 5.

User-Friendly Software

When a beginner can sit down with a software package and begin using it with little or no prior training, the program is said to be *user friendly*. It is difficult to design a program with which the user can perform complex tasks without the need for some level of training. This is primarily

---

Graphics-Based Word Processing

Graphics-based word processing programs running in a windowing environment can show you exactly what your final documents will look like when they are printed. For example, if your document is going to be printed in 10-point Helvetica type, a 10-point Helvetica "font" is shown on your computer's display, as shown in Figure 3-6. Word processors that offer this feature are sometimes called "WYSIWYG," or "what you see is what you get" programs.

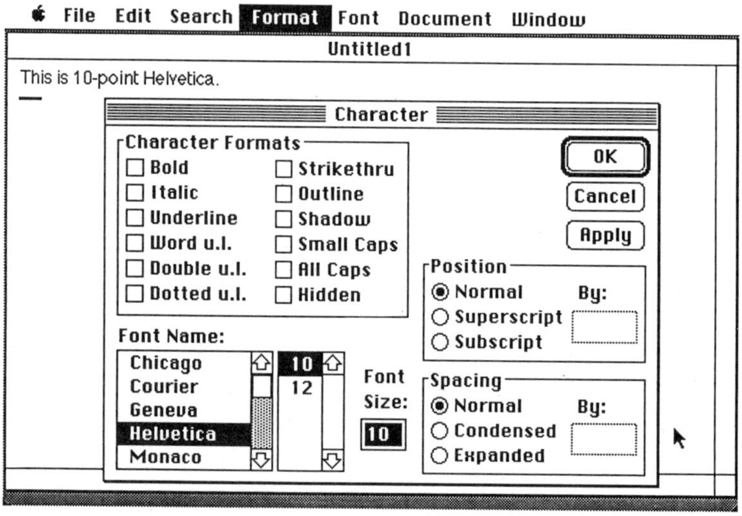

Figure 3-6.
Selecting 10-point Helvetica font in Microsoft Word for the Macintosh.

because the help information that is so useful in the beginning can become a burden once the program has been mastered.

One solution to this problem is to have ''context-based'' help that the user can request at any time while the application is running. (See Figure 3-7.) With this type of help, the program ''knows'' what step of the program you are working on and responds with help information that relates to your current activity. Most good productivity software now offers context-based *on-line* help. On-line help means that the help information is available on disk and is accessible from within the program.

Program developers assume that the user of the program will be able to understand and respond to the system-generated help information. In fact, many help prompts restate the obvious and are no more useful than a written list of the program's commands: It would be nearly impossible for programmers to anticipate every potential user error or problem. Therefore, most application developers supplement their on-line help facilities with written software documentation and other training materials.

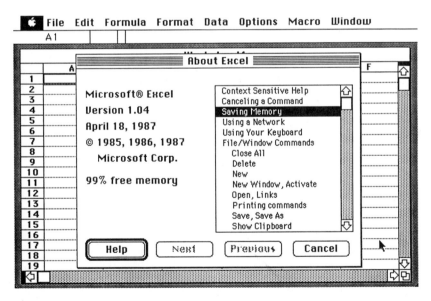

Figure 3-7.
Context-based help in Microsoft Excel for the Macintosh.

Software Documentation

Documentation is a written description of what a software application does and how it works. Good documentation does not have to be typeset on 24-pound bond, but it must be laid out clearly and should not assume that the user is a software engineer. Good documentation should also have simple amenities like tables of contents, indexes, and diagrams that clarify how the program works. If the documentation is disorganized or difficult for you to understand, you will require more support from your system supplier to implement your applications.

It usually helps to examine the introductory or overview section of the documentation first to get an idea of how the program is organized and what approach the software developer has used to automate a particular office task. Then you should examine the program's reference and tutorial sections. These should be clearly presented and should address all of the features that are supported by the program. Of course, the ultimate test of any documentation is to use it when you need help and see whether it answers your questions.

Software Training

Training is offered in many different forms. Self-training through computer-aided instruction (CAI) courses (these are also sometimes referred to as CBT, or computer-based training courses) that actually run with the application are one of the best ways to learn how to use software. CAI tutorials are included with many of the general business applications sold through retail distribution channels.

If the program you are interested in has a CAI program, you should try it out before you purchase the product. If the training materials for a software product are deficient, it will be more difficult for you to install and implement your applications, and you will have to rely more on your supplier for product support.

Computer classes are offered on topics ranging from basic computer operations to advanced programming techniques. In-store seminars are offered for many of the standard software packages sold by retail computer dealers. These seminars usually provide a good introduction to the features offered by different office automation programs. Many computer retailers and software suppliers offer classes that help their customers explore the more advanced features of their software products. Finally, many public and private colleges and trade schools offer extension classes and regular courses on just about every aspect of computers and office automation.

Software Quality and Price

A number of low-priced software packages are available that offer the same level of functionality as more-expensive products from leading software companies. You will need to consider the usability and support for each package that you evaluate to help you determine the real cost of installing and implementing each application.

For example, Lotus 1-2-3, the best-selling microcomputer spreadsheet application, has a suggested retail price of $495, while VP Planner and several other financial spreadsheet programs sell for under $150. All of these programs allow you to build complex financial worksheets and create simple business graphics; several of them have copied Lotus's user interface and offer a comparable level of functionality.

Reflex is an innovative database program that originally sold for $495, and competed with Ashton Tate's dBase III and Microrim's R:Base 5000. It did not do very well in the market. Borland International acquired the rights to Reflex and began to sell it directly to customers by mail order for $99.95. Reflex has since become a best-selling software product.

DAC Easy accounting software sells for $69.95. It is an integrated software package that contains seven modules: general ledger, accounts payable, accounts receivable, sales analysis, order entry, inventory control, and forecasting. It has been rated as one of the best software products of the year by *InfoWorld* magazine. DAC's package is adequate for the accounting needs of many small companies.

The more expensive software packages usually provide more features and are better supported than their lower-priced counterparts. However, there is not always a clear relationship between cost and quality. This is primarily because different software companies use different marketing strategies to position, support, and sell their products. As competition in the software market increases, you will find more good-quality software at low prices.

Off-the-Shelf Versus Custom Software

Years ago little software was available for business computers. If you needed to automate a particular task, you often had to write *custom software* yourself or contract out the work. These days, thousands of programs are available *off-the-shelf* to handle virtually all common business applications. Rarely do business users ever have to program their own application software.

The trade-off between off-the-shelf software and custom software is that in most cases only custom programming will exactly fit your company's current operating procedures and requirements. However, most off-the-shelf applications can be tailored, or configured, to fit common differences in business operating procedures. For example, many automated inventory-management systems can be configured to support LIFO, FIFO, or average-cost accounting.

Software can also be configured to run on different types of computer hardware. For example, the Apple Macintosh II can be configured to run with either a monochrome graphics display or a color graphics display (see Figure 3-8).

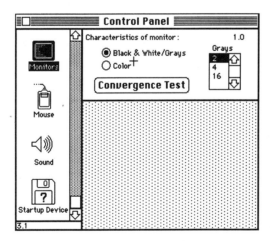

Figure 3-8.
The dialog box on the Apple Macintosh II for choosing between a color and a black-and-white monitor.

The configuring of software cannot add features or capabilities to an application unless they have already been coded into the program. If you need to add features or capabilites to an existing application, you must *modify* the software.

Modifying Software Programs

Depending on your company's requirements, you may decide to modify an existing program to add more functions, or to make it work more smoothly with your manual office systems. Modifying software is usually far less expensive than writing custom software.

Before you purchase any office automation software that you intend to modify, you should understand exactly what modifications the software supplier will allow you to make and what support will be provided to help facilitate those changes. Some software suppliers will sell you the *source code* to their program. The source code is the actual program as written by the programmer. Having the source code allows another programmer to modify the application to incorporate your changes. Unfortunately, access to source code also allows dishonest programmers to steal portions of the program for their own use.

For this reason, most software developers will not sell their programs' source code; however, they often provide enough documentation to allow a competent programmer to patch modifications into the original program's code. The caveat here is that unless the programmer who modifies the software is competent, he or she may introduce programming errors that foul up the entire program.

The consultant or programmer who will be modifying your application should establish a good rapport with a technical support person from the software company. Modifying software written by someone else is like trying to finish a song that someone else has started. Unless you are very familiar with the programming tools and techniques used by the original programmer, and unless the program's code is well documented, you may feel as though you have opened a Pandora's box.

Computer programming languages like BASIC and Pascal have been designed to make it easier to write programs. However, programming is still time-consuming and can be very complex. I strongly recommend that you employ experienced software developers rather than eager but inexperienced students whenever possible. An experienced programmer can program an application in a fraction of the time that a novice can and is much less likely to introduce bugs that would make the code unusable.

Figure 3-9 shows comparisons among off-the-shelf, system-integrator-supplied, and custom applications.

Selecting Office Productivity and Accounting Software

Software developers must compromise between writing applications that supply every possible function but that are large, slow, and difficult to work with, and writing programs that provide fewer features but are faster and easier to use. Because different users have different requirements, a number of software programs have been written to meet a wide range of needs. You will require a different type of software to perform each type of office task that you automate.

A BASIC Computer Program

The following simple program written in the BASIC programming language will print "This will print 5 times." on your screen five times. Then it will print out "That's all, folks!" and the program will end.

```
10 FOR N = 1 TO 5
20 PRINT " This will print
   5 times."
30 NEXT N
40 PRINT " That's all, folks!"
50 END
```

BASIC, Pascal, C, RPG-II, and COBOL are some of the common computer-programming languages used for business applications. These "high-level" languages are easy to use because they offer English-like commands, such as PRINT and ADD. Low-level assembly languages are much more difficult to learn and use because the programmer must pay more attention to the details of how the computer carries out each instruction. Regardless of the language used, the computer can understand only machine language (binary code), which is made up of 0s and 1s. Programs called compilers or assemblers convert the commands written by the programmer into machine language.

The more features and capabilities a program has, and the easier to use it is, the more programming is required. Most business programs have thousands of lines of code. Depending on the skills of the programmer, software can provide robust features, good performance, and ease of use, or it can be missing important features, have serious programming errors, and be slow and cumbersome to use.

Office productivity applications are programs that allow office workers and managers to increase their effectiveness by reducing the amount of time they spend on repetitive clerical tasks and by increasing the efficiency and accuracy of their work. Databases, electronic spreadsheets, and word-processing software are the major productivity software tools used in offices. Other examples of productivity software include programs for project management, job costing, business graphics, electronic mail, and time management. One or more of these applications is installed on virtually every business computer system. This type of software is discussed in much more detail in Chapter 12.

Most industries have specific requirements that office automation systems must address. For example, department stores need to have product descriptions that allow them to specify the manufacturer, type, style, color, size, and department code for each item of merchandise. Unless an automated system is set up to handle these specific requirements, it will be impossible for a business to automate its manual systems successfully or to generate useful management reports.

Standard industry applications are software packages that have been written to address the needs of a particular industry. They are often referred to as *vertical* applications. Off-the-shelf standard industry applications are available for government and educational users, professional organizations, service companies, manufacturers, distributors, and retailers.

Type of Application	Functionality	Support	Cost
Off-the-shelf standard industry applications	Generally requires some modifications; can be configured	Good	Low
VAR, or system-integrator-supplied, applications (discussed in Chapter 5)	Very close fit; can generally match all required features and some desired features	Good to excellent	Medium
Custom applications	Should match all required and desired features	Typically either excellent or inadequate	High

Figure 3-9.
A comparison of factors in selecting business software

Standard industry applications are usually based on *accounting appli-cations* that have been designed to address the needs of a particular type of business. Accounting applications are used to automate many different tasks, such as accounts payable, accounts receivable, inventory control, order entry and billing, payroll, and financial analysis. Chapter 13 discusses accounting applications in much greater detail.

Once you have decided on the software you would like to use, you can begin to evaluate the different hardware systems that will run those applications. That is the topic of the next chapter.

Software Buyer's Checklist

■ Automate only those areas of your business in which efficiency will be improved or overhead reduced. Continue to use the story worksheets to plan and justify all changes to your business operations.

■ Be sure that you are automating the simplest manual system.

■ Compare various software products using your feature lists to find an application that provides the functions you require to automate each office task. You do not have to know how the software you buy works, but you do need to understand exactly what work your software does. As you carefully compare different software products to your feature lists, check off each item that you require.

■ Evaluate standard off-the-shelf packages whenever possible. Software packages from major software companies tend to have more installed users and better user support and are usually supported by more hardware and software products from other systems suppliers.

■ Always ask for a demonstration of the exact system that you will be implementing. Compare the ease of use and the "feel" of several different software packages to see which you are more comfortable with. Demonstration software that is easy to use and is well documented usually reflects the quality of the fully functional product. However, the best way to judge the capabilities, performance, and ease of use of an application is to sit down and use the real program with real data. Real application software is rarely as simple to use or as fast as optimized demonstration programs with sample data.

■ Carefully review the program's documentation. All features in the application should be well documented.

■ Evaluate all bundled or third-party training materials that you or your personnel will be using.

■ Determine how compatible the software is with leading industry-standard software and application packages. (This will be discussed in Chapter 5.)

■ Determine whether the package can easily be configured or modified to fit your software or hardware requirements.

■ List the advantages and disadvantages of each application that meets your minimum requirements. You can "weight" each requirement according to how important you feel it is.

Operating System Software

Before we can discuss hardware requirements, one other special kind of software must be described. *Operating system software* is the "interface" between application software and your system's hardware. (See Figure 3-10.) The operating system is a set of programs containing the instructions that allow the hardware to process your application software.

Operating system software is usually loaded into the computer's main memory when the system is first started. Part of the operating system remains in the computer's memory as long as the power is on. Less frequently used parts of the operating system are loaded into main memory from disk whenever they are needed. The memory-resident portion of the operating system handles ongoing system functions; for example, it manages the computer's main memory and controls the flow of information to and from the system's different input and output devices. Special functions, such as the formatting of new disks, are handled by operating system utilities that the system loads into main memory as it needs them.

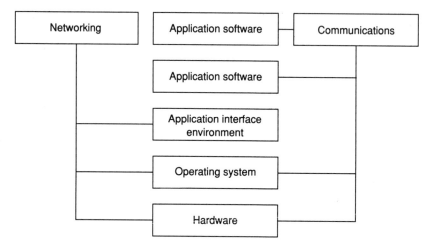

Figure 3-10.
The operating system's place in a computer system.

Part of the memory-resident operating system is hidden from the system's user and works like an invisible traffic cop, directing the system's activities. The other part of the operating system can be controlled by the user through system commands. These commands direct the computer's hardware to perform different functions, such as copying disks or directing the computer's output to a modem or printer.

Multitasking Systems

Microcomputers that use the MS-DOS version 3.x operating system are *single tasking*. This means that they can run only one program at a time. To run a second program, you need to stop the first program, load the second program into your computer's memory, and then start up the second application. Loading programs is time-consuming, and so it is inconvenient to switch back and forth between programs too often.

Microcomputers that run *multitasking* operating systems, such as OS/2, are able to run more than one program or task at the same time. For example, you could update your customer's accounts receivable files, transfer a document via a telecommunications link with your home office, and check an appointment on your electronic calendar without having to wait for each task to finish processing before you could load the next application. Multitasking operating-system software optimizes the use of your computer's time.

Multiuser Systems

Microcomputers have traditionally been single-user systems. They were created so that the individual would be able to have all of the computer system's resources for his or her own use. Minicomputers and mainframe computers allow the computer's resources to be shared among many users, each getting slices of the system's attention; this is called *time-sharing.* However, now that microcomputers are becoming as powerful as larger minicomputers were just a few years ago, it is possible for them to run *multiuser* operating systems such as UNIX or XENIX System V. Multiuser operating systems allow more than one workstation to time-share the same computer system.

Multiuser operating systems also allow more than one user to have access to the same program file simultaneously. For example, in an order-entry system in which many salespeople are taking sales orders, a multiuser operating system would allow each salesperson to enter data into the system at his or her own workstation, with the system keeping one up-to-date file of the company's current inventory.

Multiuser systems require special file protection. *File and record locking* is a software feature that allows more than one user to access the same program file simultaneously without accidentally writing over one another's work. The features of the leading microcomputer operating systems are shown in Figure 3-11.

Operating System	Single Tasking	Multi-Tasking	Single User	Multiuser
MS-DOS version 3.x*	X		X	
IBM OS/2		X	X	
XENIX System V		X		X
UNIX System V		X		X
Macintosh	X		X	

*MS-DOS versions 3.1 and later have local-area networking support

Figure 3-11.
A comparison of operating systems.

MS-DOS

The leading operating system for microcomputers is Microsoft's MS-DOS. IBM's version of MS-DOS is commonly called PC-DOS. MS-DOS is a powerful, easy-to-master operating system that is extremely well supported. Over 10 million copies of MS-DOS are currently installed on microcomputers.

Version 3.x of MS-DOS is a single-user, single-tasking operating system that has special commands built in that allow it to work with local-area networking software. Advanced versions of MS-DOS such as IBM's OS/2 offer multitasking and multiuser support.

UNIX/XENIX System V

The UNIX System V operating system is a multitasking, multiuser operating system that is licensed by AT&T. UNIX System V was originally designed to run on minicomputers but has been adapted to run on both mainframes and microcomputers. It is about 30 times as large as the MS-DOS operating system and includes a powerful system-development module and a text-formatting program that can be used for typesetting applications.

Originally, the user interface of UNIX System V was too complex for the commercial market. But improved user interfaces called *shells* have been developed to protect the user from UNIX's cryptic command language. Several companies, including Altos and Tandy Corporation, provide user-friendly, menu-oriented interfaces for their implementations of UNIX System V.

UNIX System V is more expensive to license than MS-DOS version 3.x. MS-DOS is available from IBM and virtually all other microcomputer manufacturers for less than $100 per copy. UNIX costs from 3 to 30 times as much to license but allows a number of users to share the same computer.

XENIX System V is a microcomputer adaptation of UNIX System V developed by Microsoft. A version of XENIX System V that runs on IBM-compatible microcomputers is available from Santa Cruz Operations. XENIX System V is also available from IBM, Tandy, Altos, and several other microcomputer manufacturers. Market momentum is growing for the UNIX/XENIX System V operating system. There are now over 300,000 licensed UNIX installations. Most of these licenses are for microcomputer-based systems.

DEC, Hewlett–Packard, and other minicomputer companies have implemented UNIX System V across their entire product line. This provides their customers with an excellent growth path and makes it easier for them to interconnect their computers with machines made by other manufacturers. The UNIX System V standard will help to strengthen the minicomputer market by encouraging greater software support, providing a logical migration path for microcomputer users, and facilitating interconnectivity among different types of computers.

4

Determining Hardware Requirements

At this point you are probably asking yourself, ''What kind of computer will I need to run my company's applications?'' To answer this question, you first need to determine what your specific system requirements are, and then you must gain an understanding of the types of hardware that are available to meet those needs. This chapter helps you with those tasks. You may also want to look at Chapter 10 and Chapter 11.

The analysis you use to determine your hardware requirements parallels the input-process-output cycle common to all information systems. First, you have to establish how many people will be working with your computer system simultaneously. You also have to determine whether you will need to access your computer from different physical locations within your organization. Defining these requirements will allow you to determine how many data-entry terminals, or workstations, you will need for entering, or inputting, data into your automated office system.

Once you have determined whether you will have multiple users on the system, you need to decide what type of computer to use to process your data. Then, depending on the application software that you will be using, you can determine what your printing, or output, requirements are. These issues are discussed in turn in the sections that follow.

You may choose to draw up a more detailed feature list that specifies exactly which applications you will be running, what your data-entry and output requirements are, and any special needs you may have. The more clearly you can communicate your requirements, the more easily you or your system supplier will be able to determine the most cost-effective hardware solution for your situation.

Determining Data Input Requirements

The collection of data is usually the biggest bottleneck in the information-processing cycle. In most installations, over half of the cost of using the computer is spent on data collection and entry. Well-designed data-entry programs and specialized data-entry workstations can vastly improve the efficiency and productivity of your automated system. Input devices such as point-of-sale (POS) terminals, bar-code readers, and pointing devices, like mice or light pens, can help speed up the data-entry process. Such devices are discussed in more detail in Chapter 11.

The most accurate way to estimate your data-entry requirements is to time how long it takes to enter your data into your programs. However, it is easier to estimate the minimum number of data-entry workstations you will require by using a simple "keystroke" formula. A keystroke is the press of a key.

You can easily calculate the approximate number of keystrokes entered per hour by counting the number of characters and spaces typed over a 15-minute period and multiplying it by 4. Multiply that number by 8 to arrive at the approximate number of keystrokes per day. You can then estimate your workstation requirements by dividing the number of keystrokes entered per day by 40,000 and rounding the answer up to the nearest whole number. For example, if your staff enters 75,000 keystrokes per day, you will require at least two workstations.

In other words,

Number of data-entry workstations = (number of keystrokes entered per day) / (40,000 keystrokes)

Round the answer up to the next highest integer.

You should try to schedule your workstations to allow maximum system utilization. However, if your situation requires that workstations be located in different work areas, or if it is inconvenient for some users to share terminals, you will need to use additional workstations. If you are working with a single-tasking microcomputer, you will need to set aside at least 20 percent of the system's time for printing reports and performing system maintenance functions, such as backing up data files.

Determining Data Processing Requirements

Three major classes of computers are used to automate business applications: microcomputers, minicomputers, and mainframe computers. All work in basically the same way. The main difference between them is that the more powerful computers can support a greater number of simultaneous users and can process data faster. The different types of computers are discussed in Chapter 10.

The best way to estimate the type of computer system that you will need is to begin by establishing how many workstations you will have to hook up to your computer system to enter your data. It is unlikely that your business is large enough to justify the purchase of a mainframe computer; your choice will probably be a microcomputer, microcomputer network, or minicomputer. Figure 4-1 shows the range of users for each of these types.

If you can process your data with a single workstation, you should use a microcomputer to automate your business. Microcomputers are by far the easiest and least expensive office automation solution to install and implement. If you will require a multiuser system, you can either network microcomputers or install a multiuser microcomputer or minicomputer. The following section examines the advantages and disadvantages of each alternative.

	Micro-computers	**Networked microcomputers**	**Mini-computers**
Number of users:	1 to 16	2 to 1000	1 to 128

Figure 4-1.
The range of users for the different system types.

Multiuser Microcomputers and Minicomputers

New technology has blurred the distinction between microcomputer and minicomputer technologies. In the past, processor requirements were easier to determine because multiuser microcomputers were not able to provide an adequate level of performance for more than three or four simultaneous users. However, sophisticated new microprocessors, such as the Intel 80386 chips, have given microcomputers the data processing power of small minicomputer systems. Computer systems based on advanced microprocessor technology can easily support 16 or more workstations and can run many multiuser application packages that were originally written for minicomputers.

Many of the minicomputer manufacturers have introduced ''micro'' versions of their minicomputers. Digital's Micro-Vax computer system is just one example. And microcomputer companies such as Altos, Kaypro, and Compaq have built microcomputer systems that support multiple users. Such systems feature more-powerful microprocessors and operating-systems, and they support local-area networks. The overlap between super-micro and micro-mini computer systems leaves no clearly defined choice for those automating a particular business application.

It might be difficult to find a hardware solution that allows you to run every software application you have selected to automate your office systems. Many of the best standard industry applications were originally written to run on minicomputers and have not yet been converted to work on microcomputers; on the other hand, many leading office-productivity applications run only on microcomputer systems. You might need to decide what your priorities are and select hardware that supports your key office automation applications.

The difference in initial price between a multiuser microcomputer and a small minicomputer is usually negligible. However, the difference in the cost of installing and implementing microcomputers versus that of minicomputers is often substantial. Software designed for microcomputers usually offers fewer features and is less expensive than software designed for minicomputers. For example, a well-supported accounting program designed to run on a microcomputer might cost $500, whereas a similar minicomputer program might cost $3,000 or more. Further, system support for minicomputers is usually more expensive than for microcomputer-based systems. You might need to hire a specially trained system administrator to install and support a minicomputer system.

Local-Area Networking

A computer *local-area network* comprises two or more computers that are connected to allow sharing of data and system resources. The primary advantage of *local-area networks* (LANs) is that they offer a convenient way of improving the productivity of microcomputers that are already installed in an organization. LANs allow both file and resource sharing. For example, if you will be using a word processing software package, a LAN would allow your staff to share document files that are stored on the system's "file server" and to share output devices such as laser printers. Printers are often referred to as "print servers" when they can be used by multiple users connected to a LAN. Typically, two or more microcomputers, acting as workstations, are connected to print servers and file servers. Figure 4-2 shows a simple LAN.

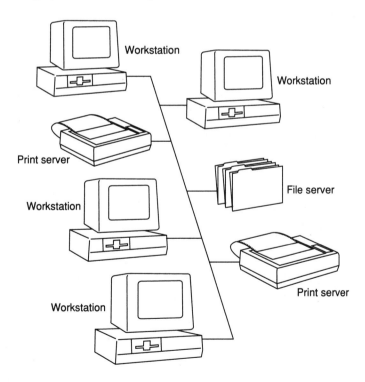

Figure 4-2.
A simple local-area network.

Currently IBM, Apple, Novell, and 3Com are the most successful suppliers of microcomputer-based local-area network software and hardware. All of these companies support standards established by Microsoft, Intel, and IBM. If you are considering networked microcomputers, evaluate the functionality and performance of these systems carefully.

Both Novell and 3Com's networks are currently faster and less expensive than IBM's Token Ring Network (TRN) while still being compatible with it. However, corporations that already have an investment in IBM equipment will probably choose IBM's network to ensure compatibility with future IBM products. Many third-party system suppliers are developing products that work with IBM's TRN.

As IBM develops the ability to connect their microcomputer-based networks to their mainframe computers, more corporations will become interested in this type of network.

Many vertical applications that were written for minicomputers have been adapted to run on microcomputer-based LANs. For example, Baby/36 is a software operating environment from California Software Products, Inc. that allows more than 4000 multiuser programs written in RPG-II to run on microcomputers connected to a Novell LAN. RPG-II is the programming language for IBM's System 36 minicomputer system. This in effect turns a Novell LAN into the equivalent of an IBM System 36.

Networked microcomputer systems can offer a cost-effective alternative to multiuser microcomputer-based and minicomputer-based systems and can provide a logical growth path for microcomputers that are already installed. To choose between a multiuser system and a networked one, you should consider two important issues. First, will your application packages perform well on the hardware configuration? And second, is there a need in your organization to use personal computers as workstations to process stand-alone office-productivity applications?

If both a minicomputer and networked microcomputers can provide equal support for your software, then you will need to evaluate the total cost and system support available for each system. We will cover these in Chapter 5 and Chapter 6.

Determining Main Memory Requirements

Main memory is usually referred to as random-access memory, or RAM, and is measured in kilobytes, abbreviated as KB. For example, a computer might have 640 KB of RAM. This means that the main computer memory can store more than 650,000 bytes (or characters) of data or programming code. (A kilobyte is 1024 bytes.)

Most off-the-shelf software clearly specifies the minimum hardware configuration necessary for the program to run properly. Many programs also indicate how much main memory is required for maximum performance and at what point increases in main memory no longer enhance performance.

The amount of main memory you need depends on the kinds of programs you will be running and on how fast you want your computer to process data. Different applications require different amounts of simultaneous processing. The more data or program code that needs to be in memory for processing to take place, the more memory will be needed to run the application.

The more memory your system has, the less often the computer will need to "swap" programs back and forth from the system's disk drives to process your work. (See Figure 4-3.) This is especially important in multitasking systems in which more than one application is running concurrently. If memory is limited, the computer will spend much of its time

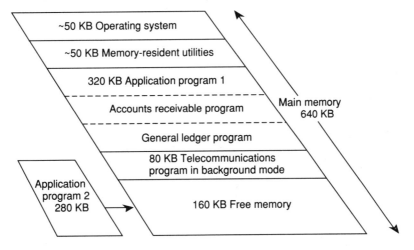

Figure 4-3.
A map of main memory.

moving the application programs out of one another's way. This phenomenon is called "thrashing" and results in poor performance.

Microcomputer-based office-productivity applications, such as electronic spreadsheets and database applications, generally require from 320 KB to 640 KB of main memory to run efficiently. Most microcomputer general-accounting applications work with 256 KB to 640 KB of main memory. Multiuser applications on minicomputers and mainframe computers sometimes require more than 1 megabyte (MB), or 1000 KB of main memory.

You can determine roughly how much main memory you will need to run your applications by drawing your own memory map. For example, if you are running a multitasking operating system on a LAN, and you will be using several programs, including one for electronic mail, a spreadsheet, a word processor, and a memory-resident utility program, you might write out the following:

Operating system software	64 KB
Networking software	128 KB
Electronic mail	180 KB
Spreadsheet	256 KB
Word processor	256 KB
Memory-resident utility	96 KB
Total memory required	980 KB

If your computer has 640 KB of main memory, you will not be able to load all of your programs at once. You will have to decide which application programs you will be using frequently enough to keep resident in main memory and load the other programs as needed. For example, you may want to keep your memory-resident utility program (perhaps an electronic calendar or a simple file manager) loaded all of the time and load your electronic spreadsheet or your word processor only when you are doing financial modeling or creating documents.

Determining Disk-Storage Requirements

Floppy-disk drives, also known as diskette drives, and hard-disk drives are used to store and transfer program and data files into and out of the computer's main memory.

The various types of drives are discussed in detail in Chapter 10. Basically, a floppy-disk drive is a slot into which you insert a floppy disk containing your program, your data, or both. To run a program from another floppy disk, you must remove the current disk and insert the new one. A hard-disk drive is a device installed inside your computer. In most cases, a large capacity hard disk can hold all of the programs and data you need in one place. Most business users will find a hard disk indispensable.

Applications that access the program files while they are executing will run faster if they are loaded from a hard disk rather than a floppy-disk drive. This is because hard-disk drives can access, read, and write data faster than floppy-disk drives can.

To compute your disk storage requirements, add the number of bytes required by the programs you will be running and the number of bytes you need to store your data, and allow enough room for a "working area" in which you can sort and move files about. This area should usually be 10 percent larger than the largest file you will have on the system.

Your data files will grow larger over time, and you may want to add more applications to your system. Thus, you should provide at least 50 to 100 percent more disk space than you currently need.

Use the following formulas to determine your disk storage needs:

Disk memory requirements = (size of all program files) + (size of all data files) + (size of work area) + (room for anticipated growth)

Program file storage = size of all (application programs) + (operating system software and utilities)

Data file storage = (master files) + (transaction files) + (working files) + (document files) + (backup files)

Work Area = size of largest file + 10 percent to allow sorting of files

Anticipated Growth = at least 50 to 100 percent of your current needs

The size of your *program files* is usually noted in a specification sheet that accompanies your software's documentation; if it is not specified, ask the manufacturer or your supplier to tell you exactly how much data is stored on the program's disks.

To compute the amount of storage you need for your accounting program's *data files,* you will have to do a bit of homework. First you need to find out from the documentation how much space is required to set up your system's *master* files. Then you need to add space for your *transaction* files and finally for any *backup* files used by the applications you will be running.

If you are running office-productivity software, you will need to estimate the size of your *work* and *document* files. Fortunately, most programs specify in their documentation how much file space to allocate given a set of parameters, such as the number of customers or perhaps the number and length of your word-processing documents.

Keeping duplicate backup copies of all of the files stored on your system's hard-disk drive is good security against accidental erasure or hardware failure. Programs or data that have been accidentally erased from your hard-disk drive can be reloaded from backup files on floppy disks or tape. Backup files can also provide an audit trail of all work done on the system.

To determine how large a hard-disk drive to buy, you will need to determine how many programs you want to keep on your system and how large your data files will be. For example, if you will be running several accounting applications and a word processing package, you might estimate the amount of hard-disk storage you require as follows:

Accounting software	1.5 MB
Accounting data files	5.5 MB
Word processing software	0.5 MB
Document files	1.5 MB
Operating system software	0.5 MB
Work area	0.5 MB
Backup files	0.5 MB
Future growth	4.5 MB to 9.5 MB
Total hard-disk storage required	15.0 MB to 20.0 MB

In this example, your system should be equipped with a 20-megabyte hard-disk drive.

Determining Data Output Requirements

The only precise way to calculate your printer requirements is to count the number of characters you will be printing and divide that number into the available printing time in your business day. This number translates into the speed at which your printer must operate to keep up with your work-load. If you are using a single-tasking microcomputer, your system will either slow down (if you have a print spooler) or stop all other computing activities when something is printing.

This formula is expressed as follows:

Speed in characters per second (cps) of the printer that you re-quire = (total number of characters on printed reports) / (total number of seconds in your workday)

For example, if on the heaviest output day your company's reports total 1000 pages, you would calculate your needs as follows:

(1000 pages) × **(65 lines / page)** = (65,000 lines)
(65,000 lines) × (an average of 65 characters per line) =
(4,225,000 characters)

One 8-hour day = 28,800 seconds

(4,225,000 characters) / **(28,800 seconds)** = 146.7 cps

Thus, you would need one 146.7-cps (characters per second) printer running nonstop to print 1000 pages in 8 hours.

A rule of thumb, depending on the printer's duty cycle, is to estimate that you can run a printer three to four continuous hours per day. Most manufacturers will supply information on the rated output of their printers and on the mean time between failures (MTBF). In our previous example, you would need at least two 160-cps printers.

Computer analysts methodically count the number of lines in the different reports that are run regularly and sum them with estimates of reports that are run occasionally to estimate computer output require-ments. However, there is actually no need to be too precise in your calcu-lations. Over time, you will probably add applications and begin generating additional management reports. It is a good idea to assume that your output needs will inevitably grow and to purchase a faster, more heavy-duty printer.

Hardware Buyer's Checklist

- Determine which software applications you will be running on your computer system. Evaluate the cost of installing and imple-menting the applications on different types of hardware.

■ Evaluate whether you will need a single-user or a multiuser system. A single-user microcomputer is the least expensive and easiest to implement office automation solution. If you require a multiuser system, you have the option of choosing a multiuser microcomputer, a minicomputer, or a local-area network using microcomputers as workstations. Chapter 10 provides additional information that will help you evaluate the benefits of different computer architectures for your business requirements.

■ Determine how much main memory (RAM) you will need to run your application software.

■ Determine how much hard-disk drive storage you will require to store and load your program and data files.

■ Determine what your data output requirements are and what type of printers or plotters will best handle your needs. These are discussed in Chapter 11.

■ Determine what your data communications requirements are. Data communications is also covered in Chapter 11.

■ Evaluate future growth requirements.

■ Request competitive proposals from system suppliers offering computer systems that meet your requirements.

It is important to choose a system from a manufacturer that offers a migration path to a system large enough to handle any foreseeable growth in your business. Converting from one automated system to another, incompatible model can be as difficult as automating a task for the first time. Many hardware manufacturers offer a migration path that allows users to move up to larger computer systems that run the same application software with little or no modification.

Recommendations

Microcomputers

Single-user microcomputers are the easiest and least expensive automated system to install and implement. A system with 640 KB or more of main memory, one or two floppy-disk drives, and a 20-megabyte to

40-megabyte hard-disk drive has become the standard configuration for single-user microcomputer-based business systems. A cassette-tape drive provides a method of backing up files that is faster and more convenient than using a floppy-disk drive, but it adds to the cost of the system.

If you are running more than one application at a time (a multitasking system), or if more than one person will be using the same program at the same time (a multiuser system) on a microcomputer, it is recommended that you purchase an IBM-compatible machine based on the Intel 80386 microprocessor. Advanced microcomputers based on this processor can address over 16 MB of main memory and can provide the computational power of a small minicomputer. Although 80386-based machines now cost about $1,500 more than comparable 80286-based machines, they offer two and a half to three times the processing power.

The Apple Macintosh family of computers represents the only successful standard, non-IBM business-oriented microcomputer system. The primary advantage of the Macintosh is that its user interface, which is similar to that of Microsoft's Windows, is powerful and easy to use. Once a user becomes familiar with the Macintosh interface, it is easier to learn new applications.

Many excellent software packages are available for general office automation tasks on the Mac, and the Macintosh system is supported by state-of-the-art desktop publishing software and laser printers. Apple's newest machines, the Macintosh SE and Macintosh II, provide a good interface to IBM's DOS-based architecture. The Macintosh SE can run MS-DOS software when a special add-on board is installed, and the Macintosh II can be modified to run both MS-DOS and UNIX System V programs. This has made the Macintosh an attractive system for general business applications.

Virtually all of the microcomputer manufacturers, with the exception of Apple, are copying, or "cloning," IBM microcomputers. To differentiate their products, these manufacturers have included additional hardware features, bundled free software, supplied more memory, included additional input and output ports, included high-performance video displays and adapters, used faster microprocessor chips, increased warranty periods, provided free on-site installation, and have even offered two-for-one promotions. The next chapter will help you evaluate these extremely competitive products.

Minicomputers

You will have to evaluate whether the greater power of a minicomputer system outweighs the greater overall total system and support costs. If a microcomputer-based software package will work for your company, it will usually be easier and less expensive to implement than a minicomputer system. If the software package that you require runs on both multiuser computers and on LANs, you will need to determine which hardware solution is most cost-effective for your needs.

Local-Area Networks

Computer networking technology is far from stable. De facto standards are just beginning to emerge as major suppliers start delivering larger volumes of networking products to the market. Different LAN products do not easily connect with one another, and programs written to run in one networked environment will usually not run without modification on another system.

Unless you are absolutely sure that you will have adequate system support, I recommend that you avoid using a microcomputer-based LAN for general accounting. However, as networking standards become more accepted and as system suppliers learn how to provide better support for LAN installations, LANs will offer more value than other comparably priced multiuser computer systems.

When more that one hardware configuration is available that will run the software applications you have chosen, you need to consider the *total* cost of installing and implementing each system. You also need to address each system's viability and compatibility and the quality of the service and support provided by the system supplier. Each of these issues is discussed in the next chapter.

5

Choosing a System Supplier

In choosing a computer-system supplier, you need to consider several issues:

- The *viability* of the hardware manufacturer, the software developer, and the system supplier.

- The *compatibility* of the system with current industry standards.

- The *quality* of the software, the hardware, and the service and support provided by the system supplier.

The previous two chapters discussed the quality of computer software and hardware. This chapter tells how to evaluate the viability, compatibility, and quality of the service and support provided by a system supplier.

Viability

The computer industry is very dynamic. Many of the system integrators and resellers that have brought leading-edge products to market have been unable to maintain their market momentum and have failed. For example, Osborne Computers, a microcomputer manufacturer that sold tens of thousands of 8-bit CP/M-based systems, was unable to develop 16-bit DOS-based systems as rapidly as some of its competitors and was driven out of business. Unfortunately, it is often difficult to service and support discontinued or obsolete computer products.

It is best to select your company's automated office system from a well-known, stable hardware or software manufacturer and to choose a system supplier that is likely to remain in business to provide your company with ongoing service and support. In choosing a system supplier, you must evaluate the company's financial stability, its commitment to the industry, the quality of its personnel, and the quality of service and support it has provided to other customers.

When the government purchases computer equipment, it generally requires that the system supplier or manufacturer be responsible for providing replacement parts and product support for at least five years. If you purchase computer equipment that has been procured by government agencies, you will probably not have difficulty obtaining service and support over the useful life of your equipment.

Compatibility

Compatibility refers to the ability of one product to work properly with another. Some computer products are designed to work together, and others are incompatible. Unfortunately, you can never assume that either software applications or hardware products from different suppliers will be compatible. For example, hard-disk drives designed to work with the Macintosh will not work properly with IBM PC-compatible systems. Even software packages from the same software developer may be incompatible. The only sure way to evaluate the compatibility of different computer products is to use them with a wide range of software packages and hardware products.

Some system suppliers have made misleading claims about the compatibility of their products. For example, several microcomputers that have been advertised as being IBM compatible will not work with TRN, IBM's local-area network. These microcomputers do work with other IBM-compatible products, and the suppliers involved assumed that they would also be compatible with future IBM products. They were wrong.

This example brings up two important issues. First, the importance of determining your current and future functional requirements cannot be overemphasized. If your company will never install IBM's TRN, you will probably never even notice whether your computers are compatible with it. And second, computer systems have become so complex that it is difficult to make them perfectly compatible with all standard computer products. However, if you purchase your system from a major system supplier, the company will generally modify or update its equipment to allow it to work correctly with other industry-standard products.

Although compatibility issues are beginning to be well understood by computer-product designers, you should never assume that different computer products will be compatible unless your system supplier has worked with the products and guarantees that they will work properly together.

Try to choose software and hardware products that are compatible with industry standards so that they will be supported by the widest range of other computer products. This will help assure that you have ongoing support for your system and that new computer products are compatible with your hardware and operating-system software.

Several national and international standards committees are responsible for setting industry-wide standards for computer-system software, computer hardware, and data-communications equipment. Unfortunately, these committees are often controlled by major computer suppliers, and it is usually in their best interest to adopt standards that are compatible with products that they have already designed or that are planned for the future. If several major suppliers have adopted incompatible technologies, multiple "standards" generally emerge that the rest of the industry must support.

However, the computer market is primarily driven by de facto standards that emerge as the result of one supplier gaining a large market share in a particular market area. The best example of a de facto standard in the microcomputer industry is the IBM Personal Computer. Over 10 million IBM-compatible microcomputers have already been installed. Literally thousands of computer manufacturers and software suppliers produce IBM-compatible products that support IBM's hardware and operating-system software.

De facto standards develop as a result of market momentum that builds on itself. Software applications usually cannot run on different types of computers without extensive modifications. Therefore, to maximize their target market, most developers design their software to run on the largest number of already-installed computer systems. Because hardware is useless without application software, most hardware manufacturers design their products to be compatible with existing hardware standards in order to take advantage of the existing base of software applications.

Support for established standards thus tends to create a kind of technological inertia that makes it difficult for smaller, innovative companies to compete with more established suppliers. Most customers are simply not willing to risk buying any new products or technology before there is a "critical mass" of industry support for them.

Both Atari and Amiga are having a difficult time trying to get major business-software developers to write programs for their non-IBM-compatible microcomputer systems. Software companies want to be convinced that new hardware products will be successful in the market before they begin to develop new applications for them, and it is very difficult for non-industry-standard hardware to become successful without a strong software base. This chicken-and-egg problem almost caused the early demise of Apple's Macintosh system.

There is no solution to the standards problem. Although making all computer products work perfectly together is a desirable goal from the end user's perspective, it is impossible for all technological breakthroughs to carry along the baggage of compatibility with older technology. Fortunately, many of the major semiconductor and microcomputer manufacturers are finding ways to improve their systems while maintaining compatibility with older technology.

Quality

In this chapter, the term "quality" refers to the level of service and support necessary to install, implement, and maintain an automated system. Products that are well designed and easy to use and that include adequate documentation and training materials will require less direct support from your system supplier during installation and implementation. However, even the best software and hardware products will generally require some level of support.

Customers are often unwilling to pay extra for the support that they need to install and implement their office automation systems. They feel that their system suppliers should provide adequate instruction to make their systems work properly. Unfortunately, most system suppliers feel that selling a small business computer does not offer enough profit for them to provide the level of customer support that most customers require. This is because the price of computer hardware and software has fallen so dramatically that support costs have become a much larger percentage of the total cost of installing and implementing an automated system.

In most cases, computer suppliers have "unbundled" support costs from the purchase price of their systems. They rely on their product's documentation and tutorials to make their hardware and software products *user installable*. A retail microcomputer customer is usually handed a stack of cartons, and it is up to the customer to transport the cartons to the workplace and read manual after manual to learn how to get the system working. Customers must decide between buying a service or support contract, which generally allows a certain amount of on-site or telephone support time; hiring an outside consultant to help them; or figuring it out for themselves from the system's documentation and tutorials. Even suppliers of larger multiuser systems expect their customers to install their systems themselves and to pay extra for any training or on-site support that they need.

It takes almost as much customer training and support to set up an accounting system on a single-user microcomputer as it does to install a large multiuser minicomputer. Assuming that they read all of the instructional materials that come with an automated office system, most business people will require between 10 and 30 hours of support and training to install and implement their first automated accounting application. It will cost between $35 and $125 per hour to hire an experienced computer consultant to help you install your system. It is easy to see how support costs can end up being higher than the cost of purchasing a microcomputer system.

Free telephone support for application software is being phased out by most major software developers. Most companies now charge at least $60 per hour to answer their customers' questions over the phone. Some software companies offer telephone-support contracts that allow the customer to make an unlimited number of support calls for a fixed yearly fee; over the useful life of the product, these fees will usually exceed the retail price of the application.

Software Updates

Major software companies, such as Lotus, Ashton-Tate, and Microsoft, offer periodic *software updates* when they want to upgrade their products by adding features, improving performance, or fixing bugs. Such updates are often included in the price of a software-support contract. Sometimes, however, you must pay extra to receive a software update. The charge is usually nominal, unless the program has had extensive modifications and many new features have been added.

Most software suppliers support only the latest version of their programs. However, if your software is working perfectly and you do not require any of the new features in the revised program, it may not pay for your company to upgrade. Revised software is not always improved; the new release may run slower, contain new programming errors, and omit old features that you like and use.

Hardware Service and Maintenance

Once you begin to maintain your company's bookkeeping records or corporate data files on your computer, you will become dependent on your system. Computer equipment is very reliable, but when something does go wrong you will need to have it fixed as soon as possible.

I strongly recommend that you get a *service contract* to cover your equipment. As a rule of thumb, a service contract to cover hardware repairs costs about 1 percent per month of the total cost of the system's hardware. This will cover on-site service calls and usually includes the cost of most replacement parts. It is desirable to have on-site rather than depot service whenever possible. Depending on your needs and your budget, the terms of your contract can range from walk-in depot service to a two-hour on-site response time.

Your hardware may be serviced directly by the manufacturer, through a computer dealer or other authorized reseller, or by a third-party service organization. Depending on the personnel involved, all of these can provide excellent support. The caveat is that in most cases support cannot be better than the hardware manufacturer's support of its own service facilities.

Xerox Americare, Sorbus, and other third-party service organizations have parts depots and support centers in virtually all major metropolitan areas. Check with your computer supplier or contact the third-party service company directly to find out how much service contracts cost for the system you are considering.

Software Training and Support

To determine the best value in office automation software, you need to evaluate carefully the *real* cost of implementing the software, including the costs of training and ongoing support and the convenience of using a well-designed program. Differences in retail price may quickly be offset by the increased power and reduced training time of a more sophisticated package. Such packages usually offer a pool of trained users and consultants who can help you implement effective solutions for your business.

When you evaluate the real costs of implementing software, industry-standard packages usually represent a good overall value. Most businesses choose software packages from leading manufacturers because they offer the best combination of functionality, performance, quality, and compatibility with other industry-standard software products.

The Real Costs of Office Automation

The real cost of a system is not just the cost of the hardware and software. You must also consider the maintenance costs, training costs, and personnel costs involved. The following list shows the different factors that contribute to the cost of an automated system.

Hardware Costs

Main computer system (including CPU, power supply, and bus)
Video board
Memory expansion board
Coprocessor boards
Disk drives and controllers
Video display monitor
Printers and plotters
Modems and other telecommunications equipment
Networking equipment
Backup power supply
Power surge protector
Floppy disks
Office supplies

Software Costs

Operating-system software
Application software packages
Training packages
Update fees

Installation Costs

Facilities planning
Running cables

Support and Service Costs

Ongoing maintenance fees for hardware
Installation of software updates
Custom software costs, if necessary
Telecommunications line charges

Training Costs

Personnel costs during training
Training classes

System Planning and Acquisition Costs

Management personnel costs
Consulting fees

Finding Application Software

There is no formula for finding good vertical application software or suppliers who work with companies in your specific industry. Many of the best vertical packages are sold by smaller system suppliers that do not have retail outlets and that do not sell enough software to justify the expense of extensive advertising or marketing campaigns. However, published reviews, guides to sources of software, industry trade associations, and major computer suppliers can help you find software packages to automate your office work.

Product reviews can help you understand the strengths and weaknesses of different application software and can save you time when you begin to compare the features and limitations of different products. Reviews published in computer magazines devoted to business software and in trade journals for your industry are usually the best source of unbiased information about comparable software packages.

Although popular office-productivity software is well reviewed, finding reviews of industry-specific application software is more difficult because the audience is more limited and because qualified reviewers are often hard to find. It is well worth a trip to the library to find out if any of the major computer or industry-specific publications have recently published reviews of the type of software you need. The magazines *PC Week, PC World, PC, InfoWorld,* and *Byte* usually have excellent review articles, and they periodically devote an entire issue to one type of application software.

A number of guides to sources of software are published. They are available at bookstores, at computer stores, through some computer manufacturers, and through on-line information services. These guides are usually six to nine months out-of-date by the time they are distributed, but they are often the only source of information about specific types of application programs.

Perhaps the best source of information about software for your type of business is your own industry's *trade association.* Many of these associations have computer advisory groups at both the state and national levels. Such groups are usually excellent sources of contacts and ''war stories.''

Most major *computer manufacturers* work closely with software developers to make sure that as much software as possible is available for the company's hardware. The manufacturer's product marketing group can usually provide up-to-date information on software developers and system integrators that sell and support vertical packages for your specific requirements. They will, of course, tell you only about software that is compatible with their computer equipment.

If any of your *competitors* (preferably ones in a different market area) have automated their operations, you can call their office supervisor or DP manager and ask how things are going with the system. People are usually either proud of their installation or very angry. It should be fairly easy to get a feel for whether or not they are happy with their system and with the support they have received from their supplier.

Computer consultants who work with different industry segments can be a great source of information and are usually well worth their fees. Make sure, however, that your consultant's fees are not really sales commissions. If the consultant is receiving commissions or referral fees from software developers or hardware suppliers, the "consulting" you are getting may be no better than the information in the manufacturer's advertising brochures. Although a consultant may appear to be professional, you should check his or her references carefully. Consultants are not required to be licensed, and they are not regulated; some are helpful, and some are disasters.

Whenever you talk with someone about a software product, be sure to ask whether he or she has actually used the product. There is a world of difference between working with a program and merely reading a review.

Locating System Suppliers

Just as there are many types of automated office systems that will meet your needs, so too are there many different system suppliers that are capable of helping you install and implement an office automation system. You need to find the system supplier that will provide the best support, service, and overall value for your automated office system.

Finding the best system supplier for your particular needs is not always easy. As Figure 5-1 shows, different suppliers usually focus their marketing efforts in different areas. However, competition has forced many suppliers to sell their products to anyone who will buy them. (This is sometimes referred to as distribution-channel conflict.) You may find the software and hardware products that you have selected being offered by retailers, system integrators, and even through discount mail-order distributors. You need to evaluate the strengths and weaknesses of each type of supplier to determine where to purchase your system. The sections that follow will help you to do this.

Supplier	Level of Support	Market Focus
Computer manufacturer	Good	Larger corporations
Computer retailer	Fair to Good	Small to mid-sized businesses
Mail-order distributor	Poor	All end users
Original equipment manufacturer (OEM)	Poor*	Value-added remarketers (VARs) and retailers
Value-added remarketer (VAR)	Good	Small to mid-sized businesses

*OEMs generally provide good support to their resellers but do not usually provide end-user support.

Figure 5-1.
Types of system suppliers.

Computer Manufacturers

Computer manufacturers usually distribute their products through several different marketing channels. They generally sell their systems directly to their largest customers, and they work with computer retailers, distributors, and system integrators — VARs and OEMs — to reach small to mid-sized companies.

Many computer manufacturers feel that they can encourage sales of their hardware by offering or recommending software packages that provide their customers with a complete, or *turnkey*, office automation solution. They therefore support some business applications directly and also work closely with independent software developers. Computer manufacturers can usually furnish a list of independent software suppliers or system integrators who sell or support turnkey packages that run on their hardware for a particular vertical market. This is one of the easiest ways for you to find out about vertical application packages that will help you automate your business.

Computer manufacturers usually state their service and support policies clearly in their printed warranties and service contracts. Some manufacturers will provide extra support under special circumstances, but you should never expect or anticipate better treatment than has been specified in your sales agreement. If you think you will need additional support, arrange for it before you order your system. After your system is installed, you will be dealing with your supplier on his or her terms.

Retailers

Computer retailers generally focus on providing single-user and smaller multiuser solutions to small and mid-sized companies that want to automate accounting or office-productivity applications. Most of the successful computer retailers have deployed outside sales forces to help them market to the local business community.

Some retail computer stores provide excellent service and support; others provide minimal service and compete primarily by offering low prices. You can generally trust your instincts about the level of support that a retailer will provide. However, unless you personally know the people involved, it is best to check with a few of the retailer's other customers to see whether they are satisfied with the service.

When you are evaluating a retail computer dealer, you should ask the same basic questions that you would ask if you were buying a car or a major appliance. For example:

- "Have you ever sold or installed this type of system before?"

- "Are you a designated service center for the products I am buying?"

- "Do you have any reference accounts that I can call?"

- "Does the sale include installation?"

- "How much training and support is included in the price of the system or software package?"

- "Do you know a software specialist who I can have modify this software application?"

- ■ "Do you have the accessories and office supplies that I will need?"
- ■ Any other question that you have about the retailer's ability or desire to help you install, implement, and service your office automation system.

If the answers to your questions indicate that the dealer wants to sell it and forget it, consider getting the product or system from a mail-order supplier and using your savings to pay for any in-house or telephone consulting that you need.

Mail-Order Suppliers

So much has been written about the perils of buying through mail order that I hesitate to go into them here. If you don't find out whether any complaints about the mail-order supplier have been filed with its local Better Business Bureau, and if you don't try to check out local references, you are simply gambling. You can lose time and money waiting for delivery.

Most mail-order companies are legitimate, but some go out of business owing a great deal of money to a lot of trusting customers. A few of the better mail-order suppliers provide excellent telephone support, but none that I have ever dealt with made house calls.

Many companies purchase their first software package from a local computer retailer and rely on the dealer's support while their key personnel become familiar with their system. They then purchase larger volumes of the same package through mail-order distributors to save money. Mail-order suppliers generally offer the best prices on microcomputer hardware and software products.

Computer retailers may be able to compete with mail-order discounters on volume purchases. If you are buying in quantity and your dealer knows that you will give your order to the lowest bidder, he or she may bid competitively to keep you as a loyal customer and to make a small profit on the work already done. Unfortunately for retail dealers, manufacturers often give hefty volume-purchase discounts. It is not always possible for retail dealers to purchase equipment through their local distributors for any less than you can through a high-volume mail-order supplier.

Original Equipment Manufacturers

An original equipment manufacturer (OEM) is a company that manufactures a product. In computer distribution channels, a company that adds a peripheral board, custom chips, or in some cases a software package to a computer system may be considered an OEM. OEMs usually focus on providing hardware solutions to value-added remarketers (VARs) or other system integrators who work directly with end users. From the end user's perspective, OEMs that sell directly to end users are the same as value-added remarketers.

Value-Added Remarketers

Value-added remarketers (VARs) are independent companies that resell hardware and software packages. Most VARs focus their marketing efforts on small to mid-sized companies that require some custom programming services, on-site support or training, or help in determining their system requirements. Most VARs specialize in installing and implementing one or more different vertical applications.

Frequently, a VAR will be the only supplier that can support both the hardware and software for your particular needs. Depending on your business and on whether you will require any custom programming, a VAR may offer the only turnkey solution. You will generally have the most "hand-holding" (customer support) when you work with a VAR, usually because you are paying for it by the hour.

Some VARs are very independent, carry many lines, and have a distributor-type relationship with their suppliers. Others make joint sales calls with their suppliers and work closely with their suppliers' support personnel. The relationship is not really important if the supplier provides good support. However, it is very important to establish exactly where your support will come from.

Checklist for Evaluating a System Supplier

1. Evaluate the quality of your system supplier's sales and support personnel. Discuss the background of the marketing and support people that will be working with you to help implement your system. Make sure that you feel comfortable with the people with whom you are going to work. Be cautious of suppliers who are flippant about issues that you bring up or who seem to have an unprofessional attitude. Your perceptions are probably on target. Look for experience,

maturity, common sense, and all of the other qualities that you would look for in an employee that you were hiring, because in a sense, that is what you are doing.

2. Evaluate the stability of the system supplier's company. Your decision will affect your company for many years. It is best if the company that supplies your equipment is going to be around for as long as you have it. Pay attention to your supplier's sales and financial status, and try to evaluate whether the business is stable. Be as careful as you would if your company was going to go into a partnership with the supplier; that is almost what you are doing.

3. Determine the willingness of the system supplier to put all agreements in writing. Dealing with a computer system supplier is like dealing with a building contractor. Misunderstandings about performance and support issues are quite common. The best way to avoid this is to have all agreements in writing.

   Most system suppliers will be more than willing to write up a *list of responsibilities* that specifies who is responsible for doing what and when it will be done. Putting together such a list can help clarify issues involving after-sale implementation and support, and it communicates to your system supplier that you are teaming up to insure a successful installation. (A sample list of responsibilities is included in Chapter 8.)

4. Evaluate the system supplier's track record. The best indicators of future performance are past sins. You should check out your supplier's track record. Ask other customers if they are happy with their equipment, their support, and their relationship with the supplier. Find out what problems they have had and whether they would buy their system from the same supplier if they could do it over again.

   Choose references at random from a list of the supplier's installed accounts. Try not to rely on names suggested by the supplier. Also, be sure to ask to visit one or two customer installations. These visits are a great opportunity to talk to business people like yourself who have automated their business and to observe how a company like your own works with automated office systems.

If you visit a customer installation, remember that the company is doing both their system supplier and you a favor. Be reasonable and considerate, and don't overstay your welcome. Do not expect to be shown around the business of a direct competitor unless they have family ties to the system supplier.

5. Find out who "turns the key." As mentioned earlier in this chapter, the term "turnkey" refers to a complete, fully operational system that is supplied and (usually) supported by one company. If you are purchasing a turnkey system, be sure that the supplier agrees in writing to be responsible for both hardware and software functionality. If multiple suppliers are involved, you still need to establish exactly which company is responsible for supporting each part of your system.

   Some questions you should ask your system supplier are:

   ■ Will the supplier have preinstallation planning and implementation meetings with your personnel?

   ■ Will they be on your site at the beginning to help with your questions and problems?

   ■ Will they provide ongoing telephone support?

   ■ Do they provide regular preventive system maintenance?

   ■ Will they help you create and then sign a list of responsibilities to clarify who is responsible for system installation and after-sale support tasks?

   ■ Which supplier will be responsible for supporting and servicing each component of your installation?

   ■ If support and maintenance are unbundled from the system, what alternative third-party sources can provide support? Be sure to evaluate third-party service companies as carefully as you do your system supplier.

6. Find out what the system will not do. Carefully evaluate the expandability of the hardware you are considering. Give yourself a migration path for your business' anticipated growth. Also, look into the compatibility of your application software with other programs that you may install in the future.

An advantage of this approach is that it frequently points to new benefits that a slightly modified system could offer. It can later save you from thinking, "If only I had known enough to ask that question."

Very experienced system suppliers sometimes have a cursory "I know what you need" attitude. By asking many questions and probing for thoughtful answers, you can assess whether or not your supplier has really thought about *your* business, your current needs, and your future office automation requirements.

7. Be realistic about the level of support that your system supplier can or will deliver. Try to have reasonable expectations of the level of support your system supplier should provide. For example, mail-order distributors will not be able to provide the level of support that a local VAR or OEM can. If you purchase your system through a mail-order supplier, do not spend your entire office automation budget for hardware and software. You will need to allocate time and money for the training and support necessary to implement your new system.

8. Become self-sufficient as soon as you can. You can educate yourself and your personnel by joining user groups, reading computer-related magazines, and going to seminars and classes. The time you invest in learning how to support your own system will be repaid by the secure feeling that you are in control of all aspects of your business.

Section II

Justifying Costs and Negotiating Contracts

This section shows you how to estimate the potential savings that automation could bring to different areas of your company. Chapter 6 gives guidelines for putting together a payback analysis report that will help you justify your decision to automate your business or department. Chapter 7 tells you how to negotiate with your system supplier and helps you draw up a request for proposal in which you specify your office automation requirements.

6

Cost Justification for Automation

The first step in justifying the cost of an office-automation system is to determine how much it costs to maintain your current manual office systems. You may already have done this as part of your analysis of the story worksheets (see "Estimating Activity Costs" in Chapter 2). If not, do so now. The next step is to evaluate the total cost of installing and implementing an office-automation system. Refer to the list in "The Real Costs of Office Automation" in Chapter 5 to be sure you have taken all costs into consideration.

This chapter helps you evaluate the potential cost benefits of automating your accounting functions and several office-productivity tasks. To do this, you compare the cost of maintaining your current manual office systems with the cost of installing an automated office system to determine what areas of your business can be automated cost-effectively.

Although it is difficult to establish the potential cost savings associated with general office automation, it is fairly easy to evaluate the potential benefits of automating specific areas of your business. This approach will be used to analyze the impact of automation at Muffin Incorporated, a combination wholesaler-retailer bakery. It represents a composite of companies that I have worked with in the restaurant and food distribution business.

The second case study involves creating a formal *payback analysis report* for the order entry and billing department of Northwest Floors, the distribution company introduced in Chapter 1. A payback-analysis report can help you describe the financial and organizational impact of automation on your company. You can use this report to help communicate your recommendations to upper management.

Determining the Real Cost of Muffin Inc.'s $30,000 Office-Automation System

As you have seen, the *real* cost of an office-automation system is the cost of the hardware and software plus the costs of training, ongoing maintenance, and support. Training and support costs generally exceed hardware and software costs over the useful life of an automated system.

Muffin Inc. has just spent $30,000 on a computer system depreciated over five years (60 months). Let's see what the real cost of that system is. The following categories are the same as those listed in "The Real Costs of Automation" in Chapter 5. Refer to that list for a breakdown of the items in each catagory.

Hardware and Software Costs. $30,000 (depreciated over five years).

Installation Costs. These will be negligible because counters and power are already installed, and no custom wiring will be required.

System Support and Service Costs. The rule of thumb for service contracts is to allow one percent of the sales price per month for services. ($30,000) × (1%) = ($300 per month for service). ($300 per month) × (60 months) = ($18,000).

Training Costs. Training costs depend on the type and number of software packages installed and on the type of computer hardware that is implemented. Your system supplier should be able to give you a fairly accurate estimate of how much time will be required to install and implement your system.

Muffin Inc. has 63 employees. Each of the four department managers will require four days of training on the system. (4 managers) × (32 hours) × ($25/hour) = ($3,200).

The two main system operators will require two weeks of training. (2 operators) × (80 hours) × ($15/hour) = ($2,400).

Each of the ten sales clerks will require two days of training. (10 salespeople) × (16 hours) × ($10/hour) = ($1,600).

All remaining employees will receive a brief two-hour overview of new company procedures relating to the computer. (47 employees) × (2 hours) × ($10/hour) = ($940).

(Total estimated preinstallation training costs) = ($8,140).

Employee turnover will require additional training time. Assuming 16 percent employee turnover per year, additional training will cost an estimated $6,860 over the five-year period.

(Total training cost for 5 years) = ($15,000).

As high as these training costs may seem, they are conservative for the implementation of a small, multiuser business computer system.

System Planning and Acquisition Costs. We have budgeted $1,000 for management personnel costs incurred in system planning and acquisition.

See Figure 6-1 on the next page for a five-year breakdown of the after-tax costs of this system.

Note: Consult your tax specialist or attorney before making any major capital expenditures.

This example does not take into account changes in federal tax laws, state or local taxes, finance charges, or the time value of money.

Muffin Inc. Cost-Justifies Office Automation

Muffin Inc., a muffin retailer, distributor, and baker, has sales of $1 million per year. Muffin Inc.'s charter is to bake up both muffins and profits.

The first step in cost-justifying Muffin Inc.'s computer system is to use simple formulas to estimate the cost savings that will result from the automation of different accounting activities. Then it will be possible to evaluate whether those savings will make a $30,000 microcomputer system worthwhile.

The Total System Cost:

Hardware and software costs:	$ 30,000
Service costs:	$ 18,000
Training costs:	$ 15,000
System planning and acquisition:	$ 1,000
Installation costs:	$ 0
Total system costs:	$ 64,000

Year	1	2	3	4	5
Cash Payments:					
Principal	$4,909	$5,197	$5,857	$6,599	$7,438
Interest	3,019	2,731	2,071	1,329	492
Maintenance	3,600	3,600	3,600	3,600	3,600
Training	8,140	1,715	1,715	1,715	1,715
Acquisition	1,000				
Total:	$20,668	$13,243	$13,243	$13,243	$13,245
Tax-Deductible Expenses:					
Depreciation	$4,275	$6,270	$5,985	$5,985	$5,985*
Interest expense	3,019	2,731	2,071	1,329	492
Maintenance	3,600	3,600	3,600	3,600	3,600
Training	8,140	1,715	1,715	1,715	1,715
Acquisition	1,000				
Total:	$20,034	$14,316	$13,371	$12,629	$11,792
Recoverable Cash:					
Income tax savings	$7,614	$5,726	$5,348	$5,052	$4,717**
Total:	$7,614	$5,726	$5,348	$5,052	$4,717
Summary of Costs:					
Total cash out	$20,668	$13,243	$13,243	$13,243	$13,245
Recoverable cash	7,614	5,726	5,348	5,052	4,717
Cost/year	13,054	7,517	7,895	8,191	8,528
Cost/month	1,088	626	658	683	711
Total cash out	73,642				
Recoverable cash	28,457				
Five-year cost	45,185				
Average monthly cost	753				

*Includes $1,500 salvage value
**Includes 40% FIT

Figure 6-1.
The after-tax cost of a $30,000 microcomputer system.

Payback Analysis for Inventory Control at Muffin Inc.

In the muffin business, profitability hinges on having the right type of muffin on the shelf. Muffins become stale in a few hours, and customers who don't find their favorite type may not come back. To maintain a high level of customer service, the bakers must have the correct baking ingredients, or muffin mix, on hand, and they must correctly forecast how many of each type of muffin to bake.

A 100 percent *customer service* level would mean that Muffin Inc. always has the muffin that their customers desired in stock for immediate sale. However, 20 percent of their muffin types (blueberry) account for over 80 percent of their sales. And although Muffin Inc. never wants to be out of muffin mix for their most popular muffins, it is almost impossible to carry every type of muffin mix without having a large quantity of mix go stale on the shelf.

An automated inventory-management system could generate reports that would help Muffin Inc. reduce the level of inventory that it must carry to maintain a high level of customer service. Automating inventory management helps most companies decrease inventory levels by 10 to 35 percent while still maintaining the same level of customer service.

Stock-status and *ABC analysis reports* can help Muffin Inc. manage its inventory. A stock-status report provides a detailed listing of current inventory. (See Figure 1-3 for an example of this type of report.) An ABC analysis report classifies each item in inventory by its sales frequency. Class A items are sold more frequently than class B or C items. (Figure 6-2 on the next page gives an example of this type of report.) An ABC analysis report will help Muffin Inc. maintain a good supply of all "A" items and reduce its inventory of "C" items.

Jack, the production manager at Muffin Inc., says that if he had an accurate summary report listing exactly what was ordered each month last year and a record of what was currently in stock, his job of reordering ingredients would be much easier. When the boss asked Jack by how much this would allow the company to reduce their current inventory levels of muffin mix, Jack replied, "Well,...lots."

I have given Jack's comment verbatim to point out that getting specific data often requires business judgment and management prerogative.

```
RUN DATE: 1/1/99              MUFFIN INCORPORATED
---------------------------------------------------------------------
              M U F F I N   A N A L Y S I S   R E P O R T
---------------------------------------------------------------------
     ITEM # RANGE: ALL
       VENDOR #: ALL
  PRODUCT CATEGORY: ALL

          CLASS A: TOP 30%   CLASS B: NEXT 30%   CLASS C: BOTTOM 30%
                      OF TOTAL INVENTORY VALUE
---------------------------------------------------------------------
-----ITEM------------------------------ CLASS    AVERAGE    YTD      YTD
   #  DESCRIPTION                                 COST     USAGE    COST

   1 BLUEBERRY MIX                        A       12.12     952   11533.48
   2 BRAN MIX                             B        7.24     735    5317.73
   3 ENGLISH MIX                          C       10.54     564    5942.30
   4 CORN MIX                             B       23.50    1120   26320.00
   5 MACADAMIA MIX                        B        8.14     521    4238.34
   6 RAISIN MIX                           C       25.53     200    5106.20
   7 HONEY MIX                            C        9.26      50     462.75
   8 CHEESE MIX                           C        0.45    1256     558.92

   8 ITEMS                                                5398   59479.71
                                                         ======  ==========
```

Figure 6-2.
Sample ABC analysis report.

"Assuming that we had this information, could we carry 20 percent less muffin mix?" asked the boss. "At least," Jack replied.

Muffin Inc.'s potential savings from improved inventory management will equal the carrying costs of the inventory it has eliminated. To estimate the percentage by which on-hand inventory could be reduced while still maintaining the same level of customer service, Muffin Inc.'s management could have done one of two things: They could have made an educated guess, which is how Muffin Inc. and most other companies estimate potential benefits, or they could have used *average-inventory-turn ratios*

Estimating Potential Inventory Reduction as a Result of Automation

The following inventory reduction formula is a good tool for estimating the value of reductions in inventory:

New sales = (estimated lost sales due to out-of-stock inventory) × (percent improvement projected from use of reports).

Savings due to inventory reduction = (value of inventory) × (carrying costs, expressed as a percentage of inventory) × (percent of inventory reduction).

To convert carrying costs into a percentage of inventory, divide the carrying costs by the value of the inventory and multiply by 100. Carrying costs ÷ Value of inventory × 100.

Carrying costs = (savings from reduced shrinkage and dead stock) + (reduced personnel costs) + (carrying cost of capital invested) + (reduced taxes and insurance on the inventory) + (lost opportunity costs for invested capital).

A typical distributor's carrying costs are between 25 and 35 percent per year.

for other muffin manufacturers to estimate how much they might be able to improve their own inventory management. Inventory-turn ratios are continually tabulated and reported in Dun and Bradstreet reports, which are available at most public libraries.

Inventory-turn ratio = ($ value of sales) / ($ value of inventory).

At Muffin Inc., the boss made an educated and informed estimate of the percentage by which inventory could be reduced. Muffin Inc.'s inventory is valued at $200,000. Carrying costs are estimated to be 25 percent and the boss estimated that Muffin Inc. would be able to reduce its inventory by 20 percent after implementing an automated inventory-management system. When these numbers are added to the inventory-reduction formula, the results are as follows: ($200,000) × (25%) × (20%) = ($10,000 per year in potential savings).

The boss at Muffin Inc. does not want to assume any improvement in sales to help justify office automation because "...business is going up anyway." Therefore, anticipated savings based on a reduction of inventory levels will be $10,000.

The 20 percent improvement in inventory management that Muffin Inc. anticipates may be higher or lower than the amount you will be able to save in your own business. You need to evaluate carefully how well your inventory has been managed manually and what inventory levels other automated businesses in your own industry carry to maintain a high customer service level. If you have not been able to manage your inventory well using a manual system, you will probably notice an even more dramatic improvement after automation; on the other hand, if your inventory has been managed very well, it may not be cost-effective to automate that area of your business.

Some automated inventory-control packages contain a *purchasing* module that contains reorder information and can generate a *purchase advice report*. A sample of this type of report is shown in Figure 6-3 on the next page. Your business might also benefit from *physical-count worksheets* (see Figure 6-4 on the next page). These can help you reduce direct labor costs when you take a physical inventory.

```
RUN DATE: 1/1/99                 MUFFIN INCORPORATED
--------------------------------------------------------------------------
              P U R C H A S I N G   A D V I C E   R E P O R T
--------------------------------------------------------------------------

BACK ORDER CONTROL CODE (BOC): B = OK TO BACK ORDER  N = NOT OK TO BACK ORDER
                               X = NO BACK ORDER CONTROL
--------------------------------------------------------------------------
                                 QTY                  QTY SOLD        HIT WENT
---ITEM---------   PRICE   COST    ON     RO    QTY ------------- BOC  RO  OUT
#  DESCRIPTION                    HAND   LEV  COMTD   PTD    YTD       LEV  STK

1 BLUEBERRY MIX   18.10   12.12   100    30    20      5    130   N    N    N
2 BRAN MIX        20.10    7.24   200    60    50     15    175   B    N    N


            2 ITEMS CHANGED STATUS
```

Figure 6-3.
Sample purchase-advice report.

```
RUN DATE: 1/1/99          MUFFIN INCORPORATED
--------------------------------------------------------------------------
              P H Y S I C A L   C O U N T   W O R K S H E E T
--------------------------------------------------------------------------
       WAREHOUSE: CENTRAL
  LOCATION RANGE: ALL
     ITEM # RANGE: ALL
       VENDOR #: ALL
PRODUCT CATEGORY: ALL
--------------------------------------------------------------------------
LOCATION  ITEM #   DESCRIPTION           SU/M      QTY     ACTUAL    CHECKED
                                                 ON HAND   COUNT         BY

0002       1       BLUEBERRY MIX          EA        20   _____   _____
0016       2       BRAN MIX               EA        60   _____   _____
0019       3       ENGLISH MIX            EA        30   _____   _____
0021       4       CORN MIX               EA       120   _____   _____
0023       5       MACADAMIA MIX          EA       750   _____   _____
0035       6       RAISIN MIX             EA        55   _____   _____
0089       7       HONEY MIX              EA       145   _____   _____
0131       8       CHEESE MIX             EA         2   _____   _____
```

Figure 6-4.
Sample physical-count worksheets.

Payback Analysis for Accounts Receivable at Muffin Inc.

Muffin Inc. is currently carrying $50,000 in outstanding receivables. Bell, the bookkeeper, sends out invoices each month, just like the phone company does. Unfortunately, unlike the phone company, Muffin Inc. sometimes has merchandise that is returned, exchanged, misshipped, or split-shipped. When the company sells muffin mix to muffin shops in a nearby county, the bills often go unpaid for months. In fact, Muffin Inc.'s average billing cycle is 78 days. And if customers don't pay up, there is no way to recover Muffin Inc.'s products; muffins are definitely consumable.

Automating its accounts-receivable department will allow Muffin Inc. to generate on demand *aged-receivables reports* that show where each customer's account stands. This credit information will allow the company to manage its daily business operations more effectively. Accounts with a bad credit history can quickly go to collection, helping to reduce bad debts, while Muffin Inc.'s well-established customers will not be mistreated for exceeding their credit limits slightly. A sample aged-receivables report is shown in Figure 6-5.

```
RUN DATE: 1/1/99              MUFFIN INCORPORATED
---------------------------------------------------------------------
     A C C O U N T S   R E C E I V A B L E   A G I N G   R E P O R T
---------------------------------------------------------------------
          AGED AS OF:3-31-99   DOES NOT INCLUDE ITEMS PAST AGING DATE
     CUSTOMER # RANGE:100       TO        300
  CUT-OFF BALANCE DUE:ALL
  CUT-OFF AGING PERIOD:ALL

  DOCUMENT TYPES:  I = INVOICE    C = CREDIT MEMO   D = DEBIT MEMO
                   B = BALANCE FORWARD   F = FINANCE CHARGE   P = PAYMENT
---------------------------------------------------------------------
---CUSTOMER----------     TERMS  BALANCE---------AGED BALANCE (DAYS)----------
  NAME          BAL-MET PHONE # CR LIMIT   CURRENT   31-60      61-90  OVER 90

21ST BAKERY            5/10 NET 10235.20   108.09 10127.11      0.00     0.00
HERB MANDEL    OPN-ITM 555-7844 20000.00

           DOC-#  TYP  APPLY-TO DUE-DATE  AMT-1      AMT-2    DOC TOTAL
           3001    B    3001    11/11/88 10127.11    0.00     10127.11
           3002    I    3002    11/11/88  715.45    69.42      784.87
           3003    C    3002    11/11/88   25.00CR   0.00       25.00CR
           3004    I    3004    11/11/88  150.00     9.00      159.00
            349    P    OPEN    11/11/88    8.90CR   0.00        8.90CR
            349    P    3002    11/11/88  375.35CR 134.52CR    509.87CR
            349    P    3004    11/11/88  115.75CR   8.25CR    124.00CR
            201    P    3002    11/11/88  250.00CR   0.00      250.00CR
           3006    D    3006    11/11/88   15.00CR   0.00       15.00
            205    P    3004    11/11/88   50.00CR   0.00       50.00CR
         993013    F    3013    11/11/88  116.99CR   0.00      116.99

BEVERLY HILLS BAKERY 2/10 NET 835.00CR   835.00CR   0.00       0.00     0.00
A. PETERS     BAL-FWD 555-9000 50000.00

           DOC-#  TYP  APPLY-TO DUE-DATE  AMT-1      AMT-2    DOC TOTAL
           3001    P            11/11/88  585.00CR 250.00CR   835.00CR

                   GRAND TOT            726.91CR 10127.11      0.00     0.00
                                        ========  ========   ======= ========
```

Figure 6-5.
Sample aged-receivables report.

The boss estimates that better customer credit checking could eliminate virtually all of Muffin Inc.'s bad debts. "We could save at least $500 per year by reducing 80 percent of our bad debts."

For our example, let's assume that the bank is charging 15 percent annual interest on Muffin Inc.'s outstanding business loans and that by automating its accounts receivable Muffin Inc. will reduce its billing cycle by 20 days—that is, from 78 to 58 days. When these numbers are used in the accounts-receivable formula, the result shows that Muffin Inc. will save $411: ($50,000 in daily receivables) × (15% per year cost of credit/365 days per year) × (20 day reduction in collection period) = ($411).

Many companies that automate their receivables begin to charge interest on overdue balances. This is easily computed by the system, which can update the customers' accounts and invoice the late charges. However, Muffin Inc. has chosen not to post interest charges. The boss wants to maintain her customers' goodwill.

Muffin Inc.'s total estimated savings for automating the accounts-receivable department are $911. "That's pretty reasonable," said the boss, "But," she added, pointing a finger at Bob, the honest computer salesman, "will this system pay for itself in one year? It takes only half an hour to bake muffins!"

Payback Analysis for Accounts Payable at Muffin Inc.

Bell, the bookkeeper, is a genius; she has discovered that by paying bills on time, no one would ever call her up to yell at her. Sometimes she would even pay bills a bit early, although the boss cautioned her against paying them too soon.

"The only way Muffin Inc. could save money on payables is to buy less muffin mix," said the boss.

"But Bell will be able to save time doing her work," countered Bob, the honest computer salesman. "The accounts-payable application will generate checks, remittance stubs, envelopes, and form letters on demand.

Estimating Improved Collections as a Result of Automation

If Muffin Inc.'s billing cycle can be shortened, its savings will equal the current interest that it is paying on its outstanding receivables balance per day multiplied by the number of days by which collections have been sped up.

Average collection-period data for different types of businesses is available from Dun and Bradstreet. This information can help you evaluate how close your own billing cycles are to industry averages.

Generating timely aged-receivables reports, reminder notices for any late accounts, and collection letters will usually improve collections dramatically. It is not unusual to reduce the collection period by 25 to 50 percent with an automated accounts receivable system.

Outstanding daily A/R = (outstanding A/R for the year) / (365 days)

Savings due to reduced billing cycle = (amount of outstanding daily A/R) × (current daily interest rate) × (number of days by which the billing cycle has been shortened)

The system will generate a *cash-requirements report* that can help Muffin Inc. manage its cash flow. And an *aged-payables report* will prevent Bell from losing discounts from vendors who bill with terms. ''And,'' Bob continued, ''you can store Muffin Inc.'s buying history from different suppliers in the programs' vendor file. That information can then be compiled in a *vendor-analysis report* that can serve as leverage when Muffin Inc. is renegotiating its contracts with major suppliers.''

Examples of each of these reports are shown in Figures 6-6 through 6-9 on this and the following two pages.

```
RUN DATE: 1/1/99              MUFFIN INCORPORATED
-----------------------------------------------------------------------------
                   C A S H   R E Q U I R E M E N T S   R E P O R T
-----------------------------------------------------------------------------
             THRU:       6/1/99
     FOR PAYMENT ON:     4/10/99
 NEXT PAYMENT DATE IS:   4/24/99
 VENDOR NUMBER RANGE:    ALL

---VENDOR------------------------   GROSS AMT VALID DISC  LOST DISC    NET AMT
 #  NAME/TERMS

100 VERMONT BAKING SUPPLY PAST DUE:      0.00    108.09       0.00       0.00
    2/10 NET 30           CURRENT:    1200.00     23.00       0.00    1177.00
                          OPTIONAL:      0.00      0.00       0.00       0.00
                          TOTAL:     1200.00     23.00       0.00    1177.00
          VCH-NO    INV #INV DATE DUE DATE  DISC DATE  PAST DUE    CURRENT
          1001 AG22401    3/15/99  4/14/99   3/25/99   -585.00    1200.00

300 RED LINE FREIGHT      PAST DUE:     68.50      0.00       0.00      68.50
    NET 30                CURRENT:     103.54      0.00       0.00     103.54
                          OPTIONAL:      0.00      0.00       0.00       0.00
                          TOTAL:      172.04      0.00       0.00     172.04
          VCH-NO    INV #INV DATE DUE DATE  DISC DATE  PAST DUE    CURRENT
          1004 44237      2/27/99  3/29/99   2/27/99     68.50
          1005 45961      3/11/99  4/10/99   3/11/99               103.54

500 E-Z REPAIRS           PAST DUE:      0.00      0.00       0.00       0.00
    NET 30                CURRENT:     232.04      0.00       0.00     232.04
                          OPTIONAL:    225.95      2.26       0.00     223.69
                          TOTAL:      457.99      2.26       0.00     455.73
          VCH-NO    INV #INV DATE DUE DATE  DISC DATE  PAST DUE    CURRENT
          1007 2357       3/2/99   5/10/99   4/10/99      0.00       0.00
          1008 2398       3/12/99  4/11/99   3/12/99      0.00      74.10
          1009 2410       3/18/99  4/17/99   3/18/99      0.00     157.94

700 PACIFIC TELEPHONE     PAST DUE:    831.77      0.00       0.00     831.77
    NET 20                CURRENT:       0.00      0.00       0.00       0.00
                          OPTIONAL:      0.00      0.00       0.00       0.00
                          TOTAL:      831.77      0.00       0.00     831.77
          VCH-NO    INV #INV DATE DUE DATE  DISC DATE  PAST DUE    CURRENT
          1012 FEB BILL   3/1/99   3/21/99   3/1/99     831.77

700 HANSON FLOUR CO.      PAST DUE:      0.00      0.00       0.00       0.00
                          CURRENT:       0.00      0.00       0.00       0.00
                          OPTIONAL:  14078.06    681.59       0.00    1396.47
                          TOTAL:    14078.06    681.59       0.00    1396.47
          VCH-NO    INV #INV DATE DUE DATE  DISC DATE  PAST DUE    CURRENT
          1003 AG22597    3/11/99  5/10/99   4/10/99      0.00       0.00
          1013 77250931   3/12/99  5/11/99   4/11/99      0.00       0.00
          1014 77489176   3/20/99  5/19/99   4/19/99      0.00       0.00

    GRAND TOTALS:         PAST DUE:    900.27      0.00       0.00     900.27
                          CURRENT:    1535.58     23.00       0.00    1512.38
                          OPTIONAL:  14304.01    683.85       0.00   13620.16
                          TOTAL:    16739.86    706.85       0.00   16033.01
```

Figure 6-6.
Sample cash-requirements report.

```
RUN DATE: 1/1/99            MUFFIN INCORPORATED
-----------------------------------------------------------------------
              A / P   O P E N   I T E M   R E P O R T
-----------------------------------------------------------------------
VENDOR # RANGE:     ALL
      AGED AS OF:   5/31/99
NOTE: ASTERISK BESIDE VOUCHER ITEM MEANS ITEM IS PERMANENTLY DEFERRED
-----------------------------------------------------------------------
VENDOR     VENDOR     VALID     VENDOR---------AGED VENDOR NET (DAYS)---------
   #        BAL.      DISC.        NET   CURRENT    31-60       61-90    OVER 90

   100     1200.00    23.00     1177.00     0.00      0.00    1177.00      0.00

   300      172.04     0.00      172.04     0.00      0.00     103.04     68.50

   400     5000.00     0.00     5000.00     0.00      0.00       0.00   5000.00

   500      457.99     0.00      457.99     0.00      0.00     457.99      0.00

   700      831.77     0.00      831.77     0.00      0.00       0.00    831.77

   800    14078.06     0.00    14078.06     0.00      0.00   14078.06      0.00

   900     1135.17    56.28     1078.89     0.00      0.00    1078.89      0.00
GRAND
TOTALS   22875.03    79.28    22795.75     0.00      0.00   16894.98   5900.27
         =========  ========  =========  ========  ========  =========  ========
```

Figure 6-7.
Sample aged-payables report.

```
RUN DATE: 1/1/99            MUFFIN INCORPORATED
-----------------------------------------------------------------------
              V E N D O R   A N A L Y S I S   R E P O R T
-----------------------------------------------------------------------
---VENDOR-----------     LAST      ---------YTD----------    -------LAST YR.-------
      NAME            PURCHASE     PURCHASES   % TOTAL     PURCHASES    % TOTAL
                        DATE

VERMONT BAKING SUPPLY   3/15/99    13700.00      8.9%       45000.00      9.5%
ACME OFFICE SUPPLY      3/5/99      2153.00      1.4%        4287.50      0.9%
RED LINE FREIGHT        3/11/99      849.08      0.6%        2365.00      0.5%
JONES PROPERTY MGMT.    3/1/99     20000.00     13.0%       50000.00     10.5%
E-Z REPAIRS             3/21/99     1134.68      0.7%         401.00      0.1%
WELLS FARGO BANK        2/28/99       83.50      0.1%         227.31      0.0%
PACIFIC TELEPHONE       3/1/99      2713.54      1.8%        4175.00      0.9%
HANSON BAKING CO.       3/20/99    93156.12     60.8%      284000.00     59.7%
REYNOLDS BREAD CO.      3/13/99    19470.34     12.7%       85000.00     17.9%

9 VENDORS    GRAND TOTALS:        153260.26    100.0%      475455.81    100.0%
                                  ==========                ==========
             AVERAGES:             17028.92                  52828.42
```

Figure 6-8.
Sample vendor-analysis report.

"None of our suppliers are complaining," replied the boss, "and Bell doesn't have enough to do now."

This dialogue highlights the need to rely on your own best assessment of your situation. There is nothing hypothetical about your Bell, your payables, or your company. You will probably find that automation does not necessarily lead to cost savings in every area of your company. It is

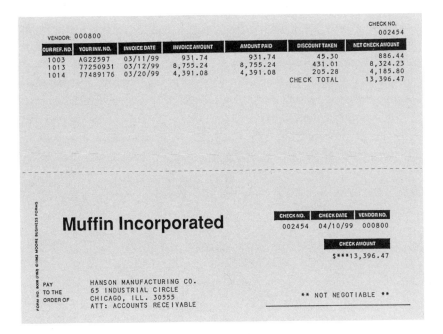

Figure 6-9.
Sample checks and stub.

usually unwise to automate things that are working well and that are cost-effective already.

If Bell was sloppy and missed payment discounts, a payables module could help her remember to take them. But Muffin Inc. works with only a few suppliers, and a simple manual filing system is completely adequate for its needs.

Payback Analysis for Order Entry and Billing at Muffin Inc.

Automated order entry would allow Muffin Inc.'s employees to enter orders directly into the accounting system, which would eliminate the need to rekey invoices into the accounts-payables, accounts-receivables, inventory, and other files. This would increase the efficiency of the clerical staff and reduce accounting errors.

If Muffin Inc.'s salespeople used special keys or codes to enter the types of muffins sold, the system could easily generate reports that would show what had sold and what would mold. This information could be entered directly into the inventory module and could help Jack predict future muffin sales more accurately.

Another reason why the boss liked the idea of an automated order-entry system was that it would allow her to reduce the number of muffin expediters. The automated system could generate a logically ordered pick list. With one cashier entering orders and several production people making and packing muffins from orders printed out in the production area, her operations would run much more smoothly. Picking savings alone might justify the installation of an automated order-entry system. Figure 6-10 shows an example of a picking list.

```
RUN DATE: 1/1/99              MUFFIN INCORPORATED
--------------------------------------------------------------------
                     P I C K I N G   T I C K E T
--------------------------------------------------------------------
   ORDER #:      101           WAREHOUSE:CENTRAL
ORDER DATE:  3/10/99

   SOLD TO:SPACE BAKERY          SHIP TO:  SPACE BAKERY
           3901 AVE. OF THE AMERICAS       3901 AVE. OF THE AMERICAS
           SUITE 360                       SUITE 360
           NEW YORK, NY 10052              NEW YORK, NY 10052

   CUST. #:    50                SALESMAN:    789
   P.O. #:  CE21-1               SHIP VIA: PARCEL POST
     TERMS:5/10 NET 25           SHIP DATE: 3/15/99
                                 DATE SHIPPED:_____
--------------------------------------------------------------------
LOC ITEM # DESCRIPTION                   QTY       QTY       QTY
                                       ORDERED   TO SHIP   SHIPPED

16      2 BRAN MIX                        5         5 DRP-SHIP

21      4 CORN MIX                        2         2 _____

23      8 CHEESE MIX                    100       100 _____

35      5 MACADAMIA MIX                  10        10 _____


        4 LINE ITEMS                             117 TOTAL QTY
```

Figure 6-10.
Sample picking list.

Rather than using typewriter-style data-entry terminals to enter retail sales, the boss wanted to use some kind of point-of-sale terminal that was better suited to Muffin Inc.'s needs. Unfortunately, holographic scanners could not read universal product codes printed on the irregular shapes of muffins, and bar code readers, although great for prepackaged cookies, tore the tops of delicate muffins. Therefore, Muffin Inc. decided to install electronic cash registers that were connected directly to the main computer system at the bakery.

The boss, using the story worksheets to analyze her business, realized that a remote printer in the back room would mean one less expediter per store and could increase customer satisfaction by getting orders filled faster. Greater customer satisfaction should lead to increased sales.

The boss estimated that she would save about $6,800 per year in direct labor costs (the muffin expediters). She also thought that sales might increase by as much as 5 percent because of better service during the lunch rush, although she decided not to mention this to Bob.

Bob had justified $17,711 in potential cost savings, and he had not even mentioned the advantages of *back-order reports*, an example of which is shown in Figure 6-11.

```
RUN DATE: 1/1/99                MUFFIN INCORPORATED
---------------------------------------------------------------------------
                  B A C K   O R D E R S   B Y   C U S T O M E R
---------------------------------------------------------------------------
FOR SELECTED CUSTOMERS ONLY

-----CUSTOMER------    -----ITEM----------    -----ORDER-----    CUSTOMER    QTY
  #  NAME             #  DESCRIPTION          #  DATE                 PO #    S/O

 600 ARIEL BAKERY      1 BLUEBERRY MIX        102  3/16/99             921     10

                       1 ITEMS ON B/O FOR ABOVE CUSTOMER
                         HAVING TOTAL EXTENDED PRICE OF:           246.70

  1    CUSTOMERS WITH BACK ORDERS HAVING GRAND TOTAL EXTENDED PRICE OF:   246.70
                                                                        ========
```

Figure 6-11.
Sample back-order report.

Payback Analysis for Muffin Inc.'s Payroll

Ms. Muffin, the boss, has 63 employees. She has been sending the payroll to an accounting service for the last five years, but she feels that Muffin Inc. is now large enough to warrant having the payroll done in-house.

She reasoned that doing the payroll in-house would be faster because her bookkeeper would not need to double-check the accounting service's figures. In fact, Muffin Inc. probably would not require any extra clerical time for its payroll. Bell, the bookkeeper, has time to burn, so it seemed more sensible for her to run a payroll program than spend time shuttling time cards and checks back and forth from the bookkeeping service. The bookkeeping service charged about $200 per month to do the payroll.

Figures 6-12 through 6-15 on the next three pages show some of the forms and reports available in a typical payroll module.

```
RUN DATE: 1/1/99              MUFFIN INCORPORATED
-----------------------------------------------------------------------
                   P A Y R O L L    R E G I S T E R
-----------------------------------------------------------------------
          FOR DEPARTMENT:                501
FOR THE PAY PERIOD ENDING:             3/1/99
EMPLOYEE TYPES: H = HOURLY   S = SALARY
CHECK TYPES: R = REGULAR   V = VACATION

FREQUENCIES USED ON THIS RUN:              THIS PAY PERIOD: W8S
VACATION CHECK 1:      W               VACATION CHECK 2:    NONE
VACATION CHECK 3:      NONE            VACATION CHECK 4:    NONE
-----------------------------------------------------------------------
DEPT     EMP# EMP-TYP   CHK-TYP      SALARY    REG-PAY    HOL-PAY    GROSS
NAME                                 WKS-WRK   OVT-PAY    SCK-PAY  YTD GROSS
         SOC-SEC-NO                  SUP-PAY   VAC-PAY    SPC-PAY

501       2        H       R          0.00     640.00      0.00     640.00
LEVINE, SUSAN M.                      2.00       0.00      0.00     640.00
         234-56-7891                  0.00       0.00      0.00


501       5        S       R          0.00     869.47      0.00    2951.75
WILKENSON, WILLIAM B.                 2.16       0.00    332.28    2951.75
                                    100.00       0.00      0.00


          OTHER EARNINGS:          1200.00  COMMISSION EARN
                                    250.00  TRAVEL EARN
                                    200.00  TRAVEL EARN

501       5        S       V          0.00       0.00      0.00     553.80
WILKENSON, WILLIAM B.                 0.00       0.00      0.00    3505.55
                                      0.00     553.80      0.00
```

```
RUN DATE: 1/1/99              MUFFIN INCORPORATED
-----------------------------------------------------------------------
                   P A Y R O L L    R E G I S T E R
-----------------------------------------------------------------------
          FOR DEPARTMENT:                501
FOR THE PAY PERIOD ENDING:             3/1/99
EMPLOYEE TYPES: H = HOURLY   S = SALARY
CHECK TYPES: R = REGULAR   V = VACATION

FREQUENCIES USED ON THIS RUN:              THIS PAY PERIOD: W8S
VACATION CHECK 1:      W               VACATION CHECK 2:    NONE
VACATION CHECK 3:      NONE            VACATION CHECK 4:    NONE
-----------------------------------------------------------------------
   3 CHECKS TO BE PRINTED              2 REGULAR            1 VACATION

DEPARTMENT TOTALS:                         YTD-IN   THIS PERIOD    YTD-OUT
           SAL-PAY:       0.00      GROSS:   0.00      4145.55     4145.55
           REG-PAY:    1509.47    FWT-GRS:   0.00      3665.55     3665.55
           OVT-PAY:       0.00       FICA:   0.00       243.76      243.76
           VAC-PAY:     553.80        FWT:   0.00      1033.94     1033.94
           HOL-PAY:       0.00        EIC:   0.00         0.00        0.00
          SICK-PAY:     332.28        SWT:   0.00       255.12      255.12
          SPEC-PAY:       0.00        OST:   0.00        21.99       21.99
          SUPP-PAY:     100.00        CWT:   0.00         0.00        0.00
                                      NET:            2364.74
        COMMISSION:    1200.00
            TRAVEL:     450.00

DEPARTMENT EMPLOYER LIABILITY TOTALS: FICA:   0.00      243.76      243.76
                                       FUI:   0.00       25.66       25.66
                                       SUI:   0.00       98.97       98.97
                                   SUP-BEN:   0.00        0.00        0.00

DEPARTMENT WORKER'S COMP TOTALS: CLASS      SUBJ-WAGES  RPTD-UNITS TOTAL-PREM
                                  PCT:    5    640.00                    3.20
                                  WEEKS                        2.16      4.32
```

Figure 6-12.
Sample payroll register.

```
RUN DATE: 1/1/99              MUFFIN INCORPORATED
-----------------------------------------------------------------------------
                  Y E A R   E N D   P A Y R O L L   R E P O R T
-----------------------------------------------------------------------------
   COMPANY:MUFFIN INCORPORATED
   ADDRESS:SOUTHERN CALIFORNIA DIVISION
           7020 WILSHIRE BOULEVARD
           LOS ANGELES, CA 90010
     FED ID:95-1135917

     STATE:CALIF. TAX CODE (MARRIED)        STATE ID:      213-4495-1
-----------------------------------------------------------------------------
SOC-SEC#   NAME/ADDRESS              1ST Q    2ND Q    3RD Q    4TH Q     YTD

456-78-9123         GRS-WAGES      1692.30     0.00     0.00     0.00  1692.30
ARNOLD J. WILSON    FWT-WAGES      1592.30     0.00     0.00     0.00  1592.30
517 HARROWSMITH ROAD FWT W/H        343.42     0.00     0.00     0.00   343.42
GLENDALE    CA      EMP-FICA-GRS   1592.30     0.00     0.00     0.00  1592.30
91055               EMP-FICA-W/H    105.89     0.00     0.00     0.00   105.89
                    SWT-GRS        1492.30     0.00     0.00     0.00  1492.30
                    SWT-WH           53.60     0.00     0.00     0.00    53.60
                    OST-GRS        1592.30     0.00     0.00     0.00  1592.30
                    OST-W/            9.55     0.00     0.00     0.00     9.55
                    CWT-GRS           0.00     0.00     0.00     0.00     0.00
                    CWT-W/H           0.00     0.00     0.00     0.00     0.00
                    EIC-GRS           0.00     0.00     0.00     0.00     0.00
                    EIC-PMNT          0.00     0.00     0.00     0.00     0.00
                    EMPR-FICA-GRS  1592.30     0.00     0.00     0.00  1592.30
                    EMPR-FICA       105.89     0.00     0.00     0.00   105.89
                    W-COMP-GRS        0.00     0.00     0.00     0.00     0.00
                    FUI-GRS        1592.30     0.00     0.00     0.00  1592.30
                    SUI-GRS        1592.30     0.00     0.00     0.00  1592.30
                    SUPP-BEN-GRS      0.00     0.00     0.00     0.00     0.00
                    RPTD-TIPS         0.00     0.00     0.00     0.00     0.00

                    REG-PAY        1000.00     0.00     0.00     0.00  1000.00
                    OVT-PAY           0.00     0.00     0.00     0.00     0.00
                    VAC-PAY          92.30     0.00     0.00     0.00    92.30
                    HOL-PAY           0.00     0.00     0.00     0.00     0.00
                    SICK-PAY          0.00     0.00     0.00     0.00     0.00
                    SPEC-PAY          0.00     0.00     0.00     0.00     0.00
                    SUPP-PAY        100.00     0.00     0.00     0.00   100.00

                    GARNIS            0.00     0.00     0.00     0.00     0.00
                    LOAN            100.00     0.00     0.00     0.00   100.00
                    UNION             0.00     0.00     0.00     0.00     0.00

                    PENSION          25.00     0.00     0.00     0.00    25.00
                    CHARITY          10.00     0.00     0.00     0.00    10.00
                    BONUS           300.00     0.00     0.00     0.00   300.00
                    COMMISSN        125.00     0.00     0.00     0.00   125.00
                    TRAVEL           75.00     0.00     0.00     0.00    75.00
```

Figure 6-13.
Sample year-end payroll report.

```
RUN DATE: 1/1/99              MUFFIN INCORPORATED
-----------------------------------------------------------------------------
                  D E D U C T I O N S   R E G I S T E R
-----------------------------------------------------------------------------
           FOR DEPARTMENT:        247
FOR THE PAY PERIOD ENDING:      3/1/99
CHECK TYPES: R = REGULAR   V = VACATION

FREQUENCIES USED ON THIS RUN:          THIS PAY PERIOD: W8S
VACATION CHECK 1:  W           VACATION CHECK 2:      NONE
VACATION CHECK 3:  NONE        VACATION CHECK 4:      NONE
-----------------------------------------------------------------------------
EMP NAME                        UNION   GARNISH------OTHER DEDUCTIONS-----   TOTAL
 #   SOC-SEC-NO  EMP-TYP  TYP LOAN               D/E-1    D/E-2    D/E-3   DEDUCT

 1  PALMER, EDWARD W.            0.00    0.00    10.00    50.00     0.00   110.00
    415-59-6091  S       R     50.00            CHARITY  PENSION
```

Figure 6-14.
Sample deduction register.

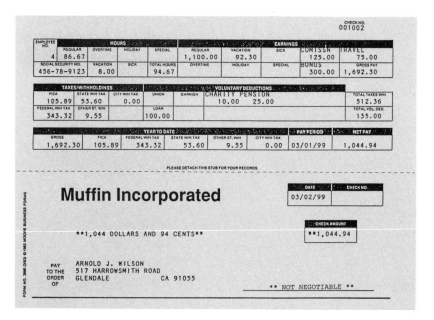

Figure 6-15.
Sample payroll check.

Payback Analysis for the General Ledger at Muffin Inc.

"If we are planning to do all of this work with the computer," asked the boss, "doesn't it make sense to run our financial statements ourselves?"

"Yes," agreed Bob. "Once you have entered all of your data into the order-entry and billing, accounts-payable, accounts-receivable, and inventory-control modules, most integrated general-ledger packages will generate your financial statements. And if you have reliable data on your cash flow and reserves, you would be able to pay off short-term notes rather than leaving surplus cash in money-market accounts. You might also be able to spot variances in departmental budgets sooner."

Ms. Muffin decided to install an automated general-ledger system. That would save another $200 per month in bookkeeping fees. "That's $22,511 in cost justification," said Bob.

Figures 6-16 through 6-19 on the next three pages illustrate some of the reports that an automated general-ledger system can generate.

```
                        MUFFIN INCORPORATED
              STATEMENT OF CHANGES IN FINANCIAL POSITION

                       YEAR TO DATE NET BALANCES
                           AS OF 3/31/99

        WORKING CAPITAL SOURCES

                                       CURRENT OPERATIONS

    NET PROFIT (LOSS)                        23845.00

    ADD EXPENSES REQUIRING NO FUNDS OUTLAY

    ACCUMULATED DEPRECIATION                  1350.00
                                            ----------
            TOTAL FROM OPERATIONS                        25195.00

        OTHER SOURCES
                                            ----------
                TOTAL OTHER SOURCES                          0.00
                                                        ---------
                TOTAL NEW WORKING CAPITAL               25195.00


        WORKING CAPITAL USES                            -4100.00
                                                        ---------
    NET INCREASE (DECREASE) WORKING CAPITAL                      21095.00
                                                            ==========
```

Figure 6-16.
Sample statement of change.

```
RUN DATE: 1/1/99              MUFFIN INCORPORATED
--------------------------------------------------------------------------------
                 G E N E R A L   L E D G E R   W O R K S H E E T
--------------------------------------------------------------------------------
      START DATE:     3/1/99
        END DATE:     3/31/99
    ACCT # RANGE:     ALL
   PROFIT CENTER:     ALL


   ---ACCOUNT------------TRIAL BALANCE-----   ---ADJUSTMENTS----   ---ADJ TRIAL BAL--
   #    DESCRIPTION    DEBITS     CREDITS     DEBITS    CREDITS    DEBITS    CREDITS

   1000 CASH ACCOUNT  380700.00    500.00    _____  _____   _____  _____

   1100 RECEIVABLES   115200.00    500.00    _____  _____   _____  _____

   1110 EMPLOYEE LOANS   5320.00     0.00    _____  _____   _____  _____

   1200 INVENTORY     186600.00     0.00     _____  _____   _____  _____

   1310 ACCUM. DEPREC.     0.00   1650.00    _____  _____   _____  _____

   2000 ACCTS PAYABLE      0.00  27600.00    _____  _____   _____  _____

   2300 MORTGAGE PAY.    500.00  55000.00    _____  _____   _____  _____

   3000 COMMON STOCK      0.00 155000.00     _____  _____   _____  _____

   3100 RET EARNINGS      0.00 447720.00     _____  _____   _____  _____

   4010 SALES-MIXES       0.00    200.00     _____  _____   _____  _____

   4020 SALES-BULK        0.00    200.00     _____  _____   _____  _____

   6000 SALARY/WAGES      0.00      0.00     _____  _____   _____  _____

   6200 DEPRECIATION     50.00      0.00     _____  _____   _____  _____

      GRAND TOTALS:  688370.00 688370.00
                    ========== ==========
```

Figure 6-17.
Sample G/L worksheet.

```
RUN DATE: 1/1/99              MUFFIN INCORPORATED
                             PROFIT & LOSS STATEMENT
                                 AS OF 3/31/99

                        CURRENT-PERIOD                 YTD
                        AMOUNT     RATIO           AMOUNT    RATIO

        REVENUE

    SALES-MIXES          80700.00   61.64%         80700.00    61.64%
    SALES-BULK           42475.00   32.44%         42475.00    32.44%
    OTHER INCOME          7750.00    5.92%          7750.00     5.92%
                        ----------                ----------
        TOT REVENUE     130925.00  100.00%        130925.00   100.00%

        COST OF GOODS SOLD

    BEGIN INVENTORY     160000.00  122.21%        160000.00   122.21%
    PURCHASES            45500.00   34.75%         45500.00    34.75%
    PURCH RET & ALLOW     -550.00   -0.42%          -550.00    -0.42%
    END INVENTORY      -154000.00 -117.62%       -154000.00  -117.62%
                        ----------                ----------
        TOT COST OF GOODS 50950.00   38.92%         50950.00    38.92%
                        ----------
        GROSS PROFIT     79975.00   61.08%         79975.00    61.08%

        OPERATING EXPENSES

    SALARIES & WAGES      5600.00    4.28%          5600.00     4.28%
    SALES COMMISSIONS    15050.00   11.50%         15050.00    11.50%
    PAYROLL TAXES         1255.00    0.96%          1255.00     0.96%
    DEPRECIATION          1350.00    1.03%          1350.00     1.03%
    INSURANCE EXPENSE      770.00    0.59%           770.00     0.59%
    ADVERTISING/PROMOTION  650.00    0.50%           650.00     0.50%
    RENT EXPENSE          3500.00    2.67%          3500.00     2.67%
                        ----------                ----------
        TOT OPERATING EXP 28175.00   21.52%         28175.00    21.52%
                        ----------                ----------
        NET INCOME (LOSS) 51800.00   39.56%         51800.00    39.56%
                        ==========                ==========

            THIS FINANCIAL STATEMENT IS UNAUDITED
            AND WITHOUT OPINION EXPRESSED BY
            ---PRINT CPA FIRM HERE---
```

Figure 6-18.
Sample profit-and-loss statement.

Payback Analysis from Sales Analysis for Muffin Inc.

"Well, Ms. Muffin," said Bob, "the next program can produce reports that will tell you everything you ever wanted to know about your sales. Sales-analysis reports can help you make good decisions, and good decisions mean higher profits for your company.

"These reports can be generated in many different formats," he continued. "They can report what has sold, what hasn't, who sold what, when they sold it, and who bought it. Sales-analysis reports allow you to spot trends by customer, territory, or item and can help you track both sales and profitability over each accounting period. And historical sales data can be used for comparative reports and forecasting models."

```
RUN DATE: 1/1/99              MUFFIN INCORPORATED
                                 BALANCE SHEET
                                AS OF 3/31/99

ASSETS                                LIABILITIES

    CURRENT ASSETS                       CURRENT LIABILITIES
CASH               468465.00      ACCTS PAYABLE        19350.00
ACCTS RECEIVABLE    71820.00      SAL/WAGES PAYABLE     1950.00
LOANS RECEIVABLE     5320.00      PENSION PAYABLE       2385.00
PREPAID INSURANCE    1480.00      GARNISH DED PAYABLE   2180.00
INVENTORY          180600.00      CHARITY DEDUCT PAYAB   525.00
                  ----------      UNION DUES PAYABLE     200.00
   TOTAL CURR ASSETS     727685.00 WITH TAX PAYABLE     1695.00
                                   EIC ADVANCES PAID     300.00
    FIXED ASSETS                   FICA TAXES PAYABLE   1055.00
FURN AND FIXTURES   85000.00      FUI TAXES PAYABLE      960.00
ACCUM DEPRECIATION  -2950.00      STATE W/H TAXES PAYA  8498.00
                  ----------      SUI TAXES PAYABLE     3780.00
   TOTAL FIX ASSETS      82050.00  SDI TAXES PAYABLE    8410.00
                        ---------- STATE TAXES PAYABLE  4775.00
                                   COUNTY TAXES PAYABLE  240.00
                                   CITY SALES TAX PAYAB  595.00
                                                      ----------
                                      TOTAL CURR LIABILITIES    56898.00

                                      LONG TERM LIABILITIES
                                   MORTGAGE PAYABLE     50900.00
                                                      ----------
                                      TOTAL LT LIABILITIES      50900.00
                                                               ----------
                                      TOTAL LIABILITIES        107798.00

                                      STOCKHOLDERS EQUITY

                                   COMMON STK, $10 PAR 155000.00
                                   RETAINED EARNINGS   495137.00
                                   NET INCOME (LOSS)    51800.00
                                                      ----------
                                      TOTAL EQUITY             701937.00
                                                               ----------
       TOTAL ASSETS     809735.00     TOTAL LIABILITIES & EQUITY 809735.00
                       ===========                             ===========
```

Figure 6-19.
Sample balance sheet.

Examples of sales reports are shown in Figures 6-20 through 6-23 on the next three pages.

"Although you can generate sales-analysis reports manually," Bob went on, "they are usually so time-consuming to produce that it is simply not practical to use them to manage operations. However, once an automated order entry and billing module is installed, virtually all of the data needed for sales-analysis reports will already be in your automated system. Muffin Inc. will be able to request up-to-date sales analysis reports on demand."

Ms. Muffin saw that by spotting trends in her customer's tastes, she would be able to respond faster and with more precision when ordering, advertising, and baking her products.

```
RUN DATE: 1/1/99                MUFFIN INCORPORATED
-----------------------------------------------------------------------------
                 S A L E S   A N A L Y S I S   B Y   C U S T O M E R
-----------------------------------------------------------------------------

---CUSTOMER----------------------    SALES      %-OF      COST-OF    PROFIT
TYP  NAME/CITY,STATE     SLSMN                  SALES     SALES

RET  HARRIS BAKERY            PTD:    0.00      0.0%        0.00       0.00
     SAN DIEGO       CA 25 YTD:       0.00      0.0%        0.00       0.00

     WASHINGTON BAKERY        PTD:    7000.00   68.0%     4000.00    3000.00
     DALLAS          TX 21 YTD:       7000.00   19.6%     4000.00    3000.00

     SPACE BAKERY             PTD:    1050.00   10.2%      535.00     515.00
     NE

     21ST CENTURY BAKERY      PTD:    2240.75   21.8%     1623.05     617.70
     SAN FRANCISCO   CA 10 YTD:      27699.51   77.5%    20137.87    7561.64

     BEVERLY HILLS BAKERY     PTD:    0.00      0.0%        0.00       0.00
     LOS ANGELES     CA 23 YTD:       0.00      0.0%        0.00       0.00

     ARIEL BAKERY             PTD:    0.00      0.0%        0.00       0.00
     LOS ANGELES     CA 23 YTD:       0.00      0.0%        0.00       0.00

          TYPE TOTALS:        PTD:   10290.75  100.0%     6158.05    4132.70
                              YTD:   35749.51  100.0%    24672.87   11076.64

WSL  ELLIOT MUFFIN SHOP       PTD:    0.00      0.0%        0.00       0.00
     GLENDALE        CA 23 YTD:      500.00     45.5%      250.00     250.00

     W.J. MUFFINS             PTD:    0.00      0.0%        0.00       0.00
     LOS ANGELES     CA 20 YTD:       0.00      0.0%        0.00       0.00

     NEPTUNE MUFFIN SHOP      PTD:    600.00   100.0%      345.00     255.00
     SANTA MARINA    CA 23 YTD:      600.00     54.5%      345.00     255.00

          TYPE TOTALS:        PTD:    600.00   100.0%      345.00     255.00
                              YTD:   1100.00   100.0%      395.00     505.00
```

Figure 6-20.
Sample sales by customer-detail report.

```
RUN DATE: 1/1/99                MUFFIN INCORPORATED
-----------------------------------------------------------------------------
                 S A L E S   A N A L Y S I S   B Y   C U S T O M E R
-----------------------------------------------------------------------------

CUST NO-OF  PCT-OF            SALES      %-OF     COST-OF     PROFIT  PCT-OF  MARGIN
TYPE CUSTS  CUSTS                        SALES    SALES               PROFIT     PCT

RET    6    60.0%  PTD:    10290.75     94.5%     6158.05    4132.70   94.2%   40.2%
                   YTD:    35749.51     97.0%    24672.87   11076.64   95.6%   31.0%

WSL    3    30.0%  PTD:      600.00      5.5%      345.00     255.00    5.8%   42.5%
                   YTD:     1100.00      3.0%      595.00     505.00    4.4%   45.9%

GRAND TOTAL 100.0% PTD:    10890.75    100.0%     6503.05    4387.70  100.0%   40.3%
     3 TYPES        YTD:    36849.51    100.0%    25267.87   11581.64  100.0%   31.4%
     9 CUSTOMERS
```

Figure 6-21.
Sample sales by customer-type summary report

```
RUN DATE: 1/1/99              MUFFIN INCORPORATED
----------------------------------------------------------------------------
                 S A L E S   A N A L Y S I S   B Y   S T A T E
----------------------------------------------------------------------------

STATE---------CUSTOMER---------------        SALES    %-OF    COST-OF   PROFIT
     #  NAME/CITY          SLSMN TYP                  SALES    SALES

CA   1 ELLIOT MUFFIN SHOP        WSL PTD:    0.00    0.0%      0.00      0.00
       GLENDALE            23        YTD:  500.00    1.7%    250.00    250.00

    10 HARRIS BAKERY           RET  PTD:     0.00    0.0%      0.00      0.00
       SAN DIEGO        JAK       YTD:       0.00    0.0%      0.00      0.00

    30 W.J. MUFFINS            WSL  PTD:     0.00    0.0%      0.00      0.00
       LOS ANGELES      20        YTD:       0.00    0.0%      0.00      0.00

   100 NEPTUNE MUFFIN SHOP     WSL  PTD:   600.00   21.1%    345.00    255.00
       SANTA MARINA     23        YTD:     600.00    2.1%    345.00    255.00

   200 21ST CENTURY BAKERY     RET  PTD:  2240.00   78.9%   1623.05    617.70
       SAN FRANCISCO    10        YTD:  27699.31   96.2%  20137.87   7561.64

   300 BEVERLY HILLS BAKERY    RET  PTD:     0.00    0.0%      0.00      0.00
       LOS ANGELES      23        YTD:       0.00    0.0%      0.00      0.00

   600 ARIEL BAKERY            RET  PTD:     0.00    0.0%      0.00      0.00
       LOS ANGELES      23        YTD:    2710.00    9.4%   2411.00      0.00

          STATE TOTALS:             PTD:  2840.75  100.0%   1968.05    872.70
                                    YTD: 28799.51  100.0%  20732.87   8066.64

NY  50 SPACE BAKERY            RET  PTD:  1050.00  100.0%    535.00       515
       NEW YORK         789       YTD:  1050.00  100.0%    535.00       515

          STATE TOTALS:             PTD:  1050.00  100.0%    535.00       515
                                    YTD:  1050.00  100.0%    535.00       515

TX  40 WASHINGTON BAKERY       RET  PTD:  7000.00  100.0%   4000.00   3000.00
       DALLAS           1         YTD:  7000.00  100.0%   4000.00   3000.00

          STATE TOTALS:             PTD:  7000.00  100.0%   4000.00   3000.00
                                    YTD:  7000.00  100.0%   4000.00   3000.00
```

```
RUN DATE: 1/1/99              MUFFIN INCORPORATED
----------------------------------------------------------------------------
                 S A L E S   A N A L Y S I S   B Y   S T A T E
----------------------------------------------------------------------------
                                SUMMARY

STATE NO-OF   PCT-OF         SALES   %-OF    COST-OF    PROFIT   PCT-OF   MARGIN
      CUSTS   CUSTS                  SALES    SALES               PROFIT    PCT

CA      7     70.0%  PTD:  2840.75   26.1%   1968.05    872.70    19.9%   30.7%
                     YTD: 28799.31   78.2%  20732.87   8066.44    69.7%   28.0%

NY      1     10.0%  PTD:  1050.00    9.6%    535.00    515.00    11.7%   49.0%
                     YTD:  1050.00    2.8%    535.00    515.00     4.4%   49.0%

TX      1     10.0%  PTD:  7000.00   64.3%   4000.00   3000.00    68.4%   42.9%
                     YTD:  7000.00   19.0%   4000.00   3000.00    25.9%   42.9%

GRAND TOTAL  100.0%  PTD: 10890.75  100.0%   6503.05   4387.70   100.0%   40.3%
  4 STATES           YTD: 36849.51  100.0%  25267.87  11581.64   100.0%   31.4%
  9 CUSTOMERS
```

Figure 6-22.
Sample sales by department or region.

```
RUN DATE: 1/1/99              MUFFIN INCORPORATED
-------------------------------------------------------------------------------
              S A L E S   A N A L Y S I S   B Y   I T E M
-------------------------------------------------------------------------------

ITEM DESCRIPTION-----------      QTY        SALES      %-OF       COST-OF    PROFIT
                                 SOLD                  SALES      SALES

   BLUEBERRY MIX        PTD:     100.00     2100.00    39.8%      1200.00    900.00
                        YTD:    1000.00    19500.00    33.7%     11000.00   8500.00

   BRAN MIX             PTD:     120.00     1380.00    26.1%       875.00    505.00
                        YTD:     800.00     8800.00    15.2%      5800.00   3000.00

   ENGLISH MIX          PTD:      16.00      248.00     4.7%       166.92     81.08
                        YTD:     281.00     4488.00     7.8%      2920.92   1567.08

   CORN MIX             PTD:      15.00      600.00    11.4%       361.00    239.00
                        YTD:     285.00    11115.00    19.2%      6669.00   4446.00

   MACADAMIA MIX        PTD:      42.00      288.00     5.5%       344.00    -56.00
                        YTD:     525.00     7350.00    12.7%      4200.00   3150.00

   RAISIN MIX           PTD:       5.00      220.00     4.2%       130.00     90.00
                        YTD:      63.00     2646.00     4.6%      1575.00   1071.00

   HONEY MIX            PTD:      20.00      300.00     5.7%       190.00    110.00
                        YTD:     265.00     2710.00     4.7%      2411.00    299.00

   CHEESE MIX           PTD:     180.00      145.00     2.7%        81.00     64.00
                        YTD:    1650.00     1200.00     2.1%       688.00    512.00

         8 ITEMS

       GRAND TOTALS:    PTD:     498.00     5281.00   100.0%      3347.92   1933.08
                        YTD:    4869.00    57809.00   100.0%     35263.92  22545.08
```

Figure 6-23.
Sample sales by product.

"I need help managing day-to-day operations," said the boss. "I haven't spent one whole weekend this year with my husband or my yacht! Up-to-date sales reports would allow me to make more-informed decisions, and I wouldn't have to run around production all day just to find out what they're baking up."

"It would cost at least $10,000 a year to hire someone to collate the data and produce usable sales reports," Bob said. "And up-to-date reports will save a great deal of your time as well."

"OK, let's figure $10,000 as additional cost justification," the boss agreed.

"We're now up to $32,511 in potential first-year savings," said Bob. "Muffin Inc.'s computer system should pay for itself in the first year of successful operation."

Figure 6-24 summarizes the areas in which automated accounting can save money.

Applications	Reduce Labor Costs	Shorten Billing Cycle	Carry Less Inventory	Increase Sales	Control Costs	Manage Cash
Order entry and billing	X	X	X	X		X
Inventory control	X		X	X	X	X
Accounts payables	X				X	X
Accounts receivable	X	X	X	X		X
General ledger	X				X	X
Payroll	X				X	

Figure 6-24.
Areas of potential cost savings for accounting applications.

Cost Justification for Office-Productivity Applications

Office-productivity applications can also justify the costs of office automation.

Cost Justification for Word Processing

Word processing is one of the easiest applications to cost-justify because it reduces the amount of clerical time spent generating written communications. In fact, in many companies you are just as likely to see a word-processing computer terminal at each workstation as you are a typewriter.

For offices in which just a small amount of word processing needs to be done, a word-processing software package can be added to the company's data-processing system to allow the staff to do occasional word-processing jobs.

As a payback example, if two secretaries each spend 50 percent of their workday doing typing tasks, one full day of secretarial time is devoted to typing every day. This activity costs $25,000 per year in salaries, benefits, and overhead.

If the secretaries spend 50 percent of their typing time creating new documents, the savings would be as follows: ($12,500 overhead) × (50% savings with an automated system) = ($6,250 annual savings).

If the secretaries spend 50 percent of their typing time revising documents, the following savings would be realized: ($12,500 overhead) × (90% savings with an automated system) = ($11,250 annual savings).

This company would save $6,250 + $11,250, or $17,500 per year in direct labor costs by installing and implementing an automated word-processing system.

As you can see, it is easy to justify two $5,000 stand-alone microcomputers or one $10,000 two-workstation word-processing system with a laser printer in an office with heavy text-processing needs.

To determine the potential cost savings for automating word processing in your business, use the following steps:

1. Estimate what percentage of your clerical personnel's time is spent creating, modifying, and retyping written documents.

2. Determine the yearly overhead for each clerical person involved with text processing. A reasonable estimate of the overhead for a secretary is currently about $25,000 per year.

3. Estimate the time savings that would result from the automation of word processing tasks. For typing that requires about 10 percent corrections, a word processor is about twice as efficient as a typewriter. For jobs that involve retyping documents or merging boilerplate into existing documents or forms, the word processor is more than ten times faster.

4. Estimate the value of using word processing equipment to help increase sales. Marketing by mail is often a cost-effective way to reach new customers. Most mail-order companies are now using computers to increase their efficiency and to handle increasing quantities of correspondence.

5. Estimate the value of organized, efficient document storage and retrieval. It is faster and easier to access and transmit documents electronically. Document storage on electronic media is also much more compact than in paper files.

Cost Justification for Electronic Spreadsheets

Electronic spreadsheets, such as Lotus 1-2-3 and Multiplan, automate the financial worksheets used by accountants and business analysts. The tasks they automate have traditionally been done manually using worksheets for financial planning and forecasting and other types of analysis.

To justify the cost of an electronic spreadsheet, you first need to establish which tasks you will automate. Then you can estimate the time savings that will result from automation. You must also consider the additional benefits, such as the value to your business of having better financial modeling information with which you can make more-informed business decisions.

1. Determine which tasks will be performed with an electronic spreadsheet.

2. Determine how long it takes to do the tasks manually and how long it will take using the electronic spreadsheet.

3. Remember to factor in the time you save by being able to ask more "what if" questions because of the ease of building and modifying the electronic spreadsheet.

4. The time savings and the added flexibility in analyzing your data represents the value of the electronic spreadsheet as a business tool.

It takes longer to create an electronic worksheet than to work through a financial worksheet with a calculator. But once you have created your electronic worksheet model, you can recalculate revised worksheets at computer speeds.

Cost Justification for an Automated Database

Database programs make it easy to store, sort, retrieve, and print out your data. It is difficult to provide a specific formula for cost-justifying database software because it can be used for virtually all applications that involve storing and printing data. However, the steps shown in "Cost Justification for an Automated Database" will give you a sense of what database capabilities may be worth to your business.

1. First, analyze your company's potential uses for database software. Some of these might be

   ■ Maintaining client lists for periodic mailings.

   ■ Managing inventory.

   ■ Tracking investments.

   ■ Managing assets.

   ■ Maintaining files of competitive data.

2. Estimate the amount of time that you would save if you had accurate information available on a computer system, as well as the value of the time you would save by using a computer rather than a manual filing system.

3. Estimate the value of having timely, accurate reports generated automatically from the data in your database.

   For example, if you will use the database to track customers' repair orders, you might estimate what improved customer service would be worth to your company in terms of additional referrals, renewed support contracts, and increased sales.

4. Factor the time that you will spend learning how to run the database software and building your data files into your estimates of potential savings. You should also take into account the time needed to maintain the data in your system's files. This will usually be less than or equal to the time this takes with a manual system.

Cost Justification for Project Management and Costing Software

In many businesses, winning one more job contract would easily justify the acquisition of automated *project-management and job-costing* software. You can also base cost justification on improved efficiency, given that the software will save management and clerical time and increase the accuracy and timeliness of management reports.

Project-management-and-costing software imposes a "computer discipline" that will increase the accuracy of your work. PERT and Gantt charts will help you avoid potential scheduling bottlenecks, and cost-estimation programs can save money by eliminating math errors and providing a costing history over time.

1. To estimate cost savings from a project management and costing system, you need to determine what your current personnel requirements for managing and costing jobs are. Once data about material and personnel costs has been entered into the system, the job-costing software will increase the efficiency of costing future jobs. This time savings is one of the main advantages of automating the job-costing process.

2. Next, estimate the amount of time spent managing project schedules. Be sure to factor in the time spent drawing and redrawing project schedules and time lines. The ability to print revised project schedules automatically will improve the efficiency of project managers.

Cost Justification for Productivity Software

Areas of potential cost savings for each type of productivity software discussed in this chapter is shown in Figure 6-25.

Applications	Reduce Labor Costs	Shorten Billing Cycle	Carry Less Inventory	Increase Sales	Control Costs	Manage Cash
Sales analysis	X		X	X	X	
Business modeling	X			X	X	X
Word processing	X			X	X	
Database applications	X			X	X	
Time billing	X	X			X	
Project-management job costing	X			X	X	X
Manufacturing requirements planning	X		X		X	

Figure 6-25.
Areas of potential cost savings for office-productivity applications.

Payback-Analysis Report

Once you have used the story worksheets to analyze your own business requirements, it should be fairly easy for you to create your own *payback-analysis report*; this report can help you justify office automation to upper management in your company.

A payback-analysis report should summarize any organizational changes that will result from automation and should clearly explain the cost justification used for the proposed system. The report format presented here is fairly generic, and you should be able to use it to document your own unique requirements.

This section uses Northwest Floors' order-entry and billing department to illustrate how to put together a payback-analysis report. The report will do the following:

- Evaluate their current manual systems.

- Suggest changes that can be made to improve their current system without the use of computers.

- Suggest possible benefits of automating their system.

- Set forth the total cost of the automated system.

- Determine the cost savings or potential for increased revenue as a direct result of automation.

- Do a simple analysis of the pros and cons of automation.

- Recommend a course of action.

Note: This report is based on the sample story worksheet prepared in Chapter 2.

A Payback-Analysis Report for Automating the Order-Entry and Billing Department of Northwest Floors

October 1, 1987
Prepared for: Al Brown, President
by: Tom Brown, Manager, order-entry department

I have put together this report to determine whether it will be cost-effective to implement an automated order-entry and billing system at Northwest Floors.

Description of Current Order-Entry and Billing System

When orders are phoned in, a four-part customer order form is filled out by a telemarketing sales representative in the sales department. The form consists of an invoice, a picking slip, a packing slip, and a shipping slip. The invoice is used for billing and internal accounting. The picking, packing, and shipping slips are sent to the warehouse. This is the only way to release merchandise to customers from inventory in the warehouse.

The sales representative is responsible for doing a credit check on the customer before the order is sent to the warehouse to be picked. On Monday mornings the sales department receives about 34 percent of the entire week's orders. There is often no time to run credit checks on established accounts. Writing up an order without doing a credit check can result in wasted time, customer confusion, and ill will when an order is subsequently held up for credit reasons. Releasing orders without credit checks can result in bad debt when merchandise is sent to customers who are over their credit limit or insolvent.

Billing notices usually go out 7 to 10 days after an order is shipped. During our peak fall season, it can take 10 to 14 working days before billing invoices are sent out to customers.

It takes about 4 days for the sales invoices to be posted to the appropriate accounts receivable files. As a result of this delay, the outstanding A/R balances are often inaccurate. There is no way for the sales representative to check credit accurately without pulling the customer's file to see if there are any unposted invoices or receipts.

The sales invoice is also used to update the stock status report and to enter back orders into the inventory control system. It takes about 4 working days for the data to be entered into the inventory control system. Therefore, warehouse personnel cannot rely on the data in their computer-generated inventory status reports and must do a physical inspection before allocating on-hand items.

The last step in the current order entry procedure is to post invoices to the sales journal, which provides information for later sales analysis and for the Sales Commissions Due report.

Areas That Might Be Improved Without Automation

One area that I feel can be improved without automating the order-entry system is credit checking. By hiring one more clerical person, the files could be updated faster, allowing most orders to be posted to the accounts-receivable files within 48 hours.

We could use a prebilling system to improve our collection turnaround time. However, our sales representatives do not have a current inventory-status report, and our customer service level is 64 percent. Reconciling invoices with actual shipments would result in many clerical adjustments, but prebilling might be worth looking into further.

(In a prebilling system, a customer invoice is sent out when an order is received. Northwest Floors currently uses a postbilling system. They send out an invoice after the merchandise has been shipped and the paperwork has been sent from the warehouse to the accounts receivable department.)

Suggested Office-Automation System

Implementing an automated order entry and billing system would require four additional data-entry terminals in the order-entry department and one additional terminal in the warehouse. The workstations and printers must be compatible with our Best minicomputer system.

We would also need to have three additional dot-matrix printers. Two of these would be in the order-entry department; one printer can support two sales representatives. We will also require one additional printer in the warehouse.

An upgrade of 512 KB of main memory will be necessary for our present computer to support the additional applications without impairing overall system performance.

We will require the order entry and billing software module that interfaces with our current Ruggy software package. Sixteen hours of custom programming will be necessary to modify the data-entry screens. This will maximize our sales representatives' utilization of the system.

Training will be provided by Ruggy Software Corporation. A two-day on-site course is included in the price of the software module.

Our present service contract can be amended to cover the additional input terminals, printers, and memory upgrade.

Ruggy Software Corporation will provide support and updates on our current contract, with an additional fee to support the new module.

Hardware Costs:

512 KB RAM upgrade board		$ 1,000
5 workstations	@ $900 ea.	$ 4,500
3 dot-matrix printers	@ $780 ea.	$ 2,340
Installation expense		$ 1,400

Software costs

Application software	$ 1,600

Training Costs:

Additional hourly personnel costs:	$ 2,400

(10 employees at an average of $15/hour for 16 hours of training)
Training classes (included in package price by supplier)
Office supplies (approximately the same as with the manual system)

Service Costs:

Yearly maintenance fees for hardware		$ 800
Yearly software update fee		$ 300
12 hours of custom programming	@ $60/hour	$ 720
Total first-year system costs		$ 15,060

Five-year system costs:

Total first-year system costs	$ 15,060
Four years of ongoing hardware and software support at $1,100 per year	$ 4,400
Total five-year system cost	$ 19,460
Yearly system costs (total/5)	$ 3,892

Potential Improvements with Automation

Automating the order entry and billing system would:

- Eliminate the need to rekey data into other departmental files.
- Provide automatic updating of stock-status files.
- Provide automatic updating of back-order files.
- Provide automatic updating of accounts-receivable files.
- Improve billing time for orders.
- Improve shipping time for orders.
- Provide on-line credit checking.

- Generate picking slips in warehouse sequence.
- Generate sales-commission reports.
- Provide automatic updating of sales-journal files.

These improvements would provide the following benefits:

1. An automated order-entry and billing system would be able to generate customer invoices automatically. This would improve our billing time.

    It currently takes about 10 working days to send out customer invoices. Automating the order-entry system and doing immediate updates to the inventory stock-status files would allow the sales representatives to know exactly what was available for same-day shipments to our customers.

    Current outstanding receivables are $500,000. By improving collection time by four days, we would realize the following savings: ($500,000 total outstanding A/R) × (12% interest/year) = ($60,000). ($60,000/year) / (365 days) = ($164.38 savings per day). ($164.38) × (4 days) = ($657.53).

    Reduced billing cycle savings are thus $658.

2. Automatic updating of the accounts-receivable files would eliminate the need to enter the orders into the A/R files manually from the invoices. This would save over 20 hours of clerical time per week. (20 hours per week) × (52 weeks) = (1040 hours). (1040 hours) × ($11 per hour) = ($11,440).

    Direct labor savings as a result of automating A/R data entry are thus $11,440.

3. The order-entry system could interface directly with the inventory-control system. This would eliminate the need to enter data into the system from the customer invoices. The stock-status report would reflect allocation of inventory on all outstanding orders.

    Having an accurate stock-status report on-line and generating picking lists in warehouse sequence would increase the productivity of the warehouse personnel. I estimate that we would save at least 15 hours per week of direct labor costs by eliminating "visual" order verifications and expediting order picking. (15 hours) × (52 weeks) = (780 hours) × ($12 per hour) = ($9,360).

Direct labor savings as a result of having up-to-date stock reports and picking lists in warehouse sequence are thus $9,360.

4. On-line credit checking would allow us to maintain the same level of customer support with one less telemarketing representative. (Average yearly cost of a sales representative, including bonus) = ($26,900).

5. Automatic posting of orders to customer's accounts will eliminate the need to post customer invoices manually to the sales journals and the general ledger. This would save about 20 hours of clerical time per week. (20 hours per week) × (52 weeks) = (1,040 hours). (1,040 hours) × ($11 per hour) = ($11,440).

Direct labor savings as a result of automating customer-invoice posting are thus $11,440.

Total expected savings as a result of implementing an automated order-entry and billing system are as follows:

Improved billing cycle	$ 658
Reduced A/R labor	$11,440
Reduced warehouse labor	$ 9,360
Reduced sales labor	$26,900
Reduced bookkeeping labor	$11,220
Expected first-year savings	$59,798

Potential Impact of Automation on Personnel

I do not anticipate any major problems implementing the order-entry and billing application. Thus far, Ruggy Software's inventory-control, accounts-receivable, and general-ledger applications have been very straightforward and reliable. Ruggy's training programs have been excellent, and we have not experienced any difficulty in working with the third-party consultants that Ruggy Software has recommended to do software modifications for us.

After installing the order-entry package, we will be able to handle the current level of sales activity with one less person in the sales department. Tom Smith, the manager of the sales department, feels that we should encourage Wanda Jones to take early retirement, with some incentive. Bill does not feel that this will cause Wanda any hardship or cause any loss of morale in his department.

I suggest moving one clerical person into the outside sales group. Phyllis Todd has expressed an interest in outside commission sales and would consider this a long-overdue promotion. Tom Smith has said that he would be glad to have Phyllis in his field sales group and that he feels she will be very successful.

We are currently running between 15 and 50 hours of overtime each week in the warehouse. We have been considering hiring one more full-time warehouse person. If we automate the system, Willy Short, the warehouse manager, feels we should be able to eliminate most or all overtime hours in the warehouse.

Potential Impact of Automation on Customers

We should be able to achieve a better level of customer service because there will be tighter control over stock levels and back-ordered items. Although our service level is currently far above average for our market, at about 64 percent, we should be able to improve that to about 70 percent with up-to-date stock-status information.

Customer satisfaction with our service will increase due to improved handling of all credit checking on customer orders.

We will offer our customers more timely billings that will be easier for them to reconcile with their orders as they arrive. However, some of our customers will be concerned about the shorter billing cycle. We can work with our major accounts on an individual basis if they have any problems with our new procedures. I anticipate that most of our customers will be positive about our reorganization.

Cost Justification

First-year cost savings:	$ 59,789
First-year system cost:	−$ 15,060
First-year savings:	$ 44,738
Five-year cost savings:	$ 298,990
Five-year system cost:	−$ 19,460
Five-year system savings:	$ 279,530

Payback-Analysis Summary

I estimate that automating the order-entry department will result in a savings of $279,530 over a five-year period. I recommend that an automated order-entry system be implemented by October 31, 1987, after our next physical inventory is completed. I request that funds be allocated for this project as soon as possible so that we can move ahead with this program before our next fiscal year.

7

Negotiating a System Acquisition

This chapter discusses some issues that will help you negotiate with your system supplier. These include whether to lease, rent, or purchase a system, as well as issues involving software licenses. You will also find information that will help you draft your own *request for proposal*, or RFP. An RFP will help system suppliers respond to your specific requirements.

Lease, Rent, or Purchase?

Once you have decided to install an automated office system, your next question is probably whether to lease, rent, or purchase your equipment.

In some cases leasing or renting can offer advantages to your business. Leasing can provide tax benefits in some situations and can reduce the initial capital outlay for the equipment. If you feel that your business may be growing extremely rapidly for some period of time, or if you feel that you would like to try out a particular piece of hardware, rental can be an attractive alternative. The following sections summarize the advantages and disadvantages of each option.

Advantages of Renting

■ You can test rented equipment in your situation to see whether it is appropriate and whether it improves your company's operations and profitability.

- Suppliers will usually let you exchange rented equipment when your requirements change or expand.

- Renting requires the least commitment emotionally, which can be very important to a new buyer.

- Renting requires the smallest up-front cash outlay.

- Short-term rental avoids equipment obsolescence.

- Maintenance of rented equipment is usually supplied by the vendor.

Disadvantages of Renting

- Renting is usually the most expensive option over the installed period.

- You do not get all of the tax benefits that you would by leasing or purchasing equipment.

Advantages of Leasing

- Leasing is an alternative way of financing a computer system. Most lease contracts specify a purchase option when the lease expires.

- Leasing generally provides all of the tax advantages of an outright purchase.

Disadvantages of Leasing

- It is more expensive to lease than to buy.

- Leasing usually requires that you maintain costly service contracts.

- Price is harder to negotiate when leasing, unless a third-party lease company is involved.

- The lessor usually does not provide support.

Advantages of Purchasing

- If you know what you want, purchasing is the least expensive way to acquire it.

- Well-managed and serviced equipment will last for years and can provide a growing organization with additional data-processing capacity over time, as new equipment is brought in.

- The purchaser accrues all tax advantages.

Disadvantages of Purchasing

- You must provide your own support and maintenance for equipment you purchase.

- You may get locked into equipment that is incompatible with future industry standards.

- The equipment can become technologically obsolete, although it should have paid for itself before this is the case.

- Purchase usually requires the largest amount of capital up-front.

- Computers have low resale value, even when they are the latest models.

Software Licenses

When you buy software, it usually comes with a *software license agreement*. This agreement protects the software company from two potentially disastrous events. The first is software piracy. This occurs when people make illegal copies of software and either give it away or resell it. The second is being sued by an end user because the program does not do what the end user thought it should or because it was misused and caused harm to the company. For example, if the people at LRK Distributors forgot to back up their system's files, and their system's hard disk crashed because of an electrical storm, their financial records could be lost. A license agreement prevents LRK Distributors from suing the software company over the loss.

A software license agreement usually limits the use of the software on multiuser systems and on networks, specifies how many backup copies of the software can be made, and states whether or not the software can be resold. It also states what the software's warranty is.

Software warranties usually do not guarantee that the program will be free of bugs. It is virtually impossible to write a complex program that has absolutely no programming errors. Software developers are generally obliged to use their best efforts to fix programming errors that prevent the program from meeting the program's specifications. For most off-the-shelf software, the product specifications consist of the accompanying reference manual. However, all that the buyer is usually entitled to if bugs in a software program cannot be fixed is a refund of the price of the program or a substitution in the form of another, comparable product.

Most software distributors are using break-the-seal or shrink-wrap software licensing agreements. The act of physically opening the disk's wrapping materials means that you accept the terms of the agreement. This method of licensing is used throughout the microcomputer industry in place of written agreements that the end user would need to sign and return to the software manufacturer. This method of acceptance has not been well tested in the courts, but most legal experts believe that it will be considered legally binding.

Figure 7-1 shows an example of a software license agreement. Read the terms and conditions of any license agreements for your software carefully. If you do not want to or for some reason cannot agree to the required conditions, try to renegotiate them with the manufacturer. Depending on how big your company is, and how big they are, the software supplier may compromise on some points or may offer your company special site licensing terms.

Larger companies often buy hundreds or thousands of copies of a software package. It is in their best interest to be able to copy the software package freely to let all of their employees use it. Standard license agreements usually do not permit any duplication of master disks,

---

Copy Protection

Copy protection is any method used to ensure that software is not copied and distributed illegally. The usual means of copy protection involves the use of special programming to prevent the user from copying the disk with the operating system's COPY command. In most cases the master disk can be copied once onto a hard-disk drive or onto a backup disk. Most copy protection schemes can be broken with special disk duplication programs, such as Copy II PC.

Copy-protected software is much less convenient to use with hard-disk–based systems than is non-copy-protected software. Many software suppliers are now using a copy protection system that no longer requires the user to insert the master, or key disk every time the program is started from the system's hard disk. However, the legal copy may be lost if the hard disk fails, is reformatted, or is accidentally erased. Most major software companies have eliminated copy protection from their software.

Many corporate users will no longer purchase copy-protected software. They feel that the only advantage to copy protection is that it reminds dishonest people who make illegal copies that they are indeed violating the software license agreement.

End User Agreement

IMPORTANT NOTICE

Before breaking the seal on the software diskette, read this agreement. If you do not consent to these conditions, return the package with an unbroken seal to the place of purchase for a full refund. Breaking the seal implies your consent to the following agreement.

1. LICENSE

XYZ Software (XYZ) grants you a license to:

Use the ABC Program (Program) and related Documentation on a single microcomputer, or on a subsequent but not additional microcomputer. If you wish to use the Program on an additional microcomputer or on a network of microcomputers, you must purchase an additional license or a multiuser license from XYZ.

You may copy the Program onto magnetic media as needed for backup copies to be used on the single microcomputer. You may not make additional copies of the documentation.

You may not use, copy, modify, or transfer the Program or the Documentation, or any portion of such items, except as expressly provided for in this agreement. You may not disassemble or decode the Program.

2. PROPRIETARY RIGHTS

The Program and the Documentation are the valuable proprietary information of XYZ. They are protected by the U.S Copyright Act (Title 17, United States Code). Unauthorized reproduction of these items constitutes infringement of XYZ's copyright. A criminal violation of the Copyright Act subjects the violator to a fine of up to $2500 and imprisonment of up to one year. (17 USC 506)

3. LIMITED WARRANTY, LIMITATION OF REMEDIES, AND LIMITATION OF LIABILITY

XYZ warrants that the Program will operate as described in the Documentation for a period of 90 days from the date you first received your copy of the Program. This warranty shall be void if you modify the Program in any way.

The entire liability of XYZ Software and your exclusive remedy in connection with the above described warranty shall be as follows:

XYZ will correct any error in the Program that XYZ can reproduce on its computer, or if XYZ is unable to correct the Program within a reasonable period of time after report of any such error, you may terminate this agreement by returning the original copies of the Program and Documentation and destroying all other copies.

After sending us an affidavit certifying that all copies have been destroyed or returned to XYZ, your money will be refunded.

The above described warranty is the only warranty regarding the Program. XYZ specifically disclaims the implied warranties of merchantability and fitness for a particular purpose. Some states do not allow the exclusion of implied warranties, so the above exclusions may not apply to you. This warranty gives you specific legal rights which vary from state to state.

XYZ does not warrant that the Program will meet your requirements or that the operation of the Program will be uninterrupted or error-free. You must assume the entire risk of using the Program. Any liability of XYZ is limited to correction of the Program as described or refund of your money.

The Program has been designed to operate on the hardware and with the operating system described in the Documentation. XYZ shall have no responsibility for use of the Program in conjunction with other hardware or operating systems.

In no event will XYZ be liable to you for any other damages (including loss of use, revenue, profit, data, or other incidental or consequential damages) arising out of the use or inability to use the Program even if XYZ has been advised of the possibility of such damages, or for any claim by any other party. Some states do not allow the limitation or exclusion of liability for incidental or consequential damages, so the above limitation may not apply to you.

4. SUPPORT AND UPDATE AGREEMENT

Upon purchase of this license and for the next 90 days, you are entitled to up to four hours of telephone support (question answering) and one free Program update if one is issued during the 90 days. After those first 90 days, telephone support and updates of the Program can be obtained by paying a fee. Read the enclosed Software Subscription Agreement or contact XYZ for details.

5. TERMINATION

This agreement shall be in effect until it is terminated in accordance with this paragraph. You may terminate it at any time by destroying the Licensed Materials together with all copies. (As used in this agreement, a "copy" means a representation of any portion of the Licensed Materials in or on any medium, whether paper, magnetic, or otherwise.) Your license to use the Licensed Materials and copy the Program will terminate automatically if you fail to comply with any term or condition of this agreement. You agree upon such termination to destroy the Licensed Materials together with all copies.

Figure 7-1.
A sample software license agreement.

except for one backup copy to be used with the same computer system as the master copy. Many large companies are also very concerned about their legal exposure if employees make unauthorized copies for internal or personal use.

Site licensing allows a software customer to make duplicate copies of a software package for use within the corporate site. Some site-licensing agreements allow the customer to duplicate disks for all on-site users; others specify a maximum number of copies that can be produced. The bottom line is that site licensing means less expensive software and fewer restrictions for the end user. Many corporate customers feel that they have enough financial leverage to demand site licenses.

Contracting for Custom Software Programming

If you contract with a software developer for custom programming services, be sure to document exactly what your applications are supposed to do. Not having a good software specification is like having a contractor build you a new house without an agreed-upon set of drawings. Verbal misunderstandings with software developers are just as common as they are with building contractors.

Even though you may not understand the specifics of how a contractor installs an electrical system, you do know where you want the outlets and how to test the system to make sure it meets your needs. Similarly, you may not know anything about programming, but in your meetings with software developers, you should communicate your requirements and evaluate the progress the developer has made in terms of how and when different tasks are implemented. For example, you can determine whether a billing module is fully functional simply by entering some sales data into the system and printing out customer statements and sales transaction reports.

Arrange to make payments to custom software developers in installments as phases of your programming project are completed. It is usually best to hold one large final payment until after your system is fully functional and offers a reasonable level of performance and usability.

I suggest that you have an attorney who specializes in computer law draft or review your agreement.

Drafting a Request for Proposal

If you are planning to purchase one microcomputer, it usually does not make sense to draft a formal request for proposal. However, if you are considering a larger purchase, such as a local-area network system that uses personal computers as workstations or a multiuser minicomputer system, it usually is helpful to draft an RFP (a request for proposal). It will spell out your needs to system suppliers and can also serve as an internal planning document and a yardstick against which to measure competitive proposals.

Many companies spend thousands of dollars on consulting fees to generate RFPs. You should be able to draft your own based on the story worksheets and the sample RFP included in this section as a model.

The following sections describe the components of a typical RFP. Figure 7-2 on the next two pages shows a sample RFP.

Once you have received proposals from the suppliers responding to your RFP, you are ready to evaluate carefully the costs, features, and specifications of the bids. You can use the criteria of viability, compatibility, quality, and overall value to help you select a system supplier.

General Information

The "General Information" section of your RFP should identify your company, describe what business you are in, and indicate any special requirements or factors that might make your company different from others in the same industry. You should also indicate who in your company the suppliers should contact if they have questions about your RFP.

Be sure to describe in detail the tasks you are interested in automating, and state why you have decided to automate these areas. It is helpful to include a brief summary of the parts of your story worksheets that a prospective system supplier would find useful.

The RFP is an opportunity to sell your company's request for assistance. It should discuss your current market position and your company's growth plans as they may relate to office-automation requirements. A supplier must spend a great deal of time to respond to an RFP. If it appears that you are only asking for help with a basic systems analysis or that you are not committed to the project, system suppliers may not be very motivated to respond.

Laurence Electronics Corporation
Electronic Instruments Division
1000 Creek Parkway
Seattle, Washington
(206) 555-1212

June 19, 1987

General Information

Laurence Electronics Corporation is a major electronic instrumentation defense contractor. The Electronic Instrument Division is located in Seattle, Washington. This division specializes in designing and manufacturing precision recording and sensing instruments for the U.S. Navy and for authorized NATO forces. Sales of the division were in excess of $285,000,000 in the last fiscal year. See the attached annual financial statement and general information overview for Laurence Electronics Corporation.

The Electronic Instruments Division has its own marketing group called the Electronic Instrument Division—Marketing Group (EID-MG). In-house computer support is provided by the Electronic Instrument Division—Information Support Group (EID-ISG). EID-ISG is directly responsible for all information system procurements.

EID-MG's management has determined that it would be cost-effective to automate job-costing and analysis functions to increase productivity of their application support engineers. EID-ISG will be acquiring a microcomputer-based job-costing system for the marketing group's use.

The job-costing system will provide accurate cost tracking for all costs incurred in the implementation of new instrument designs and the subsequent manufacture of those electronic instruments. The cost-analysis reports will be used to help the group prepare bids in response to requests for proposals and requests for quotations from government agencies and for an internal determination of the profitability of different projects.

Contact Personnel at EID-ISG

Contract specifications:	Bob Moorely ext. 4356
Technical liaison:	Thomas Richard ext. 9087
Bid coordinator:	Cheryl Borne ext. 5451
Project manager:	William Huntly ext. 6767

System Overview

EID-ISG has determined that it will use microcomputers connected to a local-area network as the basic architecture for EID-MG's system. This will allow the personnel to use their workstations for decision-management support applications, to access the main corporate computer in Washington, D.C., through telecommunication links, and to do their job-costing analysis and tracking tasks.

The job-costing package should be able to track all costs that are projected and to compare project and category costs with the actual costs incurred during the design and manufacture of electronic instruments. A link to the EID's general ledger package will satisfy this requirement. The job-costing system will then be able to generate reports that will show how accurately projects have been bid and highlight the specific areas where there have been cost overruns or unnecessary overbids.

Software Requirements

The job-costing software should:

Account for all costs for materials, subcontractors, and supplies.

Transfer all payments to the correct job classification.

Transfer all transactions to a general-ledger program for consolidation and reporting.

Generate job performance reports. These will be used to compare the actual total costs of a project to the costs that were bid in response to the government agency's original RFP.

Generate job labor analysis reports. These will compare the actual labor costs to bid estimates.

Generate job profitability reports (also called bonding reports). These will show the estimated and actual costs of a job compared with expected profitability at the completion of the job.

Generate job transaction reports. These list all cost, billing, and payment transactions for a job in date order.

Generate cost category analysis reports. These show costs by job category across all jobs, hours and labor costs across all jobs, and the ratios of costs to quantity and quantity to hours for current and prior year accounting periods.

Allow the system to maintain historical job-costing data.

Allow jobs to be closed and reopened.

Provide at least two levels of password security.

Interface with the BEST Software general-ledger program running on EID's super-minicomputer system.

Figure 7-2.
A sample request for proposal for a job-costing system (for Laurence Electronics Corporation).

Hardware Requirements

Local-Area Network

The system shall consist of a local-area network (LAN) that will comprise four IBM or compatible PC/XT-class microcomputer systems, herein referred to as "workstations," connected to a file server based on an IBM or compatible PC/AT-class microcomputer system.

The network must allow expansion to at least 36 microcomputer-based workstations.

The network should allow all users to access laser printers and all installed file servers.

The LAN system software must be compatible with Microsoft's MS-DOS version 3.2 or later and with MS-Network Manager.

Each microcomputer-based workstation:

Will be equivalent to an IBM PC/XT or compatible microcomputer system.

Will be based on an Intel 8088-family microprocessor and will be capable of running MS-DOS version 3.2 or later.

Will be supplied with at least 640 KB of main memory.

Will have at least one 360 KB (or larger) 5¼" floppy disk drive.

Will include an IBM or compatible standard Enhanced Graphics Adapter.

Will include an IBM or compatible enhanced color display monitor with at least a 12-inch diagonal screen.

Will include a turn and swivel stand for the monitor.

Will include one serial and one parallel port.

Will include all of the necessary hardware and cables to connect to the LAN.

Will include a key-lock switch accessible from the front.

The file server

Will be compatible with MS-DOS version 3.2 and MS-Network Manager.

Will have a hard-disk drive with a minimum capacity of 60 MB of storage and an average access time of 25 milliseconds or less.

Will include an IBM or compatible standard monochrome display adapter.

Will include an IBM or compatible monochrome video display.

Will be provided with a cassette tape backup storage system capable of backing up the entire file server on a maximum of three tape cassettes in less than four hours.

Printer Requirements

Laser Printer

The system will include one desktop laser printer and all necessary interconnecting cables. It must support the Epson FX-286 dot-matrix graphics command set and the Hewlett-Packard LaserJet Plus printer command set.

The laser printer shall be rated at at least six pages per minute, with at least half-page 300-dpi resolution (requires a minimum of 640 KB of RAM). The printer shall be equipped with at least a 100-page tray feed system.

Dot-Matrix Printers

The system will also include two dot-matrix printers and all necessary interconnecting cables. They must be capable of printing standard 9-by-11-inch pin-feed computer paper at a minimum of 200 cps in draft mode and 40 cps in near-letter-quality mode.

The printers must support either the Epson FX-80 or IBM Proprinter command set.

Hardware and Software Support

The supplier must provide the following:

A signed statement affirming that all proposed hardware and software is currently available and can be installed within 45 days after an order is placed with the supplier.

All technical and reference materials necessary to allow user installation of the system.

At least 24 hours of on-site training time.

A service and support contract that is renewable for at least a three-year period.

A list of reference installations that will be contacted to determine user satisfaction with services that have been provided by the supplier.

Implementation and Evaluation Schedules

All bid responses must be received by the procurement director at ISG's offices by noon on July 10, 1987.

All pricing, sample contracts, and warranty and service information must be submitted in writing with bid responses. Responses that do not include this information will not be considered.

Demonstrations and presentations will be by invitation only. These will be scheduled between July 20 and July 24.

We anticipate that a final award for this bid will be made on or before August 10, 1987.

Figure 7-2. *(continued)*

Software Requirements

In the "Software Requirements" section, you specify which types of applications you plan to implement. For example, you might list accounts receivable, accounts payable, and general ledger as your current requirements, with an option to phase in an automated payroll system in the future.

Include a list of all of the features that you require and desire in each application. The feature lists that you put together in Chapter 2 will help prospective system suppliers understand your system requirements. Use the sample feature lists in Chapter 13 to double-check that you have not left out any important features you require in your accounting applications.

Specify any features or capabilities that your company needs or would like that might require customized software. If your business requires special reports, it is a good idea to include sample reports or screen formats to help describe your requirements.

Whenever custom software or hardware configurations are necessary, it is a good idea to hold at least one formal meeting with your potential system suppliers to discuss your requirements and answer their questions.

Hardware Requirements

In this section you should specify any hardware that you have already determined you will need. For example, you might indicate that you require a remote terminal at a branch office that can be used to communicate daily sales reports to your main office.

Indicate how many individuals will be using the system, whether more than one person will need to use the system at the same time, and whether more than one person will be working with a particular application at the same time. This will help your system supplier determine your data-input requirements.

If you know what type of main processor you require, specify it. Otherwise, leave the choice open for the system supplier. For example, you might specify that you will require a multiuser system built around an IBM-compatible, Intel 80386-based microcomputer system. Otherwise, you might specify that you are, for example, a retail stereo chain with five stores and let the system supplier come up with a hardware configuration that will satisfy your company's requirements.

If you have determined your memory requirements, indicate how much main memory and how much disk storage you will require. Otherwise, leave this decision to the supplier. Different software packages often require different amounts of storage and main computer memory for similar tasks.

You should specify (or request) some method of backing up the data stored on your system. Depending on your system, your best solution might be floppy disks, tapes, or removable hard-disk drives.

You also need to determine any special output requirements that you have. For example, clarify whether you will have printers at different locations and whether dot-matrix output will suffice or if you require letter-quality output.

Hardware and Software Support

Under "Hardware and Software Support," you should request that the supplier provide you with information on the background of the companies that produce the hardware and software components that are being recommended. Ask for statistics on the number of systems of that type that have been installed, where they have been installed, and how long they have been operational.

Also request that the supplier provide you with a list of client references that you can visit or call.

Have the supplier specify whether all of the recommended equipment and software is currently available. If it is not, the supplier should indicate the expected time frame for completion and delivery. Ask for written guarantees with specific penalties for late delivery, or take your chances on your sales representative's level of optimism.

Request written copies of all guarantees and service policies and information on any additional service or support that the supplier or other third parties furnish.

If you are requesting a turnkey system, have the supplier state explicitly what installation support or training services are provided and what services are *not* provided or are billed separately.

Request information on the pricing and availability of any special services you might require, such as special training or support not usually provided by a standard system supplier.

Implementation and Evaluation Schedules

The "Implementation and Evaluation Schedules" section gives potential suppliers an idea of your time frame for choosing and installing a system. Specify when you will be reviewing the supplier's proposals, and give an expected time frame for demonstrations or vendor presentations.

Request that all pricing information and sample sales and support contracts be included in the bid response.

Specify a realistic due date for the RFP, and indicate where the system supplier should send its response. It takes time to respond to an RFP, so allow several weeks for the suppliers to pull their reports together.

State when you plan on making a buying decision and, if appropriate, whether it will be announced publicly. Also specify when you would like to begin installing the system.

Checklist for Negotiating with Your System Supplier

At this point you are ready to acquire your system. The following list of tips should help you negotiate effectively with your system supplier. These suggestions will help you to obtain the best possible terms and to build a good working relationship after your system is installed.

Use your understanding of automation and system-requirements planning to help your system suppliers evaluate your needs. It is your responsibility to communicate *all* of your requirements to your system supplier. An RFP is one of the most convenient ways of providing this information.

You can use the responses to your RFP to evaluate the relative competence of different system suppliers. Their responses should give you a good idea whether the supplier with whom you are working really understands your needs.

Use your feature list to help you evaluate different systems proposed by different suppliers. This will protect you from suppliers who want to grossly undersell or oversell you. If your feature list does not reflect your real needs, it's best to find this out before you install your system.

Buy your system from the least expensive supplier. Many computer products are manufactured by one company and resold under many brand names. The lower-cost system may actually be of a quality equal to that of more-expensive name-brand systems.

For example, the first successful laptop computer was manufactured by Kyocera in Japan. It was distributed by Tandy Corporation as the Model-100 and was also available in virtually identical packages from Olivetti and NEC. The suppliers offered slightly different features—for example, the Tandy Model-100 offered a built-in modem—and charged different prices.

Very inexpensive application programs may be adequate for your needs. In many situations, simpler, less-expensive application programs will be much easier for you to install and use. (See the section titled ''Software Quality and Price'' in Chapter 3.)

Pay for the support that you need, but do not assume that by paying more you will receive better support. ''When the insurance premiums became too high, we decided that it would pay to self-insure our company.'' This quote is from a microcomputer manager who decided to buy low-cost IBM-compatible microcomputers and a box of spare parts instead of name-brand computers.

Most business people are willing to pay a higher price for the support and reputation offered by major computer suppliers. If you are installing your first computer system or are implementing a complex office-productivity application, it generally pays to buy from a supplier who provides more support. However, for lower-risk acquisitions, such as the purchase of your company's next dozen IBM-AT compatibles, it may be more cost-effective for you to buy from the lowest-cost supplier, even if they offer minimal after-sale support.

Don't hurry; time is on your side. The cost of computer equipment is dropping continually. Although the prices of some components fluctuate, the trend for data-processing equipment has been downward, and there is no turn-around in sight. The longer you delay, the less expensive your system will be. However, the advantages of automation will not be realized until you implement your system.

Negotiate guarantees whenever possible. Most companies have official-looking printed guarantees. Just because they are in print does not mean that parties to the agreement can't simply take a pen and make changes to them. Always ask whether the product's manufacturer or your system supplier would be willing to extend warranty coverage. Many times, the supplier will make special concessions to close a sale.

Some name-brand hardware is warranted for 90 days; other less-known hardware is warranted for one or two years. If the name-brand hardware you are looking at is warranted for only 90 days, ask your supplier for a longer warranty period. Stress that the superior manufacturer should be confident enough to extend its warranty period and that this will help you to justify the higher cost of the name-brand product.

When negotiating for off-the-shelf software packages from retail computer suppliers, always ask whether training and support are included in the retail sales price. Otherwise, you should consider purchasing the products through a mail-order distributor and using your savings to help pay for the training and support you will need to install and implement them.

Third-party support organizations can offer an attractive alternative to factory maintenance. Third-party service contracts are usually less expensive than service contracts from major computer manufacturers. There is no reason to assume that factory service representatives do a better job of maintaining equipment than third-party support organizations. The major factor in good service is the people who actually do the work. A supplier with well-trained technicians and a good stock of parts can take good care of your system.

If you are installing standard software packages and ''generic'' plug-compatible computers or peripherals, you will have many reliable suppliers from which to choose for both sales and support. You can purchase general support from consultants, training and programming services from most software companies, and even have special custom programming work done by major system suppliers if you pay the going rates. There is no law that requires you to get your whole system or all of your support from one vendor.

However, there are advantages, particularly when custom hardware or software components are involved, to purchasing your entire system from one supplier who will then be responsible for the integrity and functionality of the entire system. This avoids an all-too-common practice known as ''pointing the finger at the other guy.''

Evaluate all bids on the basis of total system costs. Do not let the up-front costs confuse you. The real cost of a system, as was discussed earlier, is not only the cost of the hardware and software. Installation, personnel, training, and other factors are also expensive and time-consuming. You should be just as concerned with these hidden after-installation costs as you are with the price of your system's disk storage or workstations.

Consider purchasing used equipment. A computer has few moving parts. The boards that hold the chips, the power supply, the bus, and all mechanical assemblies are unlikely to require maintenance over the useful life of a computer. If you can find a used computer system that satisfies all of your requirements, it will probably be a good value, even after you have depreciated the moving parts, such as the keyboard and disk drives. Printers take a much harder beating than other data-processing equipment; it is best to know their life history before contemplating adoption.

Computers depreciate quickly. You can usually find excellent buys through system brokers, or, in most major cities, through classified advertisements in the newspaper. The caveat in purchasing used equipment is, of course, that it will require more service over the period that you use it. You will need to weigh the possible inconvenience of dealing with repairs over the lower initial cost of acquisition.

Consider renting equipment or obtaining it under a short-term lease. If you are anticipating changes in your business situation, you should consider renting or getting a short-term lease on your computer equipment. These alternatives offer lower entry costs and more flexibility than an outright purchase.

Time-sharing or service bureau companies can lower the risk of automating your company. Time-sharing companies and service bureaus can provide a good solution for companies that do not want to purchase computer equipment or do not want to devote their personnel's time to computer operations. The type of service offered by these businesses ranges from providing computer time on which to run your application programs to providing a complete turnkey office-automation package.

Service bureau customers send their bookkeeping to the service bureau, where it is processed on the bureau's computer system. The data that the service bureau processes is then used to generate management reports that are sent back to the clients.

Time-sharing companies are similar to service bureaus, except that the former install terminals and printers at the user's site and use telecommunications equipment to transmit data. Their clients enter data directly into the time-sharing company's computer system (over telephone lines) and print out their own reports. Time-sharing customers can usually schedule their own work and print reports on demand.

Service bureaus and time-sharing companies were most successful in the days when computers were prohibitively expensive for smaller businesses to install and maintain. These services are usually more costly than in-house data processing, and they impose a turn-around time for the processing of reports.

Read your software license agreement. Refer back to the section on software licenses. Be sure that you understand all of the limitations set forth in the software license agreement. Have any changes made *before* you agree to purchase your software.

Hold your last payment until the system works. It is always a good idea to hold a final payment until 30 days after your system is installed and fully functional. This will help motivate your system supplier to provide good installation support.

Do not purchase any equipment until you are absolutely sure that it will do what you need it to do. Fancy demonstrations have little or nothing to do with what you need to automate your business. Do not buy a system before you are absolutely convinced that you will be able to combine the hardware and software you've chosen into a fully functional system that meets all of your requirements. Failing to do this is a common mistake.

Section III

Implementing an Automated System

This section describes the tasks involved in planning for and installing an automated system. Previous sections have concentrated on the analytical aspects of the planning, such as how to prepare the story worksheets and perform a cost-benefit analysis for computerization. The first chapter of this section is oriented to the management of an automation project. It tells how to divide up the work and make sure that it gets done. Checklists are provided for you to use during the planning process.

Chapter 9 tells what to do after your computer system arrives. It describes, in general terms, how to install the computer, get your software up and running, and convert to automated procedures.

8

Managing an Automation Project

Office automation is a complex task in which you analyze your business procedures, determine whether automation will be cost-effective, and select and purchase a computer system that is right for your needs. If you will be delegating some of this job to others, you must decide how to divide up the work so that things get done smoothly and efficiently. This chapter will help you do this. It also provides checklists that you can use to make sure all of the work is completed on schedule.

Even if you will be doing all of the work yourself, you will find much of this chapter useful. The discussions of training and system security apply to any business, as does the list of responsibilities, which helps you define your role and that of the system supplier in the automation process.

Coordinating the Project

You need to decide who is going to have overall responsibility for implementing your automated office system. Depending on the size of your business and the organization of your departments, you may be faced with doing the job yourself, or you may be able to delegate part or all of the work to one or more of your employees.

The *automation project manager* responsible for overseeing the conversion from your current manual system to an automated one may or may not be the system administrator—the person responsible for day-to-day computer operations. Depending on the complexity of your office-automation system, the system administrator may be you yourself, one of your clerical personnel, a department manager, or a data processing (DP) manager who is an expert at automating office systems.

The person you choose to supervise the installation of an automated office system should have good project-management skills and the ability to pay close attention to detail. These same skills are also needed in the person who will manage day-to-day computer operations. It is not necessary for either the system administrator or the automation project manager to be a computer "guru" to be effective. It is more important that he or she be able to work constructively with the rest of your staff and understand the interface between your manual office systems and the work that the automated system does.

The automation of your accounting systems will require special attention. Unless your company's financial records are current and accurate, the information that is entered into your automated system will not be usable. (Remember, garbage in, garbage out.) The discipline imposed by the process of installing an automated accounting system can be extremely frustrating to a disorganized or poorly managed accounting department. However, if you are tenacious, you will find that your office systems (and your staff) have become well organized in the process. A flowchart for implementing a computer system is shown in Figure 8-1.

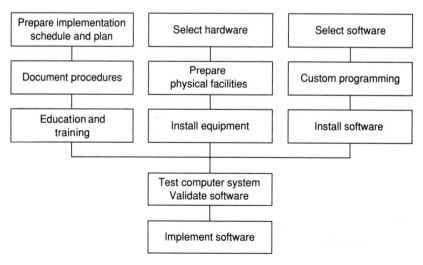

Figure 8-1.
A computer implementation flowchart.

Project Coordinator's Checklist

1. Delegate responsibility for completing the story worksheets and creating feature lists.

2. Identify each activity that you must accomplish to install your system.

3. Estimate the duration of each task to determine which ones might delay the installation or implementation of your computer system.

4. Allow adequate lead times to maintain your scheduled installation plan.

5. Establish a plan to monitor all scheduled activities.

6. Review your installation plan with your system supplier.

7. Configure or modify your software, if necessary.

8. Incorporate backup, recovery, and control considerations into your day-to-day operations.

9. Have all affected departments sign off on the feature lists and on all software applications.

10. Create data input documents. (A sample data-entry form is shown in Chapter 9.)

11. Designate someone to order and reorder specialized computer forms and other computer supplies.

12. Periodically review conversion dates for each application to ensure that they are on track.

13. Select a project manager to schedule different computer installation tasks within each automated department.

It is a good idea to use *action item checklists* to monitor all necessary office-automation installation and implementation tasks. Figure 8-2 on the next page gives an example of such a checklist. Use it as the basis for developing a format with which you are comfortable.

According to the sample action item checklist in Figure 8-2, Tom Chow has not yet ordered the software. The project manager should determine whether this will delay the installation of the system and what can be done to get the project back on schedule.

Current Status of Office Automation Project
February 15, 1988
Cc: Tom Chow, Bill Arron, Pete Wilson, Bobby Smith, the boss

Action item:	Person responsible:	Date due:	Date done:
1. Order supplies	Tom Chow	Feb. 7	Feb. 2
2. Order software	Tom Chow	Feb. 7	Pending
3. Order hardware	Tom Chow	Feb. 7	Feb. 1
4. Order desks	Bill Arron	Feb. 15	Feb. 3
5. Develop training plan	Pete Wilson	Feb. 15	Feb. 13
6. Install hardware	Bobby Smith	Feb. 19	
.	.	.	.
.	.	.	.
.	.	.	.

Figure 8-2.
A sample action item checklist.

If your system supplier is providing installation or implementation support, you should schedule regular progress meetings. This is the best way to keep the installation project on track.

The following checklist will help you plan meetings with your system supplier and with any software developers and consultants who are helping your company automate your office systems.

Checklist for Meetings with System Suppliers

1. Schedule meetings and notify participants as early as possible.

2. Keep meetings as brief as possible.

3. Select participants, not observers.

4. Designate an appropriate meeting leader.

5. Determine the status of each current action item.

6. Evaluate problems that have developed since the last meeting.

7. Allocate new resources, if necessary.

8. Assign responsibility for solving any new problems.

One of the best ways to ensure that you and your system supplier are in agreement about who is responsible for each installation and implementation task is to put together a written *list of responsibilities*. The act of drawing up this list can serve as a "reality check" for your expectations regarding system support, and it will help assure your system supplier that you are aware of the effort involved in making a successful transition to your automated system. It is usually a good idea to have your system supplier help you create a list of responsibilities before you commit to using their products or services.

Figure 8-3 gives a sample list of responsibilities. Your own list can be much more detailed. The more specific your list is, the more helpful it will be as an internal planning aid.

List of Responsibilities

System Supplier agrees to do the following:

1. Deliver and set up hardware.
2. Provide eight hours of on-site preinstallation training.
3. Provide two (2) thirty-hour user education classes at system supplier's offices.
4. Have one meeting each week to coordinate implementation of accounting modules beginning two weeks before system is installed (up to 12 meetings).
5. Review pilot results.
6. Provide ongoing warranty service and software support per agreed-upon support contract.

Customer agrees to do the following:

1. Go to training class on hardware operations.
2. Learn operating-system commands.
3. Build all system files.
4. Install application modules.
5. Pilot-test the system.
6. Do a parallel conversion.
7. Make best efforts to become self-sufficient. Will have at least three employees trained to act as system operators within 90 days.
8. Issue final system acceptance.

Approved by:

_____
Your system supplier

Approved by:

_____
Project manager

Figure 8-3.
A sample list of system supplier responsibilities.

Training

Most people are uncomfortable with things that they do not understand. This is why so many people have negative or suspicious feelings toward computers. The primary objective of your in-house computer training should be to clarify how the new system will help your staff perform its day-to-day work and how the system will be used.

People learn at different rates. You will have to be patient with yourself and the rest of your staff. It is often necessary for people to repeat computer classes or tutorials several times before they are confident of their new skills. However, you'll find that your investment in training was worthwhile when your system is running smoothly and when you and your personnel are comfortable working with it.

Consultants are often brought in to help with the transition to automation. If your finances permit, this is usually the easiest way to ensure a smooth conversion. The extent to which you need to rely on consultants will depend on the applications you are trying to automate and on the level of support and training provided by your system supplier. However, over time, you should invest in the training necessary to implement new applications yourself, rather than continuing to rely on outside consulting support.

Basic Training Plan Checklist

1. Register and attend all related classes and training programs offered by your system supplier.

2. Develop a training plan for all system operators.

3. Develop a training plan for all management personnel.

4. Determine which courses will be taken.

5. Pair up students to ensure that skills are available in the event an employee becomes incapacitated or leaves the company.

6. Determine which department is responsible for course fees.

7. Obtain self-study or computer-aided instruction, if available.

8. Evaluate how your personnel are doing in their classes.

9. Train additional backup system operators, if necessary.

10. Develop a procedure for communicating changes in company policies and procedures to everyone affected.

System Security

Computer fraud and unauthorized access to restricted data are becoming more of a problem as computers in business become more prevalent and as more employees gain access to computer terminals that are directly connected to corporate databases. It is not necessary to become fanatically concerned about computer crime or the accidental corruption or erasure of your data files. However, you should protect your electronically stored information just as vigilantly as you do your current paper records.

You can provide system security through the use of both hardware and software systems and by physically securing your computer site. Some typical security measures for business computers are as follows:

Limit physical access to computer equipment to the employees who should be using it. This is the best way to limit the opportunities for unauthorized access and potential destruction or misuse of your company's data. Some businesses implement strict sign-in procedures and have security personnel on their premises. Others require all authorized computer personnel to wear badges. At the very least, you should post a sign indicating that computer terminals are for the use of authorized personnel only. This could prevent a well-intentioned employee from accidentally corrupting data in the system.

Use keyboard locks. Many of the new desktop microcomputer systems are equipped with these locks, and you can also buy them separately. When a keyboard is locked, no inquiries or data can be entered into the system from the keyboard. This is a convenient way of preventing unauthorized users from simply walking up to a system and reading or modifying proprietary or personal files. If you feel it is a good idea to lock up your file cabinets or your desk when you leave your office, you should lock your computer as well.

Assign passwords or codes that the user must enter before he or she can access restricted files and programs. This is the most common security measure employed on business computers. Many software packages are designed to allow files to be selectively protected using different levels of passwords. For example, you could authorize an employee to read and update all accounts-receivable files but prevent that person from accessing any personnel records.

Some sophisticated database programs use passwords to restrict access to individual files, records, or fields within files. For example, a clerical person might be authorized to access the personnel file and to alter the name and address fields for individual employees' records, but not to read or make changes to the employees' salaries.

Store backup disks and tape cassettes off-site in fireproof safes. (A system for backing up your data is described in the next chapter.)

If you are concerned about electronic eavesdropping, purchase a Tempest-rated computer system. Tempest is a classified government specification for acceptable levels of electronic signal emission. This technology may not be sold outside of NATO countries and is carefully regulated by United States security agencies. This type of system is being used commercially for electronic funds transfers and other sensitive applications.

If tight data security is important to you, consider using data encryption to prevent computer fraud. Encryption systems use software or hardware "keys" to encode data before it is stored or transmitted. The recipient or user of the information must have the correct software or hardware "key" to be able to translate the coded data into meaningful, readable information. Data encryption is unnecessary in most commercial installations. It is most commonly used in the banking industry and in other areas where confidentiality is required.

Data Encryption

Vutek Corporation in San Diego, California, offers an add-on board called ENIX.SYS, designed for IBM PC-compatible microcomputers. ENIX.SYS offers password protection, special data-encryption programs, and timed access for authorized users. This means that authorized users are allowed to access information in the computer only after they have entered special passwords, and that they may access the system only during certain predetermined hours. Other users attempting to enter the system would simply be logged off after a record of their attempted access was recorded in a special file. Data files themselves are encrypted and must be decoded with the ENIX.SYS board. Telecommunications can be encrypted for transmission and then decoded by the recipient with another ENIX.SYS board.

Companies that communicate with their main computer database over telephone lines are more exposed to unauthorized system access. If this is the case in your company, you may need to take extra measures to secure your system. For example, it may be necessary to connect your incoming lines to a separate computer system that does not have direct access to secure data. This system acts as a buffer to incoming requests for information or attempts by computer "crackers" to tamper with operating-system utilities that would allow them to modify or access protected files. Callback modems are often used to dial a previously coded telephone number in response to a correct access code. This prohibits anyone who is not at an authorized site from gaining access to the system.

Your overall computer security plan should be based on a careful analysis of your company's needs and the particular hardware and software used at your installation. Many different software and hardware devices can be used to secure your system. Unfortunately, it is difficult for nontechnical business people to assess how well these security measures prevent an invasion by criminals trained in computer theory and operation. It is wise to consult with your system supplier or with a computer security specialist before implementing your security plan.

Physical Facilities

Computers can usually operate in any office environment in which your employees can work comfortably. In most cases it is not necessary to put your computer in a special air-conditioned or "clean" room. However, environmental pollution can be a serious problem. Particles of dust and dirt can get into disk drives and keyboards, causing errors and system downtime, and computers will malfunction if they overheat. Your system supplier should be able to tell you whether you will need to modify your office environment for your system.

Computers designed to be used in industrial environments, on the shop floor, or in harsh environments such as kitchens are specially built to resist heat, humidity, temperature changes, and environmental pollutants. You will need to research the environmental requirements of any equipment that you install outside of a standard office environment.

Running cables between your terminals and your computer system can be expensive and time-consuming. It is especially difficult to run cables through the walls of an older building. If you decide not to go to the trouble of doing this, there are a number of products you can use to keep the cables from looking messy and posing a hazard.

Most standard office furniture was designed before computers were invented. Standard desks are generally not wide enough to accommodate the computer display screen and a keyboard plus a mouse or other input device. Many companies are now manufacturing inexpensive computer furniture that is ergonomically designed to increase user productivity. It is much easier to concentrate during long work sessions when the computer terminal is set up properly.

Physical Facilities Planning Checklist

1. Determine who will be responsible for physical facilities planning.

2. Determine how long it will take to create a physical facilities plan.

Combating Eyestrain

Eyestrain is the most common complaint among people who work at video displays for long stretches at a time. You can do several things to help prevent eyestrain and fatigue when working with computer terminals.

1. Use a display that has at least 640-by-350-pixel resolution. (See Chapter 11 for information on display resolution.)

2. Be sure that there is no glare on the terminal's screen. A number of companies make anti-glare screens that attach to the front of the terminal. These screens will also increase the contrast, which makes the screen easier to read.

3. Avoid setting the terminal up where lighting or windows will cause reflections on the screen. Make sure that artificial lighting is at a comfortable level.

4. Provide a means of placing paper copy from which text is to be entered close to the screen. Most people find that shifting their eyes back and forth on the same level causes less eyestrain and fatigue. Special work stands are available from office supply stores to hold the work.

5. Be sure that the workstation is comfortable for the person who will be using it. An uncomfortable working position causes a person to tire much faster. Ergonomic furniture has been shown to increase worker productivity.

6. Allow anyone using the computer for long periods to take regular breaks. They should be able to get up and stretch at least twice an hour. This is one of the best ways of relieving the stress associated with a desk job.

7. Have anyone using the computer look away from the screen for a few seconds occasionally so that their eyes are not focused on the plane of the screen for too long a period. Also have them try not to stare at the screen as they type.

3. Create a physical layout chart that specifies where all equipment and cabling will be located.

4. Determine how long it will take to make site modifications.

5. Make necessary floor plan modifications.

6. Route all cabling safely.

7. Run correct power to all computer equipment.

8. Evaluate environmental factors, such as heat, air-conditioning, humidity control, dust collection, lighting, and soundproofing (especially printers).

9. Evaluate ergonomic factors, such as monitor and keyboard height and sources of glare.

10. Consider access and security issues.

11. Evaluate outside contractors, if necessary.

12. Determine how the system will physically be moved to the desired installation site.

13. Install fire protection and safety devices.

Implementation Planning Checklist

1. *Assign responsibilities for managing the conversion.* It is usually best to have someone within the affected department be responsible for implementing a given business application. For example, someone in the payroll department should be responsible for installing and implementing the payroll application.

2. *Order computer hardware and operating-system software.*

3. *Order application software packages.*

4. *Order computer supplies.* As a rule of thumb, you should order as many supplies as you think you will use in the first 90 days.

5. *Create and document a training plan.* It should include:

   ■ Management
   ■ System operators
   ■ System users
   ■ Temporary data-entry personnel

6. *Create a physical facilities plan.* It should designate:

- Overall responsibility for hardware installation
- The location of all systems and all workstations
- Power connections
- Cabling requirements for voice and data
- Environmental factors
- Computer furniture

These tasks should prepare you for the next course you must navigate as the manager of an automation project: overseeing or actually performing the installation of the system and the conversion to an automated process. That is the subject of the next chapter.

9

Installing and Implementing Your System

Your new automated office system has arrived! Now you must set it up and install the operating-system software. You will then be ready to load your application software and begin automating your manual office systems. This chapter discusses each of these tasks.

Installing the Hardware

The physical setup of a standard business computer system is quite straightforward. Most small business computers can be set up on a desk and plugged into a standard 110-volt grounded AC wall socket. Even networked microcomputers and most minicomputer systems can be set up by an average office worker with a screwdriver set and the patience to read the hardware supplier's installation guides.

The most confusing installation procedure that most business people face is adding circuit boards or memory chips to their computers. Unless you have had previous technical experience with computers or other electronics equipment, it is best to have your system supplier help you install and test add-on boards and memory upgrades.

Installing the Operating-System Software

Installing the hardware for a multiuser computer system and loading the operating-system software used to be a challenge requiring the skills of a computer technician or systems engineer. Most systems today are designed to be user-installable. Even if you are a computer novice, you should be able to install your own hardware and start up the operating-system software.

Most computer manufacturers supply *installation programs* with their systems. These programs display prompts on the screen that help you install your operating-system software. These prompts will ask you a series of questions about the input and output devices that will be connected to your system. For example, the installation program may ask how many terminals you have, whether they are color or monochrome, what the storage capacity is of any hard disks installed, whether you will be telecommunicating, what kind of and how many printers you have connected to the system, and so on. The installation program will use your responses to configure the operating-system software so that your computer's main processor will work properly with all of your system's input and output devices.

Single-user microcomputers are easy to set up. You simply insert a disk that contains the operating-system software into the disk drive and turn the machine on. The information coded onto the disk starts up the system and displays a prompt that allows you to enter operating-system commands or load your application software into the system's main memory. For example, an MS-DOS-based system displays an *A* > prompt to let you know that it is ready to load and run your application programs.

Many business computer systems provide user *shells* or application program menus that prompt you for your commands. Instead of a cryptic *A* > prompt, the screen might display something like what is shown in Figure 9-1.

It takes a minute or two to boot up a disk-based microcomputer system. "Booting up the system" means loading the operating-system software and running a diagnostic program to check out the hardware as the system gets ready to load your first application program. You boot your system each time you turn on your computer and can re-boot as needed.

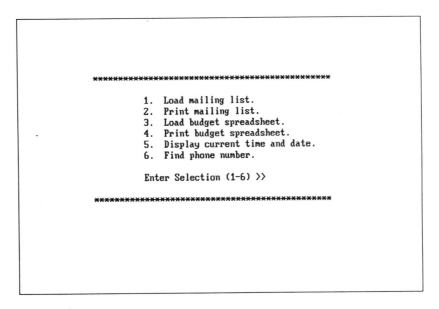

Figure 9-1.
A sample display from a business computer system shell.

If you are using a hard-disk–based system, you will need to format the hard-disk drive before you can load your programs and data files onto it. This will take 20 minutes or more, depending on the storage capacity of your drive.

Once you have formatted the hard disk and loaded your operating system and application programs onto it, you can boot your system and start up your application programs from the hard-disk drive instead of using floppy disks. Booting from a hard disk is faster than booting from a floppy disk because hard disks can access and transmit their data into the computer's main memory faster than floppy-disk drives can. (Computer operations are discussed in more detail in Chapters 10 and 11.)

Learning Operating-System Commands

Next, you need to learn how to use your computer's operating system. For example, you must learn the operating-system commands that allow you to create, rename, erase, and copy your files; format disks; and even set the system's clock. Multiuser and networked systems require you to learn more system commands, but none are really difficult. You simply have to read your operator's manuals carefully.

You may find that your documentation is incomplete or in error. If you have discovered a problem or you can't get something to work right, have a coworker with a fresh view of the problem look at what you have been doing. It is easy to repeat the same error without noticing it. If you have tried everything and your procedure or program keeps failing, call your service support representative and get some outside help. You might find you are not the first user to meet this particular problem nose to nose.

An Installation Case Study

John Derik of Derik, Peterson and Crouch, Attorneys at Law, selected an automated word-processing system that included three microcomputers, an 80-megabyte file server, a laser printer, and a dot-matrix printer connected together on a local-area network.

The sales support representative from the computer store that supplied John's system was unable to come to John's office when their system was delivered. But John was excited about the automation project and decided to begin setting up the equipment himself. He decided to install a workstation on each secretary's desk and to locate the file server and printers on a table in the copy room.

The microcomputers were easy to set up. After spending about an hour reading the system's installation guide, John removed the computers and display monitors from their packing boxes and connected the cables from the displays to the computers with a screwdriver. Then he plugged the keyboards into the microcomputers. Each microcomputer took about 15 minutes to set up.

John found that the microcomputer-based workstations were too wide to fit on the typewriter returns of his secretaries' desks. He purchased vertical computer stands and extension cables that allowed the computers to rest under the desks. This allowed him to place the display monitor and keyboard in a comfortable operator position on the typewriter returns of each desk. John also purchased anti-glare screens for each display to help reduce reflections from the office's fluorescent lighting.

The laser printer was a bit more difficult to set up. John read an 85-page manual that explained how to unpack the printer, install the toner cartridge, and plug the printer into a serial or parallel port of a microcomputer.

After reading the laser printer's user guide, John realized that it would take days to master its command programming language. He recalled, however, that the sales representative who supplied John's system had recommended a special laser-printer control-software package. This program would allow the user to select one of the laser printer's "fonts," or type styles, without using the printer's command programming language; instead, fonts could be selected from the control program's user-friendly menus.

The dot-matrix printer that John selected to print out multipart billing forms was easy to set up. He read the brief setup instructions, unboxed the printer, plugged in a print head and ribbon cartridge, and loaded pin-feed forms onto the printer's tractor feed. The dot-matrix printer allowed the selection of different fonts via switches on the front control panel.

It was much more difficult to connect the microcomputer-based workstations and printers together on the local-area network. John discovered that he had to open each microcomputer (an act which in many cases voids manufacturer's warranties) to plug in networking adapter boards. John did not feel comfortable installing computer boards, so he waited for his sales support representative to come out the following day to help him. It was fortunate that he waited. Network boards have small "dip" switches that need to be set so that the local-area network knows how to address, or send information to and from, each workstation, file server, and printer. Switches on the main computer board must also be changed to address additional memory and input/output boards that are plugged into empty slots on the computer's bus.

John eventually read the 285-page network installation manual and learned how to add more workstations and output devices to the network. The actual process was logical and simple once he understood it, but it required wading through information in the technical reference manuals. Most business people should not attempt to install or reconfigure a networked computer system without ongoing technical support from the system supplier or an experienced system administrator.

After installing the networking boards and connecting the appropriate cables, John and his sales representative were ready to install the operating system, the networking software, and the word-processing application onto the system's file server. First, they loaded the disk containing the operating system and networking software onto the file server. Then they configured the system by responding to a series of questions generated by the installation programs included with the operating system and networking software.

After loading the operating system and networking software, the sales representative double-checked that the system's hardware was connected properly and that it was fully functional by running a *diagnostic program.* This is a special program that tests hardware and software to make sure that they are working properly together.

The diagnostic program indicated that the system was not recognizing one of the microcomputers. After replacing a shorted cable and retesting the system, they loaded the word-processing application software and the laser-printer control program using an installation program that was included with the word-processing package. They then configured the word-processing program and the laser-printer control program to work with the hardware that John had selected.

The sales support representative also loaded two computer-based training programs onto the system's file server. One of the tutorials was supplied by the word-processing software company. The other was a computer-based training program called Learning MS-DOS from Microsoft that helps new users learn the MS-DOS commands.

The sales support representative showed John and his secretaries how to start up the computer system and perform basic operating-system and network-maintenance functions, such as creating, copying, and deleting files and redirecting print output from the laser printer to the dot-matrix printer. Then the sales support representative showed everyone how to use Learning MS-DOS and the word-processing tutorials, and reemphasized the importance of backing up all files.

John and his secretaries spent the next week reading their system's documentation, working through software tutorials, and creating sample documents. After they were comfortable working with the new system, they had difficulty understanding how they had previously managed their workload using standard typewriters and paper files.

Like most other business people who install multiuser or networked office-automation systems, John found that he relied heavily on his system supplier for training and technical support. John's system supplier was not the least expensive word-processing dealer, but John felt that the excellent support that was provided easily justified the premium that John's firm paid.

Automation Priorities

In most cases, automation will be more successful if different applications are automated in a planned, logical sequence. Attempting to automate too many activities at once can be self-defeating. It is important to be patient as everyone in your company gets used to the new way of doing things.

As a rule, it pays to automate the tasks that will provide the largest payback first, but you need to consider your overall business requirements and the resources available to you as you automate your business. All businesses have bottlenecks that cause a loss of productivity or profits. For example, a parts distributor might have trouble generating timely billings and late payment notices. It is helpful to identify these bottlenecks because frequently they are the areas in which automation will have the largest impact on your company's productivity.

For suggestions on the best time to automate different accounting applications, see Figure 9-2.

General ledger	Install at the beginning of the year or at the beginning of the next accounting period.
Accounts receivable	Install at the end of the (monthly) billing cycle.
Accounts payable	Install when purchase orders are at a low level or at the beginning of a buying cycle.
Billing	Install after automating inventory, accounts receivable, or both.
Inventory control	Install after doing a physical inventory.
Payroll	Install at the beginning of the year or at the beginning of the quarter.

Figure 9-2.
The best time to install accounting applications.

Installing Accounting Software

Once you have put your system together, installed the operating-system software, and learned how to use the basic operating-system commands, you are ready to install your first application software package.

Doing a Pilot Conversion

If you go out and collect all of your data, enter it into your new computer system, and then try to run your application programs, there is a good chance that you will find that something has been done incorrectly. For example, you may have collected the wrong information, or you may have entered the correct information only to discover that the program will not process your data properly or that it will not produce the reports your business requires. To avoid these problems, it is best to do a trial run with a small amount of sample data; this is called a *pilot conversion*. A pilot conversion is the best way of verifying that your office-automation system will work properly, and it is usually your last chance to ensure that the system is going to meet your office-automation needs.

Having all of the people who will be using the system involved with the pilot conversion is a great way to ensure the fewest implementation problems. Your staff can practice entering data, generating forms, and closing out accounting periods. This is a good way to begin to get everyone used to the new office procedures and paperflow. You may feel that you are wasting half a day or so, but you should consider the pilot exercise an important part of your company's training and factor it into your implementation schedule.

It is a good idea, if you have a lot of data, to develop a data-entry form like the one shown in Figure 9-3 and use it in your pilot test. These forms are used to organize the information in your company's files in a way that allows a data-entry person to enter the data into your system efficiently. Evaluate the form during your test to see if it can be improved before you use it for a full conversion.

Checklist for a Pilot Conversion

1. Budget the time and resources necessary for a pilot test.

2. Prepare the pilot test procedures.

3. Determine who will perform the test.

4. Collect test data for master and transaction files.

5. Determine who will evaluate your pilot test results.

6. Check all features and capabilities of your system.

7. Check all error conditions.

LAST NAME: ___ ___ ___ ___ ___ ___ ___ ___ ___ ___ ___

FIRST NAME: ___ ___ ___ ___ ___ ___ ___ ___ ___ ___ ___

MIDDLE INITIAL: ___

EMPLOYEE NUMBER: ___-___-___-___

DATE OF EMPLOYMENT: ___ ___/___ ___/ 19___ ___ (M/D/Y)

DEPARTMENT: ___-___-___

MONTHLY SALARY: $___-___,___-___-___.00

EXTENSION NUMBER: 1 ___-___-___-___

Figure 9-3.
A sample data-entry form.

The Importance of Parallel Conversion

Installing a computer system requires a sense of humor and a great deal of patience. Many errors will be made and repeated as everyone learns how to use the new automated system. This is why you should run your current manual office system and your automated office system in parallel until the automated system is working perfectly. Your manual office system can provide an audit trail and will safeguard the integrity of your company's records. This is known as a *parallel conversion.* A parallel conversion will build your staff's confidence, lower everyone's stress level, and greatly increase your chance of finding any bugs that were missed in the pilot conversion.

You should run in parallel for at least one accounting period. If you do not have a perfect run-through the first time, you will need to keep your manual system in place for one or more additional accounting periods. Many companies are impatient and convert to an automated system before all of the kinks have been worked out. This can result in chaos when data is lost or when your staff becomes frustrated and reluctant to use the new automated office system.

It is usually a good idea to budget extra money for hiring data-entry personnel to build your master data files. This work is tedious and can bog down an organization unless extra staff is allocated. Many companies use temporary employees to enter data and then have their regular employees verify that the data has been entered correctly into the system. Once your records are current, you should be able to handle your data-entry requirements with your regular personnel.

Checklist for a Parallel Conversion

1. Collect all necessary information.

2. Determine how long it will take to collect data.

3. Determine who will build the master files.

4. Find out whether another system is available for data entry.

5. Determine how long it will take to key data into the system.

6. Hire personnel from a temporary service, if necessary, to supplement regular data-entry personnel.

7. Verify and edit master files.

8. Convert files in batches if this makes it easier.

9. Run your manual and automated office systems in parallel.

10. Budget for the additional expense of running in parallel.

11. Allocate enough physical space to maintain both systems.

12. Reconcile your manual and automated systems after the first accounting period, and continue to do so for as long as you run the systems in parallel.

13. Schedule additional physical inventories, if necessary, to reconcile the status of your data files.

14. Determine whether the loaded (fully functional) system provides an adequate level of performance.

15. Modify your current office programs or procedures, if necessary, to work smoothly with your automated systems.

16. Plan your conversion for the least disruptive time.

Crash conversions

For a number of fairly obvious reasons, converting to an automated system without running in parallel is referred to as a *crash conversion.* You should not convert to an automated system until both your manual and automated systems are running smoothly and reports generated from the manual system agree with reports generated from the computer. As an infamous DP manager from LRK Distributors once said, "The data you lose may be your own."

Installing Office-Productivity Applications

If you will be running an office-productivity application, such as a word-processing package or an electronic spreadsheet, the best way to get started is to read the program's documentation, install it on your system, and start learning to use it. Many of the better packages have disk-based tutorials that provide on-line computer-aided instruction.

Many advanced application programs are designed so that you can do useful work with a subset of the program's available commands and then learn additional features as you need them. With practice, and really only with practice, you will become familiar and comfortable with powerful office-productivity applications.

The File-Proof Backup System

When everyone has gotten used to working with the new automated system, a strange and dangerous phenomenon will occur. This is when trust begins to develop and system users become sloppy about backing up their files. A power outage, an outraged employee, or a confused system operator can cause the loss of your company's records. This potential disaster can easily be anticipated, and the possibility of loss of data can be virtually eliminated.

I will now reveal the entirely ordinary file backup system that I have christened the File-Proof system. It is shown in Figure 9-4.

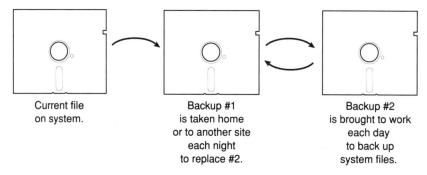

Current file
on system.

Backup #1
is taken home
or to another site
each night
to replace #2.

Backup #2
is brought to work
each day
to back up
system files.

Figure 9-4.
The File-Proof system for backing up data.

This system involves keeping two sets of backup disks. You keep one set at home or at another site and one set with the system. These sets are alternated daily to ensure that even if there is a fire or the backup disks are ruined the records from the previous backup will be available. In some cases, the off-site copy need only be switched once a week, depending on the sensitivity, volatility, and volume of data.

Rekeying even a day's worth of records can be a major inconvenience. Whenever you are entering data into your system, it is a good idea to store this data on a disk every half hour or so. This usually takes less than a minute and limits the amount of data that you can lose if a power failure or an accidental erasure occurs.

Many application programs have menu-driven backup facilities built in, and new backup tape units are available with utility programs that automatically back up any file that has been changed during a work session. Depending on your needs and your budget, these can be an inexpensive data "insurance policy."

Backup Checklist

1. Train all personnel to back up their files.

2. Determine which files will be backed up.

3. Determine how often files will be backed up.

4. Determine which backup transaction data should be printed and kept for audit.

5. Secure backup media at an off-site location.

6. Develop plans for obtaining alternate equipment in case yours becomes disabled.

7. Determine how long you can tolerate a disabled system.

8. Create a "disaster" plan for your company.

The Implementation Checklist

The following checklist summarizes the steps for converting to an automated system.

I strongly suggest that you set target dates for completing different stages of your work and manage your conversion as you would any other major project with which you were involved. Careful planning will allow you to make a smooth transition to your automated system with the least confusion and with the best chance of avoiding any major problems.

1. Install the hardware.

2. Install the operating-system software.

3. Create data-entry forms.

4. Do a pilot conversion to validate the application software.
   - Create or select live test data.
   - Load and run the test data.
   - Verify the output.
   - Do a walk-through with your staff.

5. Load and verify the master data files. Verifying data is absolutely essential. If the system has too many data errors, it will become virtually useless, and your employees will work around it whenever possible.

6. Run the application in parallel with your manual system. You should run in parallel until your personnel are comfortable with the new automated system and both your manual and automated office systems are generating exactly the same management reports.

7. Compare the computer output to your manual audit trail. Don't assume anything. It is difficult to predict which system will be correct, and it is unusual to have them come out the same. Reconciling the differences may be the best time you've had since your last IRS audit.

8. Convert to the automated system. Congratulate everybody who worked on the project and went the extra mile. Time for a bottle of champagne?

9. Back up all of your files; use off-site storage for one set of backup disks. (This may be the best piece of advice in this book.)

Checklist for Planning Future Applications

After you have installed your system, you might want to automate additional office applications. The following checklist for planning future applications will help you coordinate your planning activities.

1. Prioritize future applications.

2. Create a story worksheet for each application that you are thinking of automating.

3. Create a feature list for each application that you are considering automating.

4. Be sure that the department involved agrees with the automation plan.

5. Find out whether the current system is capable of running additional applications.

6. Find out whether additional main memory, data storage, workstations, or printers are required.

7. Create an implementation schedule for the new application.

8. Determine what additional training is required.

9. Develop an implementation plan.

Section IV

More About Hardware and Software

This section will not make you a computer wizard, but it will provide you with a basic understanding of how computers work as well as the vocabulary necessary to communicate your needs and concerns effectively to computer representatives and consultants.

The first chapter in this section describes the components that make up a computer, including chips, boards, and storage devices.

Chapter 11 describes the various ways in which you can enter data into and get results back from your computer. Here you will find information about keyboards and other data-entry devices, as well as discussions of the various types of display monitors, printers, and modems.

The final two chapters in the book provide in-depth descriptions of office productivity and accounting software. Sample feature *lists are provided for the various types of programs, and the accounting chapter includes an extensive questionnaire that you can use to determine what your business needs in an accounting package.*

You could actually skip this entire section and still be able to plan, justify, and implement an automated system for your business. However, the information it provides will give you a much better idea of what hardware and software will provide the best solution for your office automation requirements.

10

Computer Anatomy and Physiology

Basically, computers do two things:

- They tirelessly perform error-free calculations at mind-bogglingly fast speeds.

- They organize and keep track of data, making them the world's best filing cabinets.

This chapter clarifies how computers perform these functions. Once you understand how computers work, you will be much better able to evaluate the deluge of computer products available to help you automate your business.

There are two parts to every computer system: *hardware* and *software*. Computer hardware consists of the actual machines that process the data. The central processing unit, the main memory, the disk drives, and all output devices, such as printers, plotters, display monitors, and modems, are known as hardware. Computer software consists of the programs, or sets of instructions, that tell the hardware what to do with your data.

Microprocessors

The heart of the microcomputer is a special kind of integrated circuit, or chip, called a *microprocessor*. The microprocessor in a microcomputer acts as the central processing unit, or *CPU*. This is the "brain" of the computer system; it is responsible for directing all data-processing activities.

The microprocessor carries out mathematical calculations and also moves data into and out of your files.

A microprocessor comprises millions of switches known as flip-flop circuits. Each flip-flop switch has two possible values, "on" and "off." These two different electrical states (one is actually a very low voltage and the other a slightly higher voltage) represent the numbers 0 and 1. These are the only values with which computers can work. Thus, when you enter data the computer converts it into what is known as binary code, which contains only 0s and 1s. In this coding scheme, for example, the value 01000001 might represent the letter A.

Computers are able to throw their switches on and off millions of times per second. The speed at which the computer turns these switches on and off or moves data into and out of its CPU is used to determine the *clock rate* of the system. This rate is expressed in megahertz (MHz). One MHz equals one million cycles per second.

Each flip-flop represents a single *bit* of data. Eight bits in sequence is called a *byte*. Computers use eight bits, or one byte, of data to store a single alphanumeric character. Certain groups of flip-flops are called *registers*; these can hold one or more characters or computer instructions at a time. Microprocessors usually have 8-bit, 16-bit, or 32-bit registers. Therefore, the registers in microprocessors can contain one, two, or four bytes of data at a time.

Thus, depending on the register size of the microprocessor, microcomputers can process one, two, or four bytes of data at a time. This is what people mean when they talk about 8-bit, 16-bit, and 32-bit computer *architecture*. Computers that can process more bits at once can process data faster by moving and processing more information during each clock cycle.

Back in 1980, 8-bit microcomputer systems were considered the state of the art. Now, 16-bit and 32-bit microprocessors are being used in desktop microcomputers. Minicomputers used to be based on 16-bit architecture, but now most are using 32-bit architecture, and mainframe computers are using a word size of 32 to 64 bits.

Sixteen-bit and thirty-two-bit machines usually have larger *instruction sets* than do eight-bit machines, allowing them to perform certain tasks more efficiently. For example, some microprocessors have an instruction to multiply the values in two registers together during one clock cycle. A microprocessor that does not have such an instruction must multiply numbers through repeated additions, which requires more clock cycles. The microprocessor with the larger instruction set can usually do faster processing.

Intel and Motorola make the two most popular microprocessors for business systems. IBM uses the Intel 8088 in the IBM PC/XT, the 8086-2 in the PS/2 Model 30, and the faster Intel 80286 in the IBM PC/AT and the PS/2 Model 50 and Model 60. IBM is using the Intel 80386 in its latest generation of microcomputers. Apple, Atari, and Amiga have chosen the Motorola 68000 family of microprocessors.

It does not really matter which family of microprocessors you choose for a microcomputer-based system. Both Intel's and Motorola's microprocessors offer good upgrade paths and are supported by a wide range of application software. But you must make sure that the specific application programs in which you are interested are available and will perform well on the system you choose to implement.

Computers based on a new type of computer architecture involving a reduced instruction set that is actually coded into the hardware have recently been announced. This architecture gives programmers fewer instructions to work with, but it results in faster processing of those instructions. Several of the major computer manufacturers claim that this new reduced instruction set computer, or *RISC,* architecture will allow them to manufacture machines with better price-performance ratios and will ultimately speed software-development time. RISC systems should be evaluated using the same criteria you use to judge machines based on other architectures.

Computer Buses

Another important component of a computer's architecture is its *bus.* The bus consists of the electrical circuits that transfer information among the various components of the computer. Figure 10-1 is an illustration of the function of a bus.

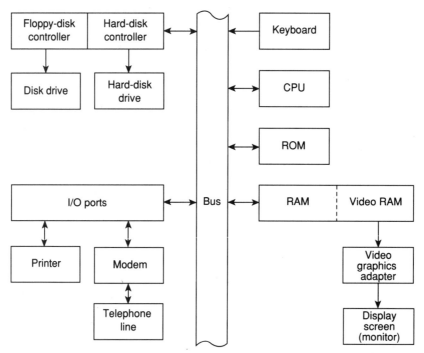

Figure 10-1.
A typical computer bus.

Comparing System Performance

The computer specification that is most often discussed is the speed of the CPU. However, different families of CPUs have different instruction sets and use different commands to do the same job. It is actually quite difficult to compare the CPU performance in different manufacturers' systems by examining their technical specification sheets.

One measure of CPU performance is the clock rate of the system, discussed previously. A 2-MHz CPU chip can process data about twice as fast as a 1-MHz chip, if the memory chips and other components in the system are designed to keep up. An Intel 80286 processor, which is used in the IBM PC/AT, runs at 6 to 16 MHz and has about twice the processing power of the Intel 8088, which is used in the IBM PC/XT and runs at 4.77 MHz.

The new 32-bit Intel 80386 processor running at 20MHz offers about two and a half to three times the processing power of the Intel 80286 chip.

However, the performance of most computer systems is limited not by the speed of the microprocessor but by the peripheral equipment attached to the system. Receiving data from the keyboard or other input devices, fetching information from memory, and outputting data to printers consumes a great deal of your CPU's time. Although large minicomputers and mainframe computers do have faster CPUs than microcomputers, their increased performance is due primarily to their ability to support many more high-performance input and output devices at the same time. If you want to improve your system's overall performance, it might make more sense to buy a faster printer or storage device, rather than upgrading your CPU.

Benchmarks, or comparison tests, are often done by suppliers and industry analysts to give an idea of the relative *throughput* of a system under conditions that simulate the ''real world'' as closely as possible. The term ''throughput'' means the amount of work that a computer system can process in a given time period. Benchmarks usually give a much better indication of actual performance than straight technical comparisons do. However, it can still be difficult to evaluate how systems with different benchmark results will function given your business tasks.

The best hardware with poor software will yield poor overall system performance, and the best software will not perform well on slow hardware. An office-automation system will perform only as well as its weakest link, and the weakest links may become apparent only after you have installed a system and are attempting to optimize its performance. This is one of the reasons why it is often best to select a turnkey system that has been optimized for the best overall system performance.

Computer Chips and Memory Storage Devices

Data is stored in a computer in special integrated circuits called memory chips. Technical advances in the design and manufacture of chips have enabled more memory to be packaged in each chip. The use of fewer chips allows systems integrators to design computers that cost less, have lower power consumption, produce less heat, and are more reliable.

There are two main types of memory storage chips: *RAM*, or random-access memory chips, which allow information to be written into them over and over; and *ROM*, or read-only memory chips, which have one set of instructions ''burned'' into their circuits and thus cannot be overwritten with new data.

Figure 10-2 illustrates the difference between short-term and long-term data storage. Short-term data storage is handled by the RAM chips in the computer. The CPU can access the RAM in the computer's main memory directly. This makes RAM access very fast. Both the application programs and the data with which the program is working are stored in the computer's main memory or on disk.

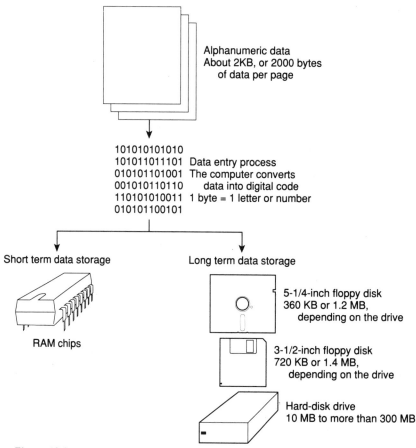

Alphanumeric data
About 2KB, or 2000 bytes
of data per page

101010101010
101011011101 Data entry process
010101101001 The computer converts
001010110110   data into digital code
110101010011 1 byte = 1 letter or number
010101100101

Short term data storage

RAM chips

Long term data storage

5-1/4-inch floppy disk
360 KB or 1.2 MB,
depending on the drive

3-1/2-inch floppy disk
720 KB or 1.4 MB,
depending on the drive

Hard-disk drive
10 MB to more than 300 MB

Figure 10-2.
Short-term and long-term data storage.

Long-term storage is typically handled by floppy-disk drives, hard-disk drives, and tape drives. There are also several removable hard-disk storage devices on the market from Bernoulli, Kodak, and other companies. Disk drives store data on magnetic surfaces that spin around. The drives contain heads that can read and write signals to the disks' magnetic media.

Whenever an application program requests data that is stored on one of the system's disk drives, the CPU transfers the data into the system's main memory to be processed. It takes longer for the CPU to access data on a disk drive than it does to access data in memory, but disks are capable of holding much more data, and the data stored on them is not lost when the computer's power is turned off. Computer memory is measured in KB (kilobytes, each of which is 1024 bytes) or in MB (megabytes, or millions of bytes) of storage.

Floppy-disk Drives

Data and program files are usually stored on floppy disks, also called floppy diskettes, diskettes, or just floppies. Their biggest advantage is their convenience in transferring and inputting data into the system. Floppy disks are also useful for backing up the files on your hard-disk drive. Most microcomputer systems offer one or two 360-KB, 1.2-MB, 720-KB, or 1.44-MB disk drives to transfer and store your programs and data files.

A standard 5¼-inch disk stores 360 KB of data. You can store from 100 to 150 typed pages on a standard 5¼-inch disk. IBM's PC/AT uses a high-density 5¼-inch disk that stores 1.2 MB of data, and the newest IBM systems work with a 3½-inch disk that stores 720 KB or 1.44 MB of data.

Unfortunately, the high-density 5¼-inch disks are not completely compatible with the standard 5¼-inch disks. High-density disk drives can read 360 KB disks but cannot reliably create them. A standard 360 KB 5¼-inch disk drive cannot be used to read or write 1.2 MB disks.

The 3½-inch disks are enclosed in a rigid plastic case that gives better protection to the magnetic media than the 5¼-inch disk's thin plastic jacket. The drives for these disks are smaller, lighter, and use less power than 5¼-inch drives. This makes them ideal for portable computer applications. Most of the new laptop computers use 3½-inch disks. IBM's PS/2 computers and the Apple Macintosh use 3½-inch disk drives.

Hard-disk Drives

Floppy disks are great for transferring program files and backing up your computer's hard-disk drive, but hard-disk drives can store much more data than a floppy disk can. One 20-MB hard disk holds as much information as 56 standard 5¼-inch disks. Hard-disk drives can also read and write information much faster than a floppy-disk drive can. Some hard-disk drives have an average access time of less than 20 milliseconds. The access time of a floppy-disk drive is typically more than 85 milliseconds.

Hard-disk drives can store from 10 MB to over 1000 MB of data. The hard-disk drives that fit into microcomputers can store more than 300 MB. Most smaller businesses will not need more than 30 MB of storage for accounting applications, unless they have enormous customer or inventory files.

Removable media, either floppy disks or removable hard-disk drives, allow you to increase the data available to your system, but you can have instant access only to the disks currently mounted in the system's drives.

Many business applications, such as database programs, require a hard-disk drive for adequate system performance. Floppy-disk drives are much slower and require you to swap disks constantly. Mounting and re-mounting disks every few minutes to find needed data can be very frustrating. A hard-disk drive is usually a worthwhile investment.

Tape Drives

Tape systems that use data cassettes or cartridges are a fast, reliable, and cost-effective way of backing up or archiving data. Although tape drives originally used open-reel tapes, most of the new units for microcomputers use data-cassette tape cartridges.

Tape drives are available in several different sizes and shapes. Smaller units for microcomputers are the same size as 3½-inch and 5¼-inch half-height disk drives. These units can store from 10 MB to 100 MB of data on each tape. Because the data is stored serially along the tape, it takes longer to access a specific piece of information on a tape drive than on a disk drive. This is why microcomputer tape drives are almost always used exclusively for backup purposes.

Laser Disks...The Future

Laser disks can store vast amounts of data. The data coded on a laser disk's surface is read by a laser beam that bounces off the spinning disk onto an electronic receptor. Data is coded onto the laser disk's surface as a series of pits, which correspond to binary 1s, and smooth areas, which correspond to binary 0s. The pits in the disk's surface cause the laser beam to be reflected differently.

Laser disks currently use two types of disk technology, read-only disks (CD ROMs) and write once, read many times disks (WORMs). Cost-effective laser-disk systems that allow data to be erased and overwritten,

---

Improving Microcomputer Performance: Coprocessor and Extended-Memory Boards

In the microcomputer environment, add-on boards containing *CPU coprocessors* are available that can be plugged into the system to improve performance. These "turbo" boards let the system's CPU continue to process input and output functions while they execute the arithmetic and other logic operations. This can dramatically improve system performance.

Intel Corporation offers the 8087, 80287, and 80387 *math coprocessor* chips to work with their 8088, 80286, and 80386 CPUs. Math coprocessors increase the speed at which mathematical operations are processed. The results are particularly dramatic with large financial modeling programs.

Extended Memory Specification (EMS) add-on boards allow an Intel 8088-based IBM PC/XT or compatible to address more than 1 MB of main memory through a technique called bank switching. Bank switching overcomes the limitation of 1 MB of main memory imposed by the data bus in the IBM PC/XT.

The IBM PC/AT runs in two modes; one emulates the IBM PC and is called real mode, and the other, known as protected mode, allows the new features of the Intel 80286 processor to be used. In protected mode, an IBM PC/AT can address several megabytes of RAM without using bank switching. When a PC/AT is running in real mode, it emulates the Intel 8088 microprocessor and thus can address only 1 MB of RAM. If your software is written for real mode, then, bank switching is necessary if you need to have your PC/AT or compatible address more main memory.

You should consider installing an EMS board in your IBM PC/XT or compatible if it is necessary to work with very large data files, such as large spreadsheets; if you are running a multitasking system; or if you use your system as a file server on a local area network. However, I strongly recommend that you use an Intel 80286 IBM PC/AT or compatible if you require more than 1 MB of RAM in your system.

as magnetic-disk drives do, are still a few years down the road. Laser disks will not replace magnetic-disk drives for at least another decade.

WORM drives capable of storing over 400 MB of data are now available for under $2,000. These drives are most commonly used to provide an audit trail of backup storage for accounting systems, for archival storage of insurance data, and for transcripts of court proceedings. Kodak has recently announced a 6800-MB, or 6.8-gigabyte, WORM drive that will be available soon.

CD ROM disks are being used to store extremely large databases, such as census information, encyclopedias, and catalogs.

Activision Corporation is shipping a CD ROM system for less than $1,000. A CD ROM edition of Grolier's Encyclopedia is bundled with Activision's CD ROM drive. The disks for this system hold more than 500 MB of data.

It will be some time before much software is available in the laser format, but microcomputer manufacturers hope that the advantage of being able to play regular audio compact disks on their CD ROM systems will help sales.

The access time of a CD ROM-disk drive is a bit slower than that of a standard 5¼-inch floppy-disk drive. Larger laser-disk drives that use 12-inch disks hold over 1000 MB of data and are as fast as hard-disk drives. However, these drives currently cost about $10,000.

Currently, there are six different sizes of laser disks and multiple formats for recording information. Although the lack of format standards may slow market acceptance, the CD ROM format appears to have strong market support. Much depends on what IBM and other major computer companies do to help build momentum for laser standards.

Anatomy of a Computer

A generic IBM PC-compatible microcomputer can be assembled from separate parts and computer boards that are readily available from many distributors and mail-order companies. Generic IBM-compatible microcomputers, or clones, are also available assembled and tested from numerous importers and distributors. Both IBM-compatible PC/XTs and

PC/ATs are now considered commodity items, and competition among the scores of suppliers has driven down system prices. Microcomputers are now available for about $500 and up, depending on the system's configuration.

Specifically, a microcomputer is composed of the key parts listed on the next page. The letters are keyed to the components shown in Figure 10-3.

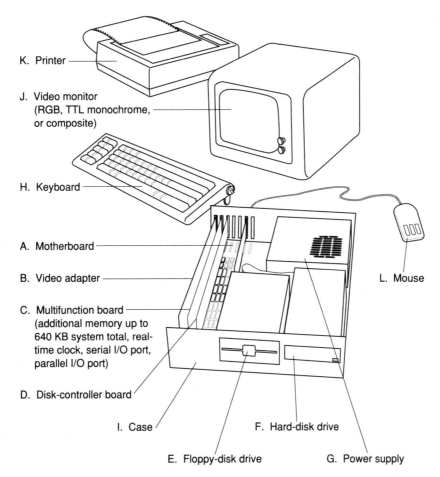

Figure 10-3.
The anatomy of a computer.

A. Motherboard. The motherboard contains the CPU; the bus, into which add-on boards are plugged; and sockets for RAM chips (usually enough to install 640 KB or more). The price of an IBM PC/XT-compatible motherboard is $100 to $300. IBM PC/AT-compatible boards currently cost about $200 more than PC/XT boards.

Be sure that the computer you select has extra slots into which you can plug add-on boards. IBM PC/XT-compatible systems usually have a total of eight slots. You will need these slots for an internal modem, an additional RAM board, a networking board, or other special-purpose boards.

You should also check to be sure that the motherboard has a socket for a math coprocessor chip.

B. Video display adapter board. This board supports the output to the video display monitor. Imported MDA, Hercules, or CGA-compatible adapters cost from $60 to $150. EGA-compatible adapters are available for about $150. Display adapters are discussed in detail in the next chapter.

C. Multifunction board. This optional board can provide a number of different features, including space for additional RAM, serial and parallel output ports, a real-time clock, game adapters for joysticks, and in some systems a floppy-disk drive controller. These boards cost from $150 to $400, depending on the features offered and the supplier.

D. Disk-controller board. This board contains the controller for the floppy-disk drives. Some boards also contain a hard-disk drive controller. Disk controllers can usually support either two or four drives. Floppy-disk drive controllers cost from $50 to $150. Combination floppy/hard-disk controllers cost about $50 more.

E. Floppy-disk drives. The disk drives are mounted on rails built into a standard microcomputer chassis. Floppy-disk drives cost between $50 and $200. Full-height drives offer no advantage over the newer half-height drives. I recommend half-height drives. Some drives are a bit noisier than others and have nicer ''doors,'' but these differences are more aesthetic than functional.

F. Hard-disk drives. Standard hard-disk drives hold 10 to 40 MB of data. A standard 20 MB hard disk with a 65-millisecond access time costs about $350. Hard-disk drives that hold more data and have faster access times can cost several thousand dollars.

G. Power supply. The power supply in a PC/XT is rated at 135 watts; the PC/AT has a 200-watt power supply. Power supplies sell for $75 to $150, depending on the manufacturer and the wattage rating.

H. Keyboard. Standard keyboards contain 93 to 104 keys. The "feel" of different keyboards varies tremendously and is very important to many users, especially experienced touch typists. Try out a few different models and select one that suits your needs and your budget. Keyboards cost from $60 to more than $300 for fancier models with built-in pointing devices.

I. Computer case or chassis. Cases for generic PCs cost between $50 and $150. A case must be designed correctly and have good electrical shielding or it will not pass FCC regulations for electronic noise and radio interference. Computers that pass class A FCC tests can be used in commercial environments; those that pass class B tests require additional shielding and are allowed to be used in the home.

J. Video display monitor. Normal televisions do not have high enough resolution to display 80 columns of readable text. I recommend higher-resolution displays for monitors that will be used primarily for business applications or text processing. If you are in any doubt about this suggestion, try reading the credits for your favorite movie on a television set.

The various types of monitors and graphic standards are discussed in some detail in the next chapter. Standard monochrome displays cost from $80 to about $250. Color monitors that support the CGA cost $250 and up, depending on the brand and the features that you choose. Color monitors that support the higher-resolution EGA and VGA cost $450 and up.

State-of-the-art "multisync" monitors can automatically adjust to support the MDA, CGA, EGA, VGA, and Hercules graphics adapters. These monitors are available discounted to about $500.

K. Hard-copy output devices. Printers and plotters are covered in the next chapter.

L. Pointing devices. Mice, joysticks, light pens, touch pads or screens, and digitizing tablets are covered in the next chapter.

Who Makes Generic Computers?

The components in virtually all of the computers on the market come from the same large component manufacturers in the United States and Asia. Computer manufacturers shop for their boards and components from the same original equipment manufacturers (OEMs) that distribute through mail-order and other distribution channels. For example, Seagate is a manufacturer that sells disk drives directly to computer manufacturers and also sells disk drives through mail-order distributors to individual buyers.

Computer manufacturers integrate these components to create a complete, functional computer system. The primary advantages of buying an assembled computer are that you get a product that is "burned in," or tested, under extreme conditions to assure functionality and that it is more convenient to go to one source for maintenance and warranty. Otherwise, prices being equal, you could just buy the items listed in the previous section and assemble your own computer.

There are many well-designed IBM-compatible computers on the market. Most of the generic computers sold through discount distributors come with money-back guarantees and free trial periods. Check the hardware product reviews in major computer magazines if you want to learn more about specific brands. Many large corporations are beginning to invest in non-name-brand computers because they are less expensive and in some cases provide excellent after-sale support through retail computer dealers and distributors.

Transportable Computers

Some applications require that a computer be moved frequently or that it be battery powered. Transportable computers, such as the Compaq II and the Kaypro 16, weigh about 20 pounds and are fully compatible with the IBM PC standard. Transportable computers are usually encased in a fairly rugged carrying case and are designed to be moved frequently and easily, with cords folding neatly into special compartments and displays integrated within the system unit. They usually feature a small 5-inch to 9-inch high-resolution display and often offer limited expandability through one or more expansion slots on the system's bus. The main advantage of transportable computers is that they are easier to move than desktop systems. The disadvantages include less expansion capability, a smaller display, and usually a price that's higher than a comparable desktop unit.

Portable "laptop" computers like the Toshiba 1200 and the Zenith 181 are battery powered so that they can be used on a person's lap without being plugged into a 110-volt AC power outlet. These computers are light—typically 9 to 15 pounds including batteries—and are small enough to fit into a standard briefcase. Laptop systems are fully compatible with IBM's microcomputers and are equipped with both floppy-disk and hard-disk drives as well as internal modems for telecommunications.

Most laptop machines use low-power LCD displays; this allows them to function for about four to eight hours without requiring a new or recharged battery. However, if you will be using your system for hours at a time and you will have access to a 110-volt AC outlet, you will be better off using a transportable computer with a higher-resolution CRT display. LCD and other flat-screen displays are being improved, but they still do not match the contrast, resolution, and legibility of CRT technology.

11

Computer Input and Output Devices

This section looks at the input and output devices you will need to enter data into your computer system, to permit data communications with other computers, and to display and print computer output, word-processed text, and management reports. I will make recommendations about different graphics hardware and have included buyer's checklists that will help you select modems and printers.

Computer Input Devices

There are many ways to enter data into a computer. The most common data-entry device is, of course, the keyboard. However, depending on the type of data that you need to record, you may wish to consider a computerized cash register or even some sort of scanning equipment.

Keyboard Data Entry

Whether you are using a microcomputer, a terminal connected to a network, or a minicomputer, you will probably enter most of your data at a keyboard. The data you enter will appear on the screen of your video display. Many keyboards have programmable command or function keys that are used in various ways by different software programs. You can buy microcomputer software that allows you to store frequently used sequences of keystrokes and then retrieve them at the press of a key. These can be real time-savers.

Pointing Devices and Digitizers

Mice, trackballs, light pens, and joysticks are devices that follow the movement of your hand, allowing you to place the cursor anywhere on the screen quickly and easily. They are sometimes called "pointing devices," and are usually connected to a computer's serial port (sometimes called an RS-232 port). An example of these types of devices is shown in Figure 11-1.

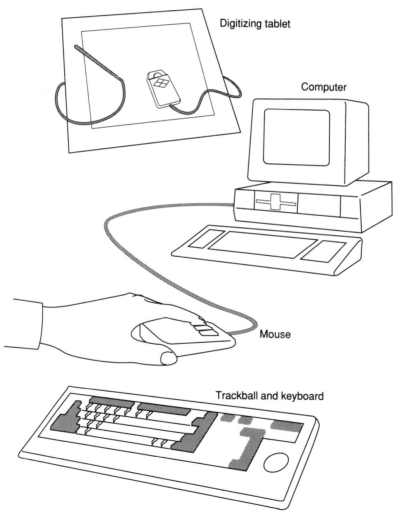

Digitizing tablet

Computer

Mouse

Trackball and keyboard

Figure 11-1.
Three types of pointing devices.

A mouse is used to select and move text and graphics. Microsoft recommends using a mouse with its word processor. Although some users are uncomfortable moving their hands away from the keyboard during data entry, a mouse is useful during editing. An Apple Macintosh computer comes equipped with a mouse; a mouse for an IBM-compatible PC is available separately for about $100.

Joysticks and trackballs do not require additional desk space for their movement, as mice do, but they are somewhat harder to control. They are used primarily for game software and for CAD applications. Light pens are used primarily to select text from menus and to select and move graphics.

Summagraphics and other companies make digitizing tablets that allow you to ''draw'' using a special stylus. The resulting graphics data is entered directly into your computer's memory. These digitizers are ideal for creating presentations and for computer-aided drafting and design applications.

Point-of-Sale (POS) Terminals

POS terminals allow you to capture sales information at the time of the sale, eliminating the need to enter it later.

Retail POS systems consist of a computer connected to cash registers or data-entry terminals. The sales information can update your company's database immediately. For example, inventory can be updated, the billing module can generate necessary invoices or receipts, and accounts receivable can do a credit check and update your customer's file when a sale is entered into a POS terminal.

POS systems often use light wands or laser scanners (you may have seen these in supermarkets) to speed data entry and improve accuracy. The wands and scanners read the bar codes (Universal Product Codes, or UPCs) that are printed on the package of most mass-market products.

POS data entry is cost-effective in many installations. As the cost of hardware goes down, many more POS systems are beginning to be installed in retail businesses. All retailers and many distributors should seriously consider a POS data-entry system.

Optical Character Recognition (OCR)

OCR equipment can scan a printed page and read, digitize, and enter the information directly into a computer with no manual rekeying. OCRs can read up to 600 pages per minute and are great for law firms and other businesses that need to enter preprinted documents into their systems.

Unfortunately, these devices have not been perfected; they can read only certain type fonts and are sensitive to dirt, smudges, and poor-quality paper. The better scanners are more forgiving and can be adjusted to read a wider range of type fonts.

Graphics-scanning devices, similar in principle to OCRs, allow graphics information to be entered directly into the computer. These are useful when you need to generate graphics for presentations or combine graphics and text on a page for a newsletter.

Prices are coming down on scanning equipment that works with microcomputers. Panasonic and other companies now offer units that will scan both text and graphics information at six pages per minute with 300-dots-per-inch resolution for less than $1,500.

Magnetic Ink Character Recognition (MICR)

The code that is printed on the bottom of your checks is printed in magnetic ink. The checks are fed into special MICR readers, which process information at the rate of more than 1500 checks per minute. This specialized technology has been cost-effective in the banking industry.

Voice Recognition and Speech Synthesis

Voice recognition is one of the most exciting and dynamic areas of computer science. Special computer chip sets and programs are available that translate the spoken word into computer code or allow computer-generated output to be translated into synthesized speech. Vocabularies are still limited, but more powerful chips are under development.

Voice recognition technology is still too expensive to be used in most general business applications, but costs are coming down as the technology improves. The ability to talk with computers should help raise the general level of computer literacy in the future!

Video Cameras

Output from a video camera can be used to enter graphics information into a computer system. You may have been to one of the novelty shops that use video output to generate a computer-drawn picture. This is usually merged with the lucky model's name or perhaps a calendar and printed out on a dot-matrix printer.

A more interesting application of digitized video output involves robotics. Video cameras can function as the "eyes" of computerized robots. Special image-processing software has been developed that allows the robot to interpret the video signals and move appropriately.

Computer Output Devices

This section discusses three kinds of computer output devices: display screens or monitors, printers and other "hard-copy" output devices, and modems, used for telecommunications.

Video Display Screens

The computer's display screen, also known as the display monitor, shows computer input and output. Some types of computers and terminals give you no choice as to the type of display you can use; with others, the choices are numerous. You can choose a monochrome display or one that offers different colors, and you can set it up to display text only or to display both text and graphics. All of these choices involve trade-offs.

The most important thing to do, if you will be selecting a display monitor for your system, is to be sure that your software, display adapter, and monitor will all work together (display adapters will be discussed later in this chapter). The documentation for your software will indicate the type of monitor and display adapter for which it is designed. Many software packages will work with a variety of display configurations.

Computer programs are either text-based or graphics-based. A text-based program will work with a text-only display adapter (the IBM Monochrome Display Adapter or compatible) and a high-resolution monochrome monitor. Graphics-based software requires a graphics adapter and an appropriate monitor. Text-based software will usually run on a graphics display, but graphics cannot run on a text-only display.

The section entitled "Computer Graphics" in Chapter 12 discusses some of the uses for graphics in business.

Display Adapter Boards

A display adapter is a board that fits inside your computer. You connect your monitor to this board, and the board acts as an intermediary, receiving data from the CPU and sending it to the monitor for display. Virtually all software developers support IBM's display adapters. IBM's standard Monochrome Display Adapter (MDA), Color Graphics Adapter (CGA), Enhanced Graphics Adapter (EGA), and Video Graphics Array (VGA) have all become de facto industry standards. The only non-IBM-compatible display adapter to have gained widespread support is the Hercules Graphics Card for monochrome graphics. Each of these boards is discussed in this section; after that discussion, I will make some recommendations.

The software you use must have a *device driver* for the display adapter you have installed in your system. Device drivers are special sections of a program that allow it to work with different input and output devices connected to the system. For example, there must be one device driver for an Epson dot-matrix printer, another for an IBM Proprinter, and other device drivers for different laser printers. Similarly, programs must have graphics drivers written to support CGA, EGA, and other graphics-display cards. Most application programs include device drivers to support only a few standard input and output devices. I strongly recommend that you select products that are compatible with well-supported industry-standard video-display adapters.

Graphics-based applications are usually configured with a special "install" utility that allows the application to work with different display adapters. The user is prompted to answer a series of questions about the system on which he or she will be running the application, and about the graphics adapter that is installed. The application then configures the correct graphics drivers to take full advantage of the hardware features that are available. For example, your program's "install" utility program might ask if you were using a CGA, EGA, or Hercules display adapter.

To understand the following discussions of graphics adapters, you must know what a *pixel* is. Basically, a pixel is just a dot of light on the screen. Every image displayed on a computer screen is made up of thousands of pixels. Each pixel is controlled by one or more bytes of video memory that contains information about where each pixel is and what color and intensity it should be. The more pixels that the screen can display, the higher the system's *resolution*. Graphics cards that individually control each pixel on the screen are sometimes referred to as *bit-mapped* graphics.

Monochrome Display Adapter (MDA). IBM's standard Monochrome Display Adapter displays 80 characters per line and 25 lines per screen of high-resolution text.

The MDA will display only text characters on the screen; it cannot display graphic images. This adapter must be used with an IBM-style (TTL) monochrome monitor.

Color Graphics Adapter (CGA). IBM's Color Graphics Adapter has two modes, a low-resolution 320-by-200-pixel color graphics mode and a 640-by-200-pixel monochrome graphics mode. The 640-by-200 monochrome graphics mode is sometimes referred to in advertisements as "high resolution." This is unfortunate, because 640-by-200-pixel displays are only medium resolution at best.

In monochrome mode, the CGA allows the display of reasonably good decision-support business graphics, although circles appear with a very jagged outline. Text displayed with the CGA has the same resolution as graphic images—that is, 640 by 200 pixels in monochrome graphics mode. The standard Monochrome Display Adapter displays the equivalent of 720 by 350 pixels of text.

Enhanced Graphics Adapter (EGA). IBM's Enhanced Graphics Adapter has rapidly become an industry standard, displacing the CGA and MDA. The main advantage of the EGA is its ability to display both legible text and high-resolution color graphics. The EGA allows the display of both high resolution 640-by-350-pixel color graphics and text. EGA technology allows you to create and display good presentation graphics with up to 16 different colors.

Microsoft, Lotus, and most other major software companies have included the necessary graphics device drivers in their software to support the EGA board.

IBM's Video Graphics Array (VGA). IBM's Video Graphics Array provides 640-by-480-pixel resolution with 16 on-screen colors from a palette of 256 colors. Text resolution is even sharper than on the EGA: 720 by 400 pixels in 16 colors or shades of gray in monochrome. Characters are composed of a 9-by-16-pixel matrix.

The VGA adapter is included with IBM's PS/2 Models 50, 60, and 80; it requires a display monitor with a horizontal frequency of 31.5 KHz. The VGA supports CGA and EGA display to maintain compatibility with existing software.

Non-IBM display adapters. Many high-resolution graphics boards operate by doubling the number of horizontal lines displayed by a standard CGA. This allows them to display high-resolution text and still run standard CGA programs. However, these adapters usually do not address the additional horizontal lines individually. Higher-resolution video adapters require the use of high-resolution color monitors that can display 640 by 400 pixels.

Some of the latest monochrome graphics adapters work with extremely high-resolution 1280-by-800-pixel displays. These boards offer "backward" compatibility with standard CGA adapters. Other new graphics adapters offer higher-resolution proprietary color graphics modes. The problem these board manufacturers have is getting software developers to include the device drivers necessary to take advantage of their special features.

Hercules Monochrome Graphics Card. The Hercules display adapter allows the display of high-resolution 720-by-350-pixel monochrome text and monochrome graphics on an IBM standard monochrome video monitor (the so-called TTL type of monitor). This has become the only non-IBM graphics standard for microcomputers. Most serious business application programs support the Hercules adapter.

Recommendations for Display Adapters

Virtually all business applications are enhanced by the use of graphics displays. But graphics applications typically run slower than text applications because they need to transfer more information onto the display. The response time for graphics programs running on the IBM PC/XT and compatible machines with floppy-disk drives has been a major concern among users. No one likes to wait for their system to redraw the screen when they are running graphics applications. However, this is becoming less of an issue as computers become more powerful and as programmers learn to adapt their programs to optimize graphics performance. On Intel 80286-based and 80386-based MS-DOS systems with a hard-disk drive, Microsoft Windows and most other graphics applications perform well.

Hercules-compatible monochrome graphics adapters now cost about the same as standard monochrome display adapters and can work with the same monitors. There is no longer any reason *not* to use a graphics adapter board. If you do not require a color display, or if you do not have a color monitor, a Hercules or compatible monochrome graphics board is the best choice. If you will be using a color monitor, I recommend an IBM EGA, VGA, or compatible board. All of these adapters offer good resolution for text and graphics and are supported by virtually all major software developers.

Video Display Monitors

You must be sure that your video display, or monitor, has high enough resolution to work correctly with your graphics adapter. The VGA requires a video display with 480 horizontal lines; the EGA requires a video display with 350 horizontal lines; and CGA monitors require the display of only 200 lines. CGA monitors can work with EGA boards but will display only 200 lines of graphics resolution.

The smaller the "dot pitch," or size of each pixel in the display, the better resolution it will have. Most CGA color monitors have a dot pitch of 0.31 millimeter or smaller. Higher-resolution VGA and EGA monitors have a dot pitch of 0.26 millimeter or 0.28 millimeter.

Several manufacturers offer special dual-mode monitors. A dual-mode monitor can display both standard monochrome text with an MDA board and monochrome graphics (using a gray scale) with a standard CGA board. The Hercules Graphics Card allows a standard monochrome video monitor to display both monochrome text and monochrome graphics. NEC has introduced a 13-inch MultiSync color display monitor that can work with MDA, CGA, Hercules, EGA, VGA, and other adapters with up to 800-by-560-pixel resolution.

Some people are convinced that amber-colored letters on a black background are best; others favor green-colored letters on black for monochrome output. I suggest getting the display you find easiest to work with.

Some color monitors have poorer resolution around the edge of the screen; the displays from major suppliers, such as IBM, Princeton, Amdek, Taxan, Zenith, Sony, and NEC, that I have evaluated all performed well.

High-resolution color monitors that can be used with IBM's EGA and VGA cards currently sell for between $400 and $700. State-of-the-art multisync monitors are available discounted to about $550. The prices on color monitors are continuing to drop as they are pushed into higher-volume production by aggressive Taiwanese and Korean companies.

Workstation Accessories

You may want to use an antiglare screen that attaches to the front of your video display and a tilt platform that allows you to raise and tilt your monitor. (Some monitors have these platforms built in.) If you spend hours looking at a screen, you will come to appreciate anything that prevents eye fatigue or neck strain.

Depending on your environment, you may also need an antistatic mat that acts as a ground. This accessory can prevent a potentially harmful high-voltage static-electricity discharge from going through your computer system.

It is also a good idea to get a surge protector to help block voltage spikes and electromagnetic interference from coming through the AC wall connection. Voltage spikes can damage your hardware and data. Surge suppressors are usually included with multiple-outlet power strips designed for computer installations.

Some users require backup power sources. These will prevent data loss in the event of a power outage. Power backup units from Elgar and other manufacturers of uninterruptible power supplies (UPS's) that work with microcomputers cost $600 and up. Depending on their rated power, UPS's can supply emergency power for more than 12 hours.

Printers for Text

A wide range of printers and plotters is available for producing hard-copy output. Choose a printer with the print quality and speed that you require.

Dot-Matrix Printers

Dot-matrix printers are inexpensive, fairly noisy, and provide output that ranges from obvious computer output, in which the letters do not have quite enough dots, to near-letter-quality (NLQ) printing that is almost as good as a typewriter. High-end dot-matrix printers use 24-pin print heads instead of 9-pin heads and as a result produce more fully formed characters. The output of some of the 24-pin dot-matrix printers is as acceptable to many users as ''letter-quality'' output. (See the next subsection of this chapter.)

Many printers allow you to choose between a draft mode that prints lower-quality text at a high speed and near-letter-quality mode that prints better-looking text but at a considerably slower pace.

Dot-matrix printers print from 80 to 400 or more characters per second (cps). They are capable of printing through multiple carbons. Good 200-cps printers are available for less than $350. Users with heavier printing requirements should consider some of the faster 300-to-400-cps dot-matrix printers available for $500 to $1,500.

Epson, IBM, and many other companies manufacture high-quality, inexpensive dot-matrix printers. I particularly like IBM's Proprinter because you can feed single envelopes or letterhead sheets into a slot in the front of the printer while pin-feed paper remains loaded.

Letter-Quality Impact Printers

Letter-quality printers produce print that looks just like that of an IBM Selectric typewriter. They are considerably slower than dot-matrix printers because they have a rotating daisy wheel or thimble that is used to strike characters onto the ribbon. These printers are generally noisy, run at about 20 to 80 cps, and range in price from $300 to $1,500.

The high end of the letter-quality printer market is being overtaken for most applications by laser-printer technology. The low end is being attacked by high-end dot-matrix printers that offer near-letter-quality output. For many applications, the small decrease in print quality offered by NLQ dot-matrix printers is more than offset by the fact that they are less expensive and can print five to ten times faster than letter-quality printers. Figure 11-2 shows a comparison of the output from a dot-matrix, a letter-quality, and a laser printer.

Dot-matrix printer   Letter-quality printer   Laser printer

Figure 11-2.
Printed output from three major types of printers.

Laser Printers

Desktop laser printers from Hewlett–Packard and other manufacturers print about 500 to 1000 characters per second, or about six to ten pages per minute. (The rated output of laser printers can be a bit misleading. I recommend that you consult reviews in major computer publications to compare the most recent performance specifications of different laser printers.) These printers are quiet, provide letter-quality output, can produce a full 8½-by-11-inch page of graphics with 300-dot-per-inch resolution, and are cost-competitive with other output devices.

Books and magazines are printed with a resolution of 1200 dots per inch (dpi). First-generation desktop laser printers print at 300 dpi; more-expensive laser printers print 400 to 600 dpi. Print resolution of 300 dpi is similar to letter-quality print from a carbon ribbon on an electric typewriter. Print resolution of 600 dpi looks almost identical to typeset text in a book or magazine.

The cost of a laser printer ranges from a bit less than $1,500 for a model with limited features to more than $6,000 for a machine that provides most of the features needed for more elaborate in-house publishing. The cost of laser printers is coming down as more companies ramp up production and drive down component costs.

Although laser printers are rapidly winning market share against the high-end dot-matrix printers as well as daisy-wheel letter-quality printers, their one major limitation is that they are nonimpact printers and thus cannot print multiple-part forms.

Most of the new laser printers allow you to load and print different type fonts. This lets you print different character sets on the same page by embedding software commands in the document you are printing. A number of third-party software companies now offer page-description languages that provide the formatting commands necessary to lay out text and graphics on the same page. This makes it easy for nontechnical users to create professional-looking documents and publications.

Drafts for this book were produced on a Hewlett–Packard laser printer. The decision to use the laser printer was based on quality of output, speed, ability to print graphics, noise level, and price. This one machine replaced three other output devices: a dot-matrix printer for rough drafts, a letter-quality printer for the final draft, and a pen plotter for graphics hard copy.

Ink-Jet and Thermal Printers

Hewlett–Packard is the leading manufacturer of ink-jet printers. These printers form letters by squirting fast-drying ink onto the paper. They are quiet, can run reasonably fast, and are moderately priced. Their output is similar to a 9-pin dot-matrix printer if special paper is used. Ink-jet printers are not well suited for many business applications because they cannot print through multiple-part forms and cannot produce letter-quality output. However, ink-jet technology is a good solution if printer noise is a problem. Hewlett–Packard advertises that you can think when their Think-Jet printer is printing; it's true.

Thermal printers are slowly becoming extinct. This is primarily because they require thermal paper, which is expensive and usually comes in inconvenient rolls. They are still used in portable terminal printers, but portable ink-jet and dot-matrix technology is winning out.

Line Printers

Line printers print from 150 to over 1200 lines per minute. They are used with minicomputers and mainframes that have large print requirements. Line printers, as their name suggests, print an entire line at a time by using a rotating print chain.

Line printers cost from several thousand dollars to over $20,000 for the fastest systems. These are the printers featured in movies where a computer goes haywire and starts spewing out reams of paper.

Print Spoolers

A print spooler is a software program that allows you to store the report or file that you want to print in a special print file. The print file can then print out your reports on your printer while you work on other tasks at the same time. This almost doubles the amount of work your system can process.

Printer Switches

A printer switch will allow you to share one printer between two or more computers, or will allow you to connect two or more printers to one microcomputer. Printer switches cost $70 and up, depending on the features they provide.

Devices for Producing Graphics Hard Copy

The current standard for graphics-output devices is still the monochrome dot-matrix printer, which produces unacceptable print quality for most presentations. Laser printers provide the only fast, high-quality hard-copy output for graphics. Laser printers have become important for presentation graphics and the desktop-publishing market.

Color Printers

Color printers based on both dot-matrix and ink-jet technology are available. Unfortunately, these printers are not well supported by standard printer-command sets. Do not assume that your software applications will work with these devices.

New color dot-matrix printers based on 24-pin technology can print over 200 cps in eight colors and can provide near-letter-quality output. These printers are more expensive than monochrome printers, but they are useful for creating visually interesting presentations.

Plotters

A plotter is a precision device that draws graphics on paper; it does so by using special felt-tip pens. Plotters are used to output analog data from test equipment and to create professional-looking presentations and overhead transparencies. If you want to make a pie chart by drawing a perfectly round circle with no jagged edges, dividing the circle into slices, coloring the slices, and then printing headings and text around the image, you need a color plotter. Plotters can have from one to over a dozen differently colored pens that can provide very-high-resolution output for CAD or business graphics. Hewlett–Packard and Tektronix are leaders in this area.

Computer-Graphics Slide-Presentation Systems

Kodak and Polaroid make systems that allow computer images to be made into color slides and prints. Graphics slide-presentation systems use two approaches. One involves actually taking a photograph of the display screen, and the other, which provides better resolution, consists of running the video output from the computer into a special monitor that has a built-in camera mechanism.

Buyer's Checklist for All Hard-Copy Output Devices

■ Be sure that the printer is supported by the software you want to run.

■ Be sure that the printer is designed to handle the volume of printing that you will require. The printer manufacturer should be able to tell you whether the printer's rated capacity is adequate for your requirements.

■ Be sure that the print quality of the printer is adequate for your needs.

■ Make sure that printer supplies are readily available at a reasonable cost. You may be surprised how expensive carbon ribbons are for letter-quality printers and how hard they are to find on Sunday in Del Mar! Also be sure that sheet feeders (devices that feed single sheets of paper) are available for letter-quality printers and that your printer has a wide-enough carriage for your printing applications.

■ Whenever possible, buy a device that supports industry-standard drivers.

 – For dot-matrix printers, the Epson/IBM command set has become a de facto standard. Epson has captured about 30 percent of the printer market; IBM's command set is nearly identical.

 – For plotters, the Hewlett–Packard and Tektronix command sets have the most software support.

 – For letter-quality printers, the Diablo, NEC, and Qume command sets have strong support from word-processing software companies.

 – Many laser printers emulate the Epson dot-matrix and the Qume, Diablo, or NEC letter-quality-printer command sets. These drivers do not allow laser printers to use all of their capabilities, however.

 – The command set for Hewlett–Packard's LaserJet printers has become a de facto standard because of its large market share.

Data Communications

Data communications over telephone lines (telecommunications) allows data to be communicated directly from one computer system to another in a remote location. (See Figure 11-3.)

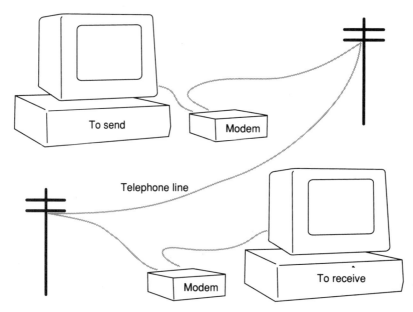

Figure 11-3.
A telecommunications connection.

Telecommunications equipment allows multiple users to access remote information services or databases, and allows traveling employees or remote information workers to access electronic mail or data files on their company's computer system. Telecommunications links can also be used to share programs or data between two machines that do not share a common disk format. For example, text files on a laptop computer can easily be downloaded to a desktop computer for reformatting.

How Telecommunications Works

To telecommunicate, you need a device called a *modem*. A modem is a signal translator that converts the computer output into tones that can be transmitted over telephone lines. When data is to be sent out, or *uploaded,* across a telephone line, it first travels through the computer's serial port to the modem, where it is translated. The modem then sends the data over the telephone line to another modem that decodes the signal and passes it along to a serial port on the receiving computer's bus. The receiving computer is then said to have *downloaded* the data. Telecommunications software controls the sending and receiving of data over a modem.

Normal phone lines allow computers to communicate at up to 2400 bits per second (bps, or baud). If you are using modems that transmit faster than 2400 bps, you should contact the telephone company to arrange for special conditioned telephone lines to be installed. Conditioned phone lines are not rerouted through noisy switches the way normal phone lines are. Because the noise on these lines is lower, they improve your chances of error-free transmission.

About Modems

Data-transfer rate: Standard modems can communicate at between 300 and 9600 bps. Most microcomputer-based systems communicate at 300, 1200, or 2400 bps. Many modems have a variable transfer rate; you change it using telecommunications software. Data transmission can take place in one direction at a time, which is called half duplex, or in both directions at once, known as full duplex. You usually specify half or full duplex in your telecommunications software.

Business users should use a modem with at least a 1200-bps data-transfer rate.

Modem command sets: The de facto industry standard for modems is the Hayes command set. Virtually all 300-, 1200-, and 2400-bps modems are Hayes-compatible. Faster 9600-bps modems are usually compatible with the CCITT (an international standards committee) V.32 standard.

Telecommunications protocols: Telecommunications protocols are standard sets of rules for data transfer. In order for data to be transmitted correctly, both modems must be set up to use the same protocol.

Modem configuration switches and telecommunications software packages allow you to set up the correct protocol. The most common protocol is the XON/XOFF, or start/stop, protocol. When the receiving machine cannot accept any more data—when its buffer is full, for example—it sends a special character called an XOFF. The other machine will not transmit any more data until it receives an XON signal, which tells it that the computer is ready to receive more data. The sending of messages back and forth to control data communications is known as handshaking.

Error-checking protocols: Error-checking protocols are built into most modems. These protocols provide ways of detecting transmission errors and requesting a retransmission of any portion of the incoming message that has been dropped or garbled during transmission.

The most common error-checking protocols are the Xmodem and Kermit protocols. There are also many proprietary error-checking protocols. Different telecommunication protocols are not compatible, so you need to make sure that the sending and receiving modems have at least one protocol in common. Xmodem is currently the most common error-checking protocol in the microcomputer environment.

Some 2400-bps modems use a technique known as adaptive equalization. This program adapts the modem to the characteristics of the phone connection. Adaptive equalization allows 2400-bps modems to maintain error rates equal to or lower than 1200-bps modems that do not have this feature.

External versus internal modems: Modems are available as standalone units that connect to a serial port, or as add-on boards that plug into the computer's bus. Both full-length and half-length boards are available, as are modems bundled on boards with additional features, such as serial and parallel ports. If you can spare a slot in your computer, it is usually more convenient to use an internal modem.

Special Modem Features

- A carrier-detect indicator (on external modems only) that lights up when the modem is on-line.

- A built-in speaker that lets you hear ringing and busy signals.

- Automatic redial that retries a busy telephone number a specified number of times.

- Message buffering that allows the incoming file to be put into a block of memory called a "buffer" so that it can be downloaded into your system.

■ Unattended transmission and receipt of messages, so that you can automatically send messages at a certain time, and answer incoming calls automatically.

■ A voice/data switch that allows you to switch your line between voice and data communications.

Recommendations for Modems

I recommend that you use Hayes or compatible modems. Hayes has become the de facto standard modem in the microcomputer industry. Virtually all the current telecommunications software runs on Hayes-compatible modems.

Modems cost from $100 to more than $700 depending on the supplier and the transmission speed (300 to 9600 bps). Modems from most of the major manufacturers are reliable and easy to use.

If you need to send a great deal of information over telephone lines, I recommend using a 2400-bps modem. The increased transmission speed can save you a great deal of money in long-distance telephone charges.

Popular Telecommunications Software

Smartcom II from Hayes and Crosstalk XVI from Microstuf are two of the most popular telecommunications software packages. These packages are easy to use and powerful enough to handle virtually all telecommunication requirements. They are also well documented and have tens of thousands of users.

Microsoft Access is a new program that has powerful features that allow rapid and accurate access to information services and electronic mail. If you are doing complex searches over different information sources or rely heavily on electronic mail, you might want to consider this program.

PC-Talk III, a telecommunications package by Andrew Flugelman, is a good example of "shareware." Shareware is software placed into the public domain without copy protection. The author asks for a contribution of $25 if you use and like the program. PC-Talk III runs on a standard IBM PC/XT or PC/AT or compatible system. The documentation is on the disk in a file that you can print.

Electronic Mail

Several companies now offer an electronic mail (e-mail) service. This service will let you send electronic mail messages to other subscribers and receive messages from them via a telecommunications connection to the service's computer network.

Many electronic mail services provide a nationwide communications network that allows you to dial a local phone number to access the service. You can send messages to people all over the country. This service provides an audit trail of all messages, helps eliminate "telephone tag," and reduces long-distance telephone charges.

Many companies are now attempting to convince their customers to use electronic mail for all day-to-day business communications. E-mail can save time, is more accurate than verbal phone orders, and is much less expensive than sending letters via an overnight delivery service. A 500-word e-mail letter costs about 50 cents to send; longer letters are about $1.

MCI and Western Union are two of the companies offering a nationwide network for electronic mail and other telecommunications services. Their addresses are given below. If you have further interest, you should look into at least two different offerings. The services and prices differ, and one may be better suited to your company's needs.

MCI Mail
1900 M Street
Box 1001
Washington, DC 20036
(800) MCI-2255

Western Union - Easylink
One Lake Street
Upper Saddle River, NJ 07458
(800) 982-2737

Electronic mail can also be set up on a local-area network. Although most companies don't have terminals on everyone's desk, many companies are finding that this level of office automation can dramatically increase office productivity. For many businesses, electronic mail alone can justify the cost of installing a network.

Information Services

Information-service companies provide access via telecommunications to dozens of different databases. On-line information services allow you to request quotations on your favorite stocks, check your competitor's credit rating with Dun and Bradstreet, consult wine reviews, and read the latest articles in the *Harvard Business Review*. You can also access on-line news services, join computer buying clubs, and post or retrieve messages on electronic bulletin boards. Many of these services also offer private electronic mail.

Attorneys, physicians, pharmacists, financial analysts, and other professionals use information services to provide themselves with up-to-date, industry-specific information. For example, attorneys can use Lexis and Westlaw to help them do legal research. These services offer sophisticated query languages that allow legal practitioners to perform complex searches using keywords or case names.

Three of the most popular database information sources are as follows:
CompuServe
5000 Arlington Centre Blvd.
P.O. Box 20212
Columbus, OH 43220
(800) 848-8199
(614) 457-0802 (In Ohio)

The Source
1616 Anderson Road
McLean, VA 22102
(800) 336-3366
(703) 734-7500

Dow Jones News Retrieval Service
P.O. Box 300
Princeton, NJ 08540
(800) 257-5114
(609) 452-1511

Initial subscription fees to use information services range from $10 to $50 and include one or more hours of connect time to learn how to use the database's different options and search commands. Line-connect charges on information services vary widely, from about $6 per hour during low-usage time to $12 or more per hour during normal business hours.

Connect charges also vary depending on the databases you access after you have signed on to one of the information services. Some specialized databases have access fees of hundreds of dollars per hour. You may feel that these access fees are quite reasonable compared to the costs of doing your own marketing research or hiring consultants.

Information services generally charge higher connect fees for users with high-speed modems. However, it still pays to use higher-speed modems if you will be downloading very much information. For example, The Source currently charges

	Nights and Weekends	**Prime Time**
300 bps	$8.40 per hour	$21.60 per hour
1200 bps	$10.80 per hour	$25.80 per hour
2400 bps	$12.00 per hour	$27.60 per hour

There is a $10 minimum monthly service charge.

The connect time is charged for your entry and query time as well as the computer's search and report time. Therefore, even though the 2400-bps modem seems to be exactly four times faster for less than 50 percent additional fees, in reality the disparity in charges is not quite as great.

According to The Source, a recent study showed that a user using 2400-bps communications for 10 hours per month would save more than $1,000 per year over the same person using a 300-bps connection.

Electronic Bulletin Boards

There are thousands of electronic bulletin boards. Many of these are targeted to the specialized needs of the business community. Some of these on-line bulletin boards require subscription or usage charges, but most are free to all interested subscribers. User groups, hobbyists, and system suppliers sponsor many of these services.

Electronic bulletin boards (also known as BBS's) allow users to post messages that other users can read and respond to. Some bulletin boards are oriented toward interactive dialogue about different current events or computer topics; others are more free-form. They can be a great way for you to meet other computer users with similar interests.

Many BBS systems require passwords, but the systems will usually issue passwords (often for free) on-line when you first call in. Most local computer user groups have lists of BBS phone numbers and will be able to tell you which are the most active, the most interesting, or just the most fun.

Voice-Data Communications

Voice-data communication systems, such as Northern Telecom's new Meridian DV-1 system, allow one digital communications channel to communicate both voice and computer data. For example, two managers could discuss a project while simultaneously reviewing a market forecast that has been transmitted over the same phone link. The managers could review the forecast information on their microcomputer screens, make changes, and store the information for later review. By discussing their ideas and being able to work together on the forecast, the managers may have saved the time and expense of a face-to-face meeting.

This level of office automation is still quite expensive, but it should gain momentum rapidly as more business people learn how to adapt this technology to solve their business problems.

12

More About Productivity Software

This chapter will give you a good idea of how computers can help you automate general office tasks, such as word processing, financial analysis, file management, and interoffice communication, to improve your office productivity.

Database-Management Programs

Most organizations have documents or files that are used during the workday. Much of this information can be stored electronically in a computer. One of the principal benefits of using computers for this is their ability to manipulate and retrieve electronically stored data at high speeds.

Database programs are designed to help you to manage data stored in your computer's files. The advantage of a database-management program is that you can use it to store, rearrange, and retrieve data in special database files without knowing anything about computer programming.

Database programs provide special input screens that you use to enter data into the computer files. They also offer different ways of rearranging, or sorting, that data to generate reports. Many database programs include powerful report generators that allow you not only to list what is in a file but to rearrange the information into presentation-quality reports.

Like most other automated processes, database programs follow the input-process-output cycle. Data must first be entered, or input, into the system. The database program then processes the data by updating existing files. After that, it is ready to output reports on demand.

It does take time to enter your data into the database files, but once it has been entered, most database programs let you use query techniques to get the information and reports that you need. The system will analyze your query and respond by calling up the data you need and arranging it in a reasonable report format.

A typical database query might be, "List all of the salespeople who are over quota for their year-to-date sales." The more English-like and less cryptic the commands for the program are, the easier it will be to use. In less-sophisticated databases, you have to query in something more closely resembling the computer's view of the world, for example, "LIST ALL SLSMN1 TO SLSMN100 > 100% QUOTA" or even "LIST SLSMN=1–100 AND SLSMN=>100% QUOTA." Learning time is valuable; better-designed databases with good documentation and a user-friendly interface are well worth their price.

Building a Database

To build a database, you first need to set up your database files. Database files comprise records, which in turn contain different fields of data. A field is the smallest amount of information that can be entered, sorted, and retrieved by a database program.

Database programs have special utility programs that make it easy to set up the database. Usually, the program presents a blank table that lets you specify how you want to set up your files. You then simply respond to the prompts generated by the program. Figure 12-1 shows an example of this type of screen. The "key field" that it mentions will be discussed shortly.

The next step is to enter your data into the files. Most database programs have special data-entry screens that are created automatically from your original file definitions.

Figure 12-2 shows a sample data-entry screen. Such screens are often set up with a special program called a screen-design utility. This type of program generally requires you to respond to a series of prompts, after which it generates custom input and output screens that you then use to

```
Name of Data File:       SALES FILE
Number of Records:          100
Key Field:                   1

Field 1 Name of Field:             SALESNUM
        Type (alpha or numeric):       N
        Number of Characters:          2

Field 2 Name of Field:             QUOTA
        Type (alpha or numeric):       N
        Number of Characters:          2

Field 3 Name of Field:             SALESPERF
        Type (alpha or numeric):       N
        Number of Characters:          9

Field 4 Name of Field:             %QUOTA
        Type (alpha or numeric):       N
        Number of Characters:          3
```

Figure 12-1.
A file-definition screen.

```
File Name: SALES FILE

Salesperson Number:

Sales Quota        $     .00

Sales Performance  $     .00

% of Quota               %

Fill in screen with appropriate response, then use
command keys to execute:

F1=Enter  F2=Delete  F3=Edit  F4=Read/List  F5=Exit
```

Figure 12-2.
A data-entry screen.

create the database files and to format custom reports from the data in the files.

Once your data has been entered, most database-management programs allow you either to print standard reports or to create your own reports. The program will ask you to list the fields of data that you want included in your report. It will prompt you for information about where on the report the data fields should appear and what mathematical relationships should be built in for financial summaries. You can usually specify beginning and ending dates for the report so that it will include only data for that period.

Figures 12-3 and 12-4 show two sample data files. Let's see how a database program would work with these files. The personnel file and sales file are each made up of three records. Each record has four fields of information. These records can be sorted by any of the fields.

If you want to put together a report that will allow the sales manager to review the performance of the sales staff, you will probably want to use the salesperson's name rather than just his or her employee number.

```
          Field 1   Field 2          Field 3     Field 4
Record 1  Jones     1075 Adams St.   555-9090       32
Record 2  Smith     890 Paulino St.  555-0001       56
Record 3  Peterson  118 Filbert St.  555-0987       23

Field 1 = Name
Field 2 = Address
Field 3 = Phone number
Field 4 = Salesperson number
```

Figure 12-3.
A sample personnel file.

```
          Field 1    Field 2    Field 3     Field 4
Record 1      32     $10000     $5000        50%
Record 2      56     $14000     $9000        64%
Record 3      23     $12000     $16000       133%

Field 1 = Salesperson number
Field 2 = Quota
Field 3 = Sales performance to date
Field 4 = Percent of quota attained
```

Figure 12-4.
A sample sales file.

To do this, it will be necessary to retrieve data from both of the files. You need to combine the name field from the personnel file with the fields containing sales information in the sales file. A database-management program will take care of this for you.

How does the program know what name should go with each sales record? Here is where the key field comes in. The two files have one field in common—the salesperson number (field 4 in the personnel file and field 1 in the sales file). The program uses this field to link the records in the personnel file to their counterparts in the sales file. Any field used to relate records in different files is known as a key field. The ability to link files easily is one of the features that make database programs so powerful.

It is not difficult to use a database. However, databases must be updated continually to maintain the accuracy of the system's data. Database reports reflect the information that you put into your files. Remember, garbage in, garbage out.

Relational Database Programs

Many database suppliers claim that their products are ''relational'' databases. Fully relational databases allow every field to be related to every other field in the database. This is an elegant structure, but in reality a tremendous amount of computer overhead is needed to provide this capability. In other words, the computer system must be incredibly fast to be able to use this type of database architecture. The databases currently available for microcomputers are not fully relational, but they attempt to approach this level of functionality.

My advice is not to be concerned with the design of the database product but simply to make sure that whatever database you are considering has the features and ease of use that you require to automate your tasks.

dBASE III Plus, R:BASE System V, and Paradox

dBASE, a microcomputer-based database program from Ashton–Tate Corporation, has the largest installed base of trained users and programmers. Over 1 million copies of the dBASE program have been sold.

dBASE III Plus is the most recent version of dBASE. It has a built-in application-development language to help you build your database applications, and a menu-driven interface that makes it easy to store and retrieve your data. Another important feature of dBASE III Plus is a screen-design utility that saves a great deal of time when you are developing a new screen format for inputting or displaying data.

R:BASE from Microrim Corporation has been dBASE's major competitor. R:BASE System V works with another program from Microrim called Clout, which incorporates a sophisticated natural query language. You can program Clout to allow the database to respond to commands with sentences that are quite close to plain English. For example, you could ask for a report that lists sales by region for the last six months, and the system would create a database query and generate a report for you.

Paradox from Ansa Software has a user interface similar to a Lotus 1-2-3 spreadsheet. Because more than 2 million people are using Lotus 1-2-3, it made good sense to capitalize on the experience of Lotus's customers. The major advantage Paradox offers is that its program application language called PAL makes it extremely easy to program.

Entire accounting systems can be designed with general database programs. However, this requires extensive programming and is certainly not a project for a novice computer user. Several companies, including SBT Corporation, market accounting systems based on dBASE files; these programs are available with source code to allow the more advanced user to customize the accounting modules.

Multiuser and Networked Database Products

Paradox, R:BASE System V, and dBASE III Plus are available in special versions that run on networked microcomputers.

Revelation, a database system from Cosmos, is a powerful database system that runs on both microcomputer and minicomputer systems. If your organization requires a flexible package that can easily migrate to larger hardware configurations, you should evaluate the Revelation system. It is well supported, and its structure will be familiar to those users of larger systems who have worked with data dictionaries.

File Managers

On the lower end of the database market are products known as file managers. These programs are designed to make it easy to build data files and to access the information in them. They usually do not include powerful report-generation programs, application-development languages, screen-design utilities, or natural language capabilities. However, as file managers become more feature-oriented, they are beginning to be more like database programs.

PFS:File and PFS:Report, from Software Publishing Corporation, provide an easy-to-use, inexpensive file-management system that is excellent for managing files of information and generating simple reports. Over 650,000 copies of these programs have been sold. IBM resells the PFS series under the IBM label.

Ashton–Tate's Rapidfile is a combination file-management program and basic word processor. The program allows the user to select either Ashton–Tate's pull-down menu interface, or one similar to Lotus 1-2-3's horizontal menu interface. This flexible interface, combined with an on-disk tutorial, interactively teaches the program's basic operations. Rapidfile is currently the most sophisticated file-management program available.

Checklist of Database Software Features

Database-management software is the heart of most business data-processing systems. Be sure that the database program you select has the features that you require and is easy to use.

- Before you purchase a database program or start to build your files, be sure that the program will do *everything* you need it to.

- The power of a database program is its ability to make data storage and retrieval simple and fast. If these functions are awkward or if you cannot get the information formatted exactly the way you want, you are probably using the wrong product.

- Demonstrations are helpful, but if possible try building a simple database and generating a few reports yourself with the product that you are considering installing. You will find that some database products are much easier to use than others and that most database products have restrictions that will limit your ability to set up and manage your files exactly as you would like.

  Although this exercise will take you a few hours or even a day, the time will be well spent. You will learn about the capabilities of each system and will be better prepared to commit yourself to spending the week or more necessary to master a sophisticated database product.

■ Be sure that your database program provides enough characters per field, fields per record, and records per file for your needs. Few things are more aggravating than running out of space in a database. It is usually extremely inconvenient to break a database into two or more segments.

■ Many databases include a data-checking facility that helps prevent entry errors. Compare competitive products to determine which will be easiest for you or your data-entry operators to use.

■ Be sure that the database program you choose will allow you to do all of the calculations you will need in numerical fields. This is much more convenient than trying to export your database files to another program to do simple calculations for reports.

■ Determine whether there is adequate security for your database files. This is most important on multiuser and networked systems. Most multiuser database programs offer at least two levels of password security.

■ For some applications it is important to be able to keep a permanent audit trail of all changes to the database files. If this is necessary, be sure that the database program has this capability.

■ Some integrated database products have spreadsheet, graphics, and text-processing functions built in. If these are not available, be sure that you can easily export your files to other productivity software so that you can use your database files for reports, forecasting, and other tasks.

Electronic Spreadsheets

As I pointed out earlier, computers can do super-fast, accurate numerical computations. The electronic spreadsheet is a great format for entering numerical data and then building mathematical relationships between the different entries. One of the primary uses of electronic spreadsheets is for building forecasting models.

	1	2 January	3 February	4 March (proj.)
1				
2				
3	Total Sales	100.00	150.00	200.00
4	Cost of Goods Sold	50.00	75.00	?
5	Net Profit	50.00	75.00	?

Figure 12-5.
A sample spreadsheet.

The electronic spreadsheet is analogous to an accountant's worksheet. The spreadsheet allows data to be formatted logically, and new values to be plugged in and analyzed for comparisons and projections. The fields in a spreadsheet are called cells, and they can be filled with either numeric values or alphanumeric labels. Figure 12-5 shows an example of a spreadsheet.

Like an accountant's worksheet, an electronic spreadsheet is arranged in columns and rows. Mathematical formulas can be assigned to the cells in the spreadsheet to link them and to cause the values in them to be recalculated when a change is made in a related cell.

In Figure 12-5, two formulas are built into the worksheet to allow forecasting. First, columns 2 through 4 are set up so that Total Sales – Cost of Goods Sold = Net Profit. The formula might be entered into the program as (Row1 ColumnX) – (Row2 ColumnX) = (Row3 ColumnX), where "X" is any column from 2 through 4 in the spreadsheet.

The other formula tells the spreadsheet that Cost of Goods Sold = 50 percent of Total Sales, and instructs it to build that formula across columns 2 through 4. The important concept to understand about formulas in spreadsheets is that values in one cell can be based on the values in other cells.

With these relationships built into the spreadsheet, it will calculate Net Profit based on any value you select for Total Sales. For example, if you project that Total Sales in March will be $200, the profit will be calculated at $100. If you assign monthly sales the value of $300, the spreadsheet will calculate a value of $150 for Net Profit. This is, of course, a very simple example; real-world examples are much less obvious and much more useful.

Once you have done a forecast with a spreadsheet you will never willingly go back to using a calculator and pencil. Each time one number is changed in a forecast or other spreadsheet model, *all* of the values need to be recomputed. Once you have built the model, the electronic spreadsheet does this at an amazing speed. A change that would take you many hours to compute manually can be done in seconds. With the computer you can quickly and accurately analyze change after change in your spreadsheet model to do "what if?" planning.

VisiCalc, Multiplan, SuperCalc, and Microsoft Excel

VisiCalc, the first electronic spreadsheet, helped justify the cost of microcomputers for anyone involved with financial analysis. VisiCalc helped launch Apple Computer and the microcomputer revolution. Both SuperCalc and Multiplan improved on some of VisiCalc's features and rapidly gained market share.

Multiplan allows the user to link spreadsheets together using cells similar to key fields in a database. This is useful for building large financial models. SuperCalc allows data from the spreadsheet to be used to generate simple charts. Graphic displays of the data help to summarize and highlight important trends.

Both of these products have been through several revisions and are powerful and well-documented.

Microsoft Excel is the best-selling electronic spreadsheet in the Macintosh environment.

Lotus 1-2-3

Lotus 1-2-3 is a sophisticated electronic spreadsheet that allows you to create graphs from data in the spreadsheets and to build small data files. These powerful features, coupled with an excellent user interface and superb marketing, have made Lotus 1-2-3 the top-selling business application program on the market.

Because it has become the de facto standard for financial analysis software in corporate America, the Lotus 1-2-3 package has excellent third-party support. Many software companies have produced application packages and templates based on the Lotus 1-2-3 program. Several companies are marketing products that use Lotus 1-2-3 to analyze data files downloaded from mainframe computers to microcomputers.

Literally dozens of books about Lotus 1-2-3 have been published, although the documentation is so good that you are not likely to need any additional materials to master the program. Many night schools, computer stores, and business colleges offer classes on Lotus 1-2-3.

Checklist of Electronic Spreadsheet Features

While shopping for an electronic spreadsheet program, keep the following recommendations in mind:

- Look for a program that has a logical user interface and on-screen help facilities.

- Be sure the program allows easy, rapid movement of the cursor by means of command keys or a pointing device such as a mouse. The program should allow easy correction of typing errors and deletion or modification of any portion of the worksheet.

- The program should allow use of names instead of codes to refer to individual cells in the worksheet. Using logical cell names, such as ''gross sales'' or ''January forecast,'' makes understanding relationships within your worksheet easier.

- The program should be able to upload data from other programs and export data to other office-productivity programs such as databases and graphics packages.

- You'll likely need to link worksheets together. Linking allows changes in one worksheet to be reflected in another worksheet.

- Many spreadsheets offer macros, which let you store frequently used keystroke sequences in a cell of the worksheet. By using a macro instead of typing out an entire sequence of keystrokes, you can let the macro type the keystrokes for you.

- The program should recalculate worksheets as fast as possible. Adding additional RAM to your system will improve performance if you are working with very large worksheets; using a math coprocessor chip will speed up all calculations.

- Many spreadsheet programs have an audit feature that prints out a report on all references and formulas within a worksheet. These reports can help you debug large electronic worksheets.

- Some electronic worksheets allow you to open windows or to split screens to view, edit, or transfer data to multiple worksheets simultaneously.

- Most electronic worksheets back up your work when you are finished working with the program. It is also important to be able to save a worksheet without exiting the program.

- Some electronic worksheets can create charts from the numbers in a spreadsheet and can pass data to integrated file managers and word-processing programs.

Word Processing

Word-processing software can easily justify the cost of a microcomputer. If one or more of your employees spends much time revising or composing text or generating mailing lists, a word processor can be a fantastic office-productivity tool.

A number of excellent dedicated stand-alone word-processing systems are available, but for most applications, a microcomputer running a good word-processing software package is a more flexible alternative. Word-processing programs for microcomputers are differentiated by the features they offer and the ease with which you can enter and change your text files.

Many of the major companies producing word-processing software offer different levels of their software. They might offer an inexpensive system with limited capability for $100 to $150 and a full-featured system for $300 to $500. There are literally scores of word-processing programs available. Many of them are easy to use, are well supported, and offer powerful text-processing features.

A full-featured word-processing package will usually include a spelling checker, on-line thesaurus, outlining capability, math feature, automatic indexing, table of contents generation, and glossaries. A particularly helpful feature that some word-processing packages offer is mailmerge, which allows the information from a file containing address information to be merged into form letters.

High-End Word Processors

Microsoft Word is a good example of a sophisticated word processor. It is easy to learn, easy to use, and has excellent laser printer support. Word is a graphics-based program, meaning that it can offer a WYSIWYG, or "what you see is what you get," display. On a graphics monitor, special type fonts are displayed on the screen; no embedded command codes are visible. For example, italics and boldface print appear correctly on the computer's video display.

Word performs best with a mouse, which you use to move the cursor around on the screen. A mouse speeds up editing functions such as insertion and deletion of text. Editing is facilitated through the use of "windows" that can divide the screen into several work areas. Each window can contain portions of one or more different documents. Word includes an on-line dictionary, a thesaurus, and a sophisticated outlining program. This book was written using Microsoft Word. Word is available both for the Macintosh and for IBM and IBM-compatible computers.

WordStar is a good, tried-and-true product. More users have been trained on WordStar than on any other word processor. The program uses many command keys to execute different word-processing functions. This makes it a bit more complicated to learn than some of the other word processors.

WordPerfect is another excellent product. It is intuitive and has excellent documentation. It is one of the easier full-featured word processors to use. WordPerfect and Microsoft Word are currently the two best-selling word-processing packages on the market.

MultiMate makes a word processor that has a command set and a user interface very similar to those of the Wang word-processing system. MultiMate is one of the more popular word processors in corporate environments because it is easy for users who have been trained on Wang word-processing systems to learn.

IBM offers DisplayWrite 4, a modified version of the software that runs on the discontinued stand-alone word processor called the DisplayWriter. It is a good product and has been successful through IBM's powerful marketing efforts.

Word Processing for the Casual User

Many people who use a word processor simply want an electronic typewriter that makes it easy to correct mistakes and store documents. A number of word-processing packages are available for less than $100 that are completely adequate for this casual user.

MicroPro, MultiMate, WordPerfect, and others offer entry-level programs that are straightforward and easy to use. The features that you generally give up are things like automatic footnotes, different type fonts, style sheets, and glossaries. In addition, the low-end word processors usually do not have built-in spelling checkers.

If your spelling skills are like mine, an on-line dictionary can really help you catch both misspellings and those insidious text bugs known as "typos." Some of the new spelling checkers are memory resident and will highlight (in inverse video) suspected typos as you type your document. If you are in doubt, you can ask to see alternate spellings, and if you are still not satisfied, you can call up an on-line thesaurus to suggest synonyms.

Multiuser Word Processors

Some of the major microcomputer software suppliers offer special licensing arrangements that allow users to run their software on networked and multiuser computer systems.

Many of the manufacturers of minicomputer and mainframe computer systems offer integrated office-automation solutions that incorporate proprietary word-processing software packages. Digital Equipment Corporation (DEC), Altos, Hewlett–Packard, IBM, and other companies offer packages targeted toward legal firms and other organizations with heavy word-processing requirements.

Checklist of Word-Processing Features

In deciding on word-processing software, consider the following features:

- Be sure the program you choose allows easy, rapid movement of the cursor by means of command keys or a pointing device such as a mouse.

- Block text manipulation requires an easy, intuitive method of selecting text. Be sure your program can easily delete and move words, sentences, and paragraphs using a minimum number of keystrokes. An undo command, which countermands your latest editing action, is extrememly helpful and can save you from redoing accidentally erased work.

■ The ability to select and change fonts, or type styles, and pitch allows you to create better-looking documents. Your word-processing requirements may include other options, such as the ability to produce boldface, underlined, double-underlined, italic, superscript, and subscript characters; double-spaced, triple-spaced, centered, justified, numbered, and automatically hyphenated lines; and numbered pages.

■ Automatic paragraph indention, automatic page reformatting, decimal tabs, multiple margin settings, justified text, micro justification, right-aligned text with a ragged left margin, user-specified page breaks, tabs and margins, multicolumn formatting, newspaper-style columns, and variable-width columns can help your documents appear more professional.

■ The ability to search for a particular sequence, or string, of characters and globally replace the string with another character, word, or phrase can save a great deal of time when a change must be made throughout a document.

■ Many manuscripts require headers (text that appears at the top of each page) or footers (text at the bottom). It is also useful to have automatic or user-specified page numbering within a header or footer.

■ Footnotes are often used in academic and technical papers. In-text footnotes, automatic numbering and endnotes are helpful features.

■ Spelling checkers can correct spelling errors and incorrect capitalizations. They can also display misspelled words in context and suggest correct spellings. Some spelling checkers include, or are bundled with, a thesaurus.

A spelling checker must have a large vocabulary, or dictionary, to be useful; several are available with over 100,000 listings. Specialized dictionaries are available for the legal and medical professions.

- Mailmerge allows you to generate personalized form letters. The mailmerge programs merge a list of names, addresses, or other data into a boilerplate letter or document.

- Many word processors, database programs and file managers can output a standard ASCII (American Standard Code for Information Interchange) file that can be merged into your documents. ASCII files have no special formatting commands; they are composed of characters and numbers.

- Moving a word-processing document from one type of system to another is not always easy. This is because different word processors use different file formats. IBM uses a format called DCA (Document Content Architecture), Wang uses WANG WPS, WordStar uses the WordStar format, Ashton–Tate uses .dbf files and several other programs use DIF (Data Interchange Format). Fortunately, many programs allow you to import and export ASCII files. Be sure that you can transfer your files into whatever formats you require.

- Be sure that your word processor supports your printer's features. For example, some word processors support proportional spacing and others provide a typewriter mode that prints like a typewriter as you enter data. If your word-processing program tells your printer to perform one of these functions and your printer can't do it, the printer will either ignore the request or simply stop printing and send you an error message.

- Some word processors allow you to print documents in background mode. Programs with this useful feature queue documents to print one after another while you work on other tasks.

- Some word processors allow you to open windows or to split screens to make it easy to view, edit, and copy between two or more documents simultaneously.

- Most word processors back up documents when you stop working on them. It is also important to be able to save a document without exiting the program.

- Some word processors allow addition and subtraction of numbers in horizontal and vertical columns, provide password protection, do simple line and box drawings, and provide a word count for your document file. The word-count feature is particularly helpful for professional writers in determining the length of a document.

■ Some word processors let you embed invisible print-format commands in your documents, while others display each print-format command. Invisible print-format commands make it easier to work with your files.

Desktop Publishing

Desktop-publishing software lets you create laser-printed documents that look as if they were laid out in a print shop. It is one of the fastest-growing computer applications. More than half a million laser printers have been sold; most of these are used by small businesses or work groups for desktop publishing.

Some word-processing programs integrate some of the features of desktop publishing and word processing. For example, Microsoft Word supports the Hewlett–Packard LaserJet fonts. But specialized desktop-publishing software allows a great deal more flexibility in how documents are laid out. For example, Aldus Pagemaker allows you to electronically paste together in the same document both text generated by a word processor and optically scanned graphics images.

Desktop-publishing programs use a page-description language (PDL) to describe the shape and position of the text and graphics sent to the laser printer. The three leading PDLs are: Postscript from Adobe Systems, which is used in Pagemaker; Interpress from Xerox, used in the Ventura Publisher product; and Document Description Language (DDL) from Imagen, which is licensed by Hewlett–Packard. Both IBM and Apple have announced products that work with Postscript.

The printer that you select for your desktop-publishing system must be designed to work with the PDL of the software that you will be using. You cannot print documents created with Postscript on a printer that supports only Interpress.

Fortunately, most desktop-publishing software supports multiple PDLs. For example, Xerox's Ventura Publisher supports both Interpress and Postscript. To further remedy the situation, some of the printer companies are adding multiple PDL support to their printers.

Many businesses can justify the cost of a desktop-publishing system by the cost savings and the improved turn-around time of creating sales materials, manuals, and newsletters internally.

Computer Graphics

Microcomputer graphics have three main applications: *decision-support graphics, presentation graphics,* and *computer-aided design.*

Decision-support graphics are used to display in graphic form information from database, financial modeling, and other office-productivity applications. Such graphics can improve the quality of internal and external communications. A chart or graph can often highlight or summarize the important facts in a sea of data. Decision-support graphics can help you spot important trends, problem areas, and potential opportunities in your management reports. Electronic spreadsheet packages, such as Lotus 1-2-3 and Ashton–Tate's Framework II, provide limited business graphics and charting capabilities.

Computer graphics are also used to generate presentation graphics, in which high-quality hard-copy output is produced for marketing and other types of presentations. The graphics images can be output to high-resolution printers, laser printers, or plotters.

Software packages for presentation graphics, such as Micrographix Windows Draw and Microsoft Chart, have facilities for importing data from other office-productivity applications, such as Lotus 1-2-3 and dBASE III. Paint and draw programs also allow you to input graphics data by using a mouse, digitizing tablet, light pen, or scanning device. These programs make it easy to create presentations that combine text and pictures. For example, you might create slides for a presentation that combine text from a management report, charts from your office-productivity applications, and pictures input from an optical scanning device.

Many low-cost computer-aided design, or CAD, application packages now run on microcomputers. These allow architects, engineers, and civil planners to do complex design and drafting tasks. CAD systems are expensive but may be justified in businesses that do labor-intensive design and drafting work.

CAD systems usually require specialized graphics-input hardware and high-resolution video displays. They also require specialized software that allows graphics designs to be modified and created from libraries of symbols and patterns already entered into the CAD system. Specialized CAD programs can easily perform powerful mathematical and graphic manipulations of graphics images that would be almost impossibly time-consuming to generate manually.

If you need a CAD system, it is well worth the time to learn how to use several different software packages to compare their strengths and weaknesses. A business graphics or CAD system that provides 95 percent of the functionality that you need may be almost worthless.

Project Management

If your business requires the scheduling of materials, shipments, personnel, or projects, project-management software can be quite helpful. This type of software helps you schedule and plan events and estimate job costs for projects and programs that must be completed over a certain time frame. Most of these programs use what is called the critical-path method to help you track your project's status and will indicate when additional resources need to be focused in a particular area to avoid project delays.

Some project-management software allows you to schedule multiple projects by small increments of time and to track personnel costs. Be sure that the program you select allows you to track all of the variables that your business requires. It is often impossible to work around the limitations of a scheduling program. For example, if you need to schedule your workers on a food-production line according to the number of seconds each task takes, a program that allows you to schedule personnel in hourly increments will not do you any good at all.

Project management packages offer:

- Critical-path scheduling.

- The ability to track interrelated tasks.

- Automatic recalculation of costs and times when changes are made to the schedule.

- Generation of status reports and charts.

■ Generation of Gantt charts. (A Gantt chart is a time line that shows how different tasks in a project interrelate. See Figure 12-6.)

■ Generation of PERT charts. (This is another scheduling model. See Figure 12-6.)

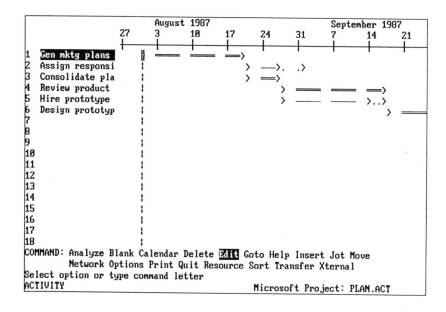

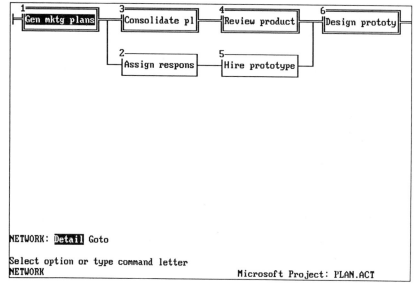

Figure 12-6.
A sample screen from a project-management program.

■ Generation of cost-estimation reports.

■ Generation of personnel-requirement reports.

Memory-Resident Utility Programs

There are many memory-resident utility programs on the market. These programs allow you to suspend a currently running application and use a convenient utility, such as a telephone dialer, calendar, or outline processor, at the press of a key. When you are finished with your "pop-up" program, you can press another key to return to the program with which you were working. Figure 12-7 shows a screen from a pop-up utility.

You should allow only programs that you use regularly to reside in your computer's main memory. Memory-resident utilities tie up portions of main memory and can slow down the execution of some of your other programs. You can always use the computer's operating system to bring up different applications as they are needed.

SideKick from Borland International is a good example of a memory-resident utility. SideKick is currently the most popular desktop organizer

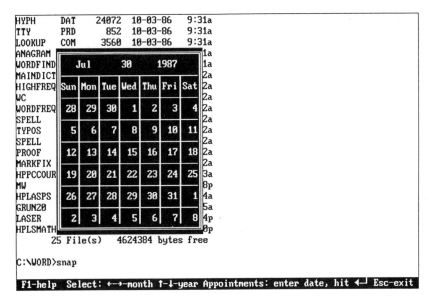

Figure 12-7.
A sample screen from a memory-resident utility.

program; it has an electronic calendar, a standard calculator, a phone dialer, and a notepad built in. These programs pop up when you press a command key. SideKick can help you organize your "electronic" desktop. Over 500,000 people are using SideKick.

Most memory-resident utilities sell for less than $100. If you dedicate your system to running only one or two programs or are using your system strictly for accounting applications, it is unlikely that you will benefit from memory-resident applications.

Integrated Software

Office-automation packages fall into two broad categories: stand-alone applications, which automate one task, and integrated applications, in which a variety of compatible modules perform multiple tasks. This section discusses the advantages and disadvantages of integrated applications software.

An integrated program is one consisting of several different applications that work with one another. Program integration is desirable for several reasons:

- It can provide program data compatibility—the ability to move data from one application module or program to another and use it without having to reenter data.

- It can provide user interface compatibility. If programs use the same commands and the same type of graphics interface, it is easier for the user to learn and use different applications.

- It can improve the programs' performance. Users are concerned with both the power of the individual programs in an integrated package and with the extent of the interaction between them. Different programs allow varying degrees of interconnection among different tasks.

There are two approaches to the integration of software applications. One is to design one large *application program* that has integrated modules, each of which performs a general task and can share its information with the other modules within the program. The other approach is to design an *application environment* that can be shared by different programs. The application environment allows different programs to have a

common user interface and allows data to be moved easily between them.
Figure 12-8 illustrates the difference between application programs and

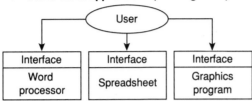

Stand-alone applications (no integration)

- User must learn each program's user interface and command set.
- Programs have different data structures, making it difficult to share data.

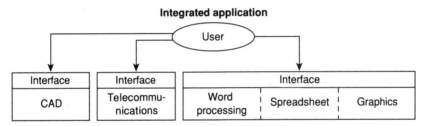

Integrated application

- User has to learn only one user interface.
- Program modules can easily share data.
- Limited to modules within the application.

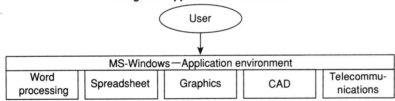

Integrated application environment

- User has to learn only one user interface.
- All programs written to run in the environment can share data.
- Programmers can use the application environment to help them write graphics-based applications. Much of the code for the user interface and for handling data structures is built into the application environment.

Figure 12-8.
A nonintegrated system and the two approaches to integration.

application environments. The integrated application program will be discussed first.

Is Integrated Software for You?

Back in 1984, when Lotus Corporation's Symphony and Ashton–Tate Corporation's Framework products were announced, it looked as though integrated applications would take over a large share of the productivity software market. Both of these products offered word processing, graphics, electronic spreadsheets, and data communications. Even though these programs were powerful and well designed, the needs of the market have become differentiated to the point that integrated packages are not the best solution for many users.

Although these packages are usually suited for typical business managers, they may not have the depth required by so-called power users. For example, financial analysts may require as much flexibility as possible in a business graphics program. Individual graphics programs currently offer more power than any of the major integrated products on the market. Similarly, professional writers may require the flexibility and features of a stand-alone word-processing software package.

Advantages of Integrated Software

- Integrated applications allow better integration of the different application modules. This means that the programs can share information that is set up in a common format.

- Integrated applications are easier to learn because they have a similar command structure and a common user interface.

- Some integrated software programs are very powerful. Integrated packages can move information from one task to another very rapidly. For example, data in a spreadsheet can be used to generate a chart or graph of the data automatically; the data from the electronic spreadsheet does not need to be reentered or loaded into the graphics program. Further, when new values are entered into the spreadsheet, the program can update the charts or graphs based on that data.

- Integrated packages are generally less expensive than the sum of their stand-alone versions.

Disadvantages of Integrated Software

- The modules you need may not be available in an integrated package. For example, you may need a terminal emulation program or a graphics package that can do computer-aided design. These may not be available in an integrated package that supports your other requirements.

- Integrated packages are usually less powerful than the best stand-alone applications. Most integrated applications do not offer the depth in terms of features and options that different stand-alone applications do.

- Integrated packages may have modules that you do not need or that duplicate other software that you are already using and are satisfied with.

Integrated Application Environments

Integrated application environments offer the advantages of both integrated and stand-alone applications; that is, they allow powerful individual applications to work together. However, in order for an application program to work in an integrated application environment, the program must be written to use a standard graphics interface. Not just any program can run in this type of environment.

Both Microsoft Windows and the Macintosh provide an integrated application environment that allows a common graphics-based user interface under which programs from different manufacturers can share information. The Macintosh and Windows in the MS-DOS environment have been supported by most of the major software developers. This standardization should make it easier for new companies with good ideas to bring powerful, industry-compatible products to the market.

13

More About Accounting Software

Automated accounting systems parallel the accounting procedures that you are currently performing manually. This makes using well-designed accounting software very intuitive and straightforward. You should be able to install and implement most well-designed accounting applications fairly easily *if* they are designed to handle your specific requirements.

A number of the accounting packages on the market assume only a basic knowledge of accounting and computer principles. Some of these packages include tutorials on basic bookkeeping skills as well as ones on the products themselves. I strongly recommend that you master basic bookkeeping before attempting to install an automated accounting system. The better organized your books are, the easier and less risky it will be for you to automate.

The example in this section focuses on a typical distribution business. However, with minor modifications, you can use the sample feature lists and flowcharts to create your own feature lists, payback-analysis reports, and requests for proposals for your own accounting applications.

In the example system, updates are made to all related files as soon as data is entered into the system. This is called *real-time* processing. Older *batch-processing* systems required batches of input documents to be entered together as a file called a batch file. The batch file was then processed by various programs that updated each related file.

Order Entry and Billing

The flowchart in Figure 13-1 shows a four-part customer order form moving through a typical distribution company. The customer's credit can be checked when the order is entered into the system. Picking, packing, and shipping forms are generated by the system and are sent over to the warehouse.

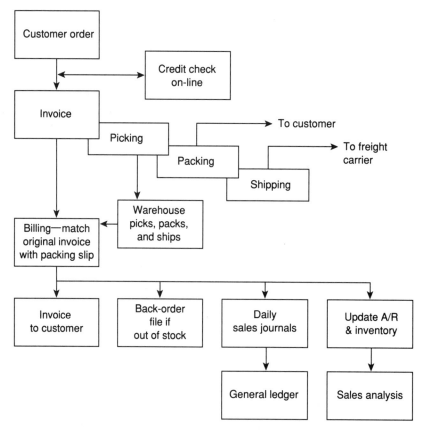

Figure 13-1.
An order-entry and billing flowchart.

In the billing department, the original order is matched with the picking slip from the warehouse, and an invoice is generated for the customer or a back order is reported. The software can update the sales journal, accounts-receivable files, and inventory files. The general ledger is updated each month, and sales-analysis reports can be run at any time.

The sales-cycle flowchart in Figure 13-2 gives an overview of how order entry and billing interfaces with the accounts-receivable, inventory-control, and sales-analysis modules.

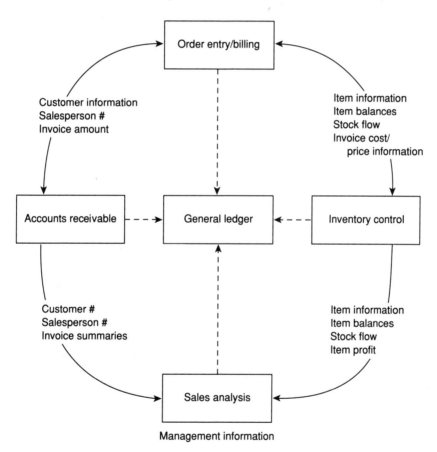

Figure 13-2.
A sales-cycle flowchart.

Advantages of Automated Order Entry and Invoicing

- Remote printers can print out orders in picking sequence.
- Picking accuracy and efficiency is increased because of legible picking lists.
- Warehouse personnel can usually be reduced.
- Invoices are produced almost instantaneously.
- Invoices go with the shipment.
- The system posts orders to accounts receivable.
- Credit can be checked at order entry.
- Order takers are more productive, and customer service is improved.
- Operators can be faster and provide more accurate information because there is less redundant data entry.
- Inventory is updated after each transaction.
- Back orders are posted immediately.

Feature List for an Order-Entry and Billing Module

When shopping for an order-entry and billing package, look for one that will:

- Allow order entry and editing with the order-entry list.
- Print invoices and picking, shipping, and packing slips.
- Allow orders to be invoiced when they are entered, or allow them to be held as open orders for later billing.
- Interface with an inventory module to update inventory records.
- Interface with an accounts-receivable module to update customer accounts.
- Handle credit memos.
- Handle a back-order file, and print back-order reports.
- Interface to general ledger and sales analysis via accounts-receivable and inventory modules.

Order-Entry and Invoicing Questionnaire

The following questions will help you and your system supplier determine whether an automated system will meet your needs.

- How many orders are taken per day?
- What is the average number of items or lines per order?
- Are orders placed, picked, and then shipped?
- Are orders placed and then reserved?
- Are orders put up for call?
- Are orders set up for route delivery?
- Do you invoice and extend orders when they are received?
- How long does it take to invoice an order after it is placed?
- Do you keep an invoice register?
- Do you allow charge as well as cash orders to be placed?
- Do you calculate discounts from invoices?
- Do you need to send out picking tickets?
- How are you advised when customer shipments are made?
- Do you invoice multiple shipments on the same order?
- How do you handle short shipments or temporarily out-of-stock situations?
- Do you keep an up-to-date order-status report?
- How do you do an order inquiry?
- Do you sell by different units of measure than you stock?
- Do you include shipping weights on your invoices?
- Do you issue credit memos with returns to inventory?
- Do you issue credit memos without returns to inventory?
- Do you require space on invoices for explanations or notices?
- Do you send out marketing materials with your invoices?
- Do you require multiple tax codes on your invoices?

- Do you offer discounts or terms on your invoices?

- Do you put any noninventory items on invoices?

- Do any other requirements need to be taken into account to handle your specific order-entry and invoicing requirements?

Inventory Control

Figure 13-3 shows an inventory-control flowchart. The receiving report is used to update the inventory-control files when merchandise is received. All invoices, adjustments, and purchase orders are entered into the system and update the inventory files. A stock-status report can be run on demand, and the inventory's status is posted to the general ledger at the end of the month.

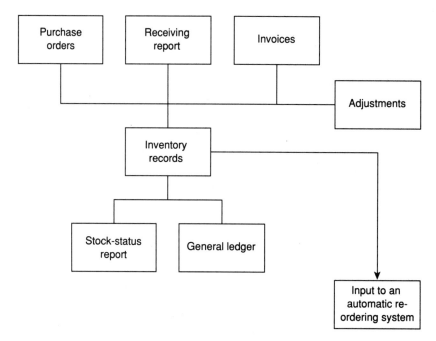

Figure 13-3.
An inventory-control flowchart.

Advantages of Automated Inventory Control

■ Management reports help reduce inventory.

■ Customer service is improved.

■ Fewer stock-outs occur.

■ Current inventory reports are available on demand.

■ Improved and speedier reordering is possible.

■ Inventory lists make physical inventories more efficient.

■ Pricing and availability information is always current.

■ Inventory can be allocated from the order-entry module.

■ The program can search for specific inventory items.

■ Receipts are posted to stock immediately.

Feature List for an Inventory-Control Module

In deciding on an inventory-control module, try to find one that will:

■ Provide for the maintenance and listing of all inventory items in the master inventory file.

■ Allow inventory costing by the standard cost, average cost, FIFO, or LIFO methods.

■ Provide multiwarehouse capability.

■ Provide flexible pricing methods, and allow for price changes.

■ Allow for the entry, editing, and posting of inventory transactions.

■ Print price lists, stock status reports, inventory value reports, usage reports, and physical count worksheets for periodic inventories.

■ Print reorder reports.

■ Print ABC analysis reports that list all ''A'' items, ''B'' items, and ''C'' items to help evaluate product mix. (''A'' items are those most frequently sold, and ''C'' items sell the least.)

Inventory-Control Questionnaire

The following questions will help you and your supplier decide whether a system is adequate for you.

- How many different items do you have in your inventory?

- How many different items do you think you will have in your inventory in two to three years?

- How many characters (spaces) do you have in your product codes?

- What kind of structure do you use for pricing?

- Do you use a printed price list?

- Do you resell nonstocked items?

- Do you have vendors ship directly to your customers?

- Do you group your inventory by category?

- Do you group your inventory by supplier?

- Do you require inventory, sales, and profitability reports?

- Do you require a stock-status report?

- How often do you take physical inventories?

- Do you create physical-count worksheets?

- Do you create a count and variance report?

- Do you make adjustments to your inventory reports and your sales journals?

- Do you require the ability to make inquiries as to whether items are in stock?

- Do you look up items with an alphabetic key?

- Do you have more than one warehouse?

- Do you use the serial identification numbers of some or all of your inventory items?

- Do you have a bill-of-materials requirement?

- Do any other requirements need to be taken into account to handle your specific inventory-control requirements?

Automated Purchasing Questionnaire

A purchasing module may be included or be available separately with some inventory-accounting packages. In selecting one, ask yourself the following questions:

- How many purchase orders do you write per month?
- How many lines does your average purchase order require?
- How many vendors do you order from?
- Do you require your system to print out your purchase orders?
- Do you create a receiving report? If not, how do you track received orders?
- Do you use cost-change reports?
- Do you create a suggested purchase report?
- Who originates purchase-order requests?
- Do you use multiple vendors for the same item?
- Do you create an open purchase-order report?
- Do you have a list of names and addresses of current vendors?
- Is a broker listing required on your purchase orders?
- Do you have a way of tracking and inquiring about open purchases by item?
- Do you require detailed purchase-order reports on demand?
- Do you require an automatic item-reorder feature?
- Do any other requirements need to be taken into account to handle your specific purchase requirements?

Accounts Receivable

Figure 13-4 on the next page shows an accounts-receivable flowchart. The accounts-receivable program updates the customer file and generates the cash-receipts journal, the A/R journal, and the daily A/R control sheet. The daily A/R control sheet is posted to the general ledger and supports the generation of customer statements.

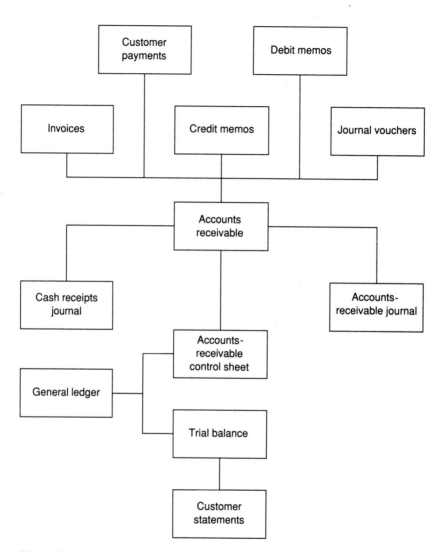

Figure 13-4.
An accounts-receivable flowchart.

The information in the accounts-receivable files can also generate aged accounts-receivable reports and the sales journal. The accounts-receivable files can also be used to report sales commissions on paid accounts if your business requires this.

Advantages of Automated Accounts Receivable

- Outstanding accounts receivable can be reduced.

- Late charges can easily be added to overdue invoices.

- Credit is easier to manage because current outstanding customer balances are always available for review.

- Collections are easier to manage.

- Statements can go out faster.

- Many systems will handle both open-item and balance-forward accounts within the same package.

- Posting errors can be reduced.

- Accounts receivable can be posted to the general ledger.

Feature List for an Accounts-Receivable Module

In selecting an accounts-receivable package, try to find one that will:

- Handle both open-item and balance-forward customers if necessary.

- Provide lists from the customer file and the salesperson file.

- Allow editing and posting of sales transactions to the sales journal.

- Print aged accounts-receivable statements and reports.

- Allow on-line customer account inquiries for editing or credit checking.

- Calculate and post finance charges.

- Generate sales-commission reports.

- Provide a report showing accounts-receivable distributions to the general ledger.

- Interface with order entry and billing, general ledger, and sales analysis.

Accounts-Receivable Questionnaire

Use the following questions to help you and your supplier find a system that meets your needs.

- How many active customers do you have?

- If you are in a retail business, do you track who your customers are?

- How many outstanding invoices do you have?
- Do you offer different terms to different classes of customers?
- Do you require different "bill to" and "ship to" addresses?
- Do you have retail sales?
- Do you have wholesale sales?
- Do you create aged accounts-receivable reports?
- Do you require variable aging periods?
- Do you create a past due report by invoice number?
- Do you create a past due report by account?
- Do you keep a cash-receipts journal?
- Do you keep a miscellaneous transactions journal?
- Do you do statement pricing?
- Do you invoice selected accounts only?
- Do you require a customer name and address list?
- Do you need to know current customer account status on demand?
- Do you check your customers' credit histories?
- Do any other requirements need to be taken into account to handle your specific accounts-receivable requirements?

Accounts Payable

The accounts-payable department interfaces with the company's vendors and handles all purchase requests from within the organization. Figure 13-5 shows an accounts-payable flowchart. All purchase requests from the company result in the generation of purchase orders. These must eventually be validated against the goods that the company has received.

The purchase order is compared with the invoice and the receiving report, generating a cash-requirements report. This, in turn, is used to create a check for the vendor and is posted to a disbursements journal. The disbursements journal is used to update the general ledger.

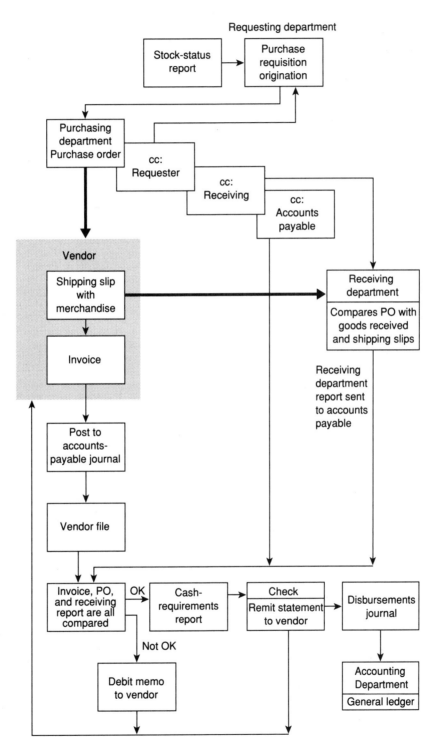

Figure 13-5.
An accounts-payable flowchart.

Advantages of Automated Accounts Payable

- Cash-flow reports provide an overview of future cash requirements.

- Aged payables can be used to take advantage of discounts from vendors who bill with terms.

- Checks, stubs, envelopes, and form letters can be generated on demand.

- The company's buying history from different vendors can be stored in the vendor file.

Feature List for an Accounts-Payable Module

In shopping for an accounts-payable package, try to find one that will:

- Use the accrual accounting method.

- Provide maintenance and editing of master customer file.

- Allow entry and posting of payables, adjustments, cancellations, prepaid orders, and all other transactions.

- Print accounts-payable checks and check register.

- Generate an open-item report.

- Allow on-line vendor account inquiries.

- Generate a cash-requirements report.

- Permit and account for all partial payments.

- Generate a vendor-analysis report.

- Interface with the general ledger.

- Generate a report showing accounts-payable distributions to the general ledger.

Accounts-Payable Questionnaire

The following questions will help you clarify your accounts-payable needs.

- How many accounts-payable control accounts do you have in your general ledger?

- How many alphanumeric characters (spaces) do you assign in your vendor numbers?

- How many general ledger control accounts are referenced by the accounts-payable module?
- How many one-time entries do you have per accounting period?
- How many recurring entries do you have per accounting period?
- How many invoices do you process per batch and per period?
- How many checks do you process per batch and per period?
- How many checking accounts do you have?
- What is the maximum dollar amount of an invoice?
- What is the total dollar amount that is handled each period?
- How many lines are required for voucher descriptions?
- Do you require on-screen, summary, or detailed aged reports by
  - All vendors?
  - Selected vendors?
  - Due date?
  - Amount owed?
  - Future amounts due?
  - Any other format?
- Do you use an alphabetic or numeric vendor roster?
- Do you use your vendor roster to generate mailing labels?
- Do you require automatic check printing?
- Does your check register flag breaks in number sequence?
- Does your check register flag voided checks?
- Does your check register list manually prepared checks?
- Do you require reports for
  - Outstanding-check listings?
  - Vendor analysis?
  - Discounts lost?
  - Detailed journal entries?
  - Summary journal entries?
  - Vendor ledger?

■ Do you make payments by

- Vendor name?

- Aging?

- Vendor number?

- Invoice number?

- Due date?

- Exception?

■ Do any other requirements need to be taken into account to handle your specific accounts-payable requirements?

Payroll

Figure 13-6 shows a flowchart for a payroll system. You will have to update your payroll program each year to reflect changes in the tax laws. The information in these tax files is combined with data from each employee's weekly or biweekly time card and his or her employee payroll file. The

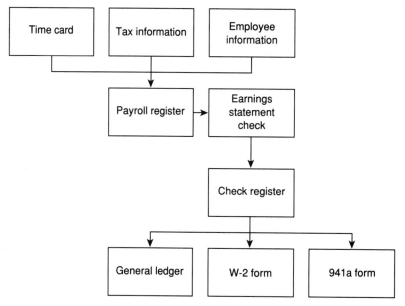

Figure 13-6.
A payroll flowchart.

payroll program then generates an earnings statement (the check stub) and payroll check and updates the employee's payroll file to reflect the year-to-date fields.

The employee payroll files are used to update the check register and the general ledger and to generate W-2 forms (employee earnings statements) and 941a (quarterly business tax) forms.

To keep from reentering data, make sure that your payroll software interfaces with your general ledger and accounts-payable applications. I recommend implementing an automated payroll after the general-ledger and accounts-payable packages are fully functional.

Advantages of Automated Payroll

- Computes taxes and deductions automatically.

- Reduces data-entry and bookkeeping time.

- Improves accuracy of payroll.

- Prints payroll checks, earnings statements, and payroll history.

Feature List for a Payroll Module

In selecting a payroll package, try to find one that will:

- Provide lists from the employee file.

- Handle hourly and salaried employees on daily, biweekly, monthly, and bimonthly pay periods.

- Handle multistate payrolls.

- Generate a payroll worksheet to help confirm all wages.

- Allow interactive editing of attendance records, and generate an edit list.

- Handle all special deductions.

- Calculate the payroll for each pay period.

- Allow easy update of the tax tables when tax regulations change.

- Print a payroll register and a deductions register.

- Print the paychecks and check register.

- Allow manual posting of adjustments.

- Print a history report showing union, insurance, and other deductions.

- Print quarterly 941a reports and year-end 1099 (nonemployee compensation) and W-2 forms.

- Interface to the general-ledger module.

Payroll Questionnaire

Use the following questions to help you select a payroll package that meets your needs.

- Do you use weekly, biweekly, monthly, or other pay periods?

- What is the maximum number of employees to be paid?

- What is the maximum paycheck amount?

- How many optional deductions are required?

- What is your total payroll each period?

- Which of the following reports and forms do you require?
  - Checks with fixed format
  - Checks with variable format
  - Check register
  - Payroll summary
  - Pre-check-printing report
  - 1099 forms
  - 941a forms
  - W-2 forms
  - Outstanding check listing
  - Employee register
  - Employee inquiry with all details
  - Wage reports
  - Detail journal entries

- Do you have hourly employees?

- Do you have salaried employees?

- Do you have commissioned employees?

- Do you have employees on other pay plans?
- Do you pay holiday, vacation, sick leave, or other types of compensation?
- Do you prepare payroll checks manually?
- Do you make automatic payroll deductions for union dues, loans, garnishments, health insurance, or other miscellaneous items?
- Do terminated employees receive W-2s immediately?
- Do you give out pay advances?
- Do you pay employees from other states?
- Do any other requirements need to be taken into account to handle your specific payroll requirements?

General Ledger

Figure 13-7 shows a general-ledger flowchart. Business transactions are entered daily into the general ledger from accounts payable, accounts receivable, payroll, and inventory. These are posted to the daily journal. A trial balance is generated each month from the journal and the amounts are then posted to the general ledger.

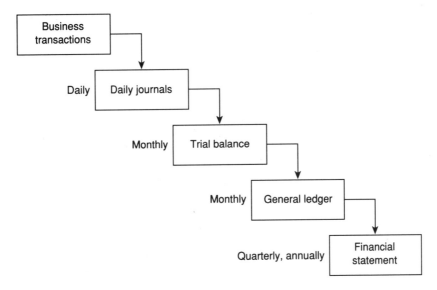

Figure 13-7.
A general-ledger flowchart.

The general-journal transaction register is posted to the general-ledger worksheet. The monthly trial balance serves as an audit trail for all posted transactions. The general-ledger worksheet is used to generate the company's financial statements, including the profit and loss statement and balance sheet.

Many automated general-ledger packages produce financial statements on demand. Some, however, will only print out financial reports when they close out an accounting period.

Feature List for a General-Ledger Module

In selecting a general-ledger package, look for one that will:

- Cover 13 rather than 12 accounting periods.

- Support multiple companies, and multiple profit centers within an organization.

- Provide an easy way to edit the chart of accounts.

- Allow manual entry of general journal transactions and manual posting.

- Generate the general-ledger worksheet and trial-balance reports.

- Allow on-line inquiries.

- Print financial reports in user-defined formats.

- Allow the transaction-detail history file to be kept on-line if disk space is available.

- Interface with accounts receivable, accounts payable, payroll, and inventory control.

General-Ledger Questionnaire

The following questions will help you in selecting a general-ledger package that meets your needs.

- Is your account number structure alphanumeric?

- How many digits are there in the main account numbers?

- How many subaccounts or department digits do you use?

- How many characters are there in your description fields?

- How many accounts are there in your chart of accounts?

- How many journal entries do you process per batch?

- How many journal entries do you process per period?
- How many companies do you handle?
- How many departments do you handle?
- How many journals do you handle?
- Which of the following statements and reports do you require?
  - Balance sheet
  - Balance sheet with prior year comparisons
  - Income statement
  - Income statement with departments included
  - Income statement with monthly budget comparisons
  - Income statement with prior year comparisons
  - Statement of changes in financial position
  - Subsidiary schedules to financial statements
- Do you require any other financial reports?
- Do you require a special format for your financial statements?
- Do you use a cash or accrual method of accounting?
- Do you require automatic posting of recurring entries?
- Do you require automatic allocation of expenses?
- Do you require automatic refreshing of journal entries?
- Do you need to be able to correct entries already posted to prior periods or prior years?
- Which of the following accounting modules do you plan on installing now and in the future?
  - General-ledger
  - Accounts-receivable
  - Accounts-payable with check writing
  - Payroll with check writing
  - Purchase-order
  - Order-entry and billing

- Inventory-control
- Bill-of-materials inventory
- Sales-analysis
- Income-tax and client-writeup (for CPAs)
- Fixed-asset with depreciation
- Job-costing
- Professional-time and billing
- Project-management
- Others

■ Do any other requirements need to be taken into account to handle your specific general-ledger requirements?

Sales Analysis

Once information has been entered into an automated accounting system, it is fairly easy to generate customized reports that specifically address your management needs. This is particularly helpful when individuals in different departments need to access information in different formats for different tasks.

Sales-analysis packages provide sales reports by customer, supplier, item, item category, dollar value, sales representative, and virtually any other logical format.

Advantages of Automating Sales Analysis

■ Sales reports can be generated automatically in virtually any logical format.

■ Trends can be spotted by customer, territory, or item.

■ Programs can analyze profits as well as sales trends over a yearly accounting period.

■ Historical data can remain on file to aid forecasting.

Sales-Analysis Questionnaire

The following questions, which also serve as a feature list, will help you clarify your sales-analysis needs.

- Do you require customer analysis by
    - Gross sales?
    - Inventory item sales?
    - Comparative sales?
    - Product category?
    - Profitability?

- Do you require salesperson or territory analysis by
    - Gross sales?
    - Item or product category?
    - Comparative sales?
    - Customer?
    - Customer type?

- Do you require product or inventory analysis by
    - Gross sales?
    - Unit sales?
    - Profitability?
    - Vendor or supplier?
    - Product type or category?
    - Customer?
    - Seasonal movement?
    - Average velocity of sales?
- Do you require a sales tax report?
- Do you require information from prior years?
- Do you require weekly or daily profit recap reports?
- On average, how many products does a customer buy from you?
- Do any other requirements need to be taken into account to handle your specific sales-analysis requirements?

Income Tax Preparation

Most individuals with complex tax returns rely on the expertise of their CPA or tax attorney to help them understand and interpret the ever-changing tax codes. If you are currently going to a tax specialist for advice, you will still need that advice to file an "automated" tax return correctly. Tax-preparation programs assume that you are capable of doing your taxes manually. They automate the arithmetic calculations, but you must know what numbers to put in the blanks.

Tax preparation is a good example of an application that is usually not cost-effective to automate. This is because tax preparation is not a repetitive task. An individual's learning curve is much longer if he or she must learn how to do taxes *and* use a tax-preparation program. And the cost of tax-preparation software is usually about the same as a professional tax preparer's fees.

Howardsoft Corporation publishes Tax Preparer, a well-designed, easy-to-use package that is comprehensive enough for virtually any small business or corporation. Tax Preparer has an expert mode for professional tax preparers that allows them to prepare multiple client returns. I highly recommend this type of program for tax specialists.

Feature List for a Tax-Preparation Module

The tax-preparation package you select should:

- Conform to the latest IRS regulations.

- Have updates available from the supplier as soon as the rules or laws change.

- Contain and print out all of the necessary federal and state tax forms.

- Allow on-line, interactive data entry.

- Permit the preparation of corporation, partnership, and individual returns.

- Use last year's records to automatically update depreciation schedules, capital gains, and other items that carry forward to the new year.

A Final Word

IBM's Executive Education Classes stress that the single most important element in predicting a successful computer installation is a positive and supportive attitude from upper management. The fact that you have taken the time to read this book is a good indication that you will provide the support and encouragement necessary for your organization to successfully implement an office-automation system.

Index

DOUG DAYTON

Doug Dayton is the president of Dayton Associates, a firm that consults on office automation for small to midsized businesses. He has worked in the marketing and sales departments at IBM and Microsoft and is the author of several articles on office automation. Dayton currently lives in Bellevue, Washington.

The manuscript for this book was prepared and submitted to Microsoft
Press in electronic form. Text files were processed and formatted using
Microsoft Word.

Cover design by Greg Hickman
Interior text design by the staff of Microsoft Press
Illustrations by Nick Gregoric
Principal typography by Ruth Pettis

Text and display composition by Microsoft Press in Times Roman, using
the Magna composition system and the Linotronic 300 laser imagesetter.